AF506683

Mindfulness

A Do-It-Yourself Guide to Inner Peace

BLISS WOOD

Mindfulness

A Do-It-Yourself Guide to Inner Peace

Foreword by
Reverend Donna Michael
Ordained Minister, International Forgiveness Coach,
Spiritual Counselor

Publisher: Bliss Wood

Email: just4bliss@gmail.com

Website: www.just4bliss.com

ISBN: 979-8-9949892-1-0

First edition: March 2026

Instagram: @Just4BlissPublishing

Printing: Amazon

For inquiries regarding this book, please contact the publisher at the contact details provided above.

Website: www.just4bliss.com

The information and techniques in this book are intended for educational purposes and are not a substitute for professional medical advice, diagnosis, or treatment. Consult with your healthcare provider before starting any new wellness practice, especially if you have any pre-existing conditions. While these techniques have helped many people, everyone's journey is unique. The author and publisher cannot be held responsible for any injuries, losses, or damages resulting from the use of this material. Listen to your body, use common sense, and ask for help when needed.

Dedication

This book is lovingly dedicated to **Thich Nhat Hanh**, *one of the greatest teachers of mindfulness the world has ever known. Born in central Vietnam in 1926 and ordained a Buddhist monk at the age of sixteen, he lived a life anchored in compassion, courage, and the unshakable belief that peace begins with each of us. During the Vietnam War, he emerged as a guiding force for nonviolent action, illuminating a path of reconciliation when the world was shrouded in suffering.*

In 1967, Martin Luther King Jr. nominated him for the Nobel Peace Prize, recognizing the extraordinary impact of his tireless work. Over the course of his life and until his passing in 2022, Thich Nhat Hanh traveled the world, gently reminding humanity how to breathe, how to walk with intention, and how to return home to the present moment.

To Thich Nhat Hanh, whose saintly wisdom continues to ripple through the world long after his passing, I offer my deepest gratitude. May his legacy of mindful living illuminate our collective path, reminding us that every moment holds the potential for peace.

May each of us, in our own quiet way, dedicate our present-moment awareness to the lineage of love, compassion, and profound stillness that he so beautifully embodied.

"With mindfulness, you can establish yourself
in the present in order to touch the wonders of life
that are available in that moment."
—THICH NHAT HANH

Contents

Contents

Contents

Contents

Foreword

Feeling overwhelmed trying to learn how to live more mindfully?

You aren't alone. In our ever-increasing efforts to pursue peace, we often end up perturbed, perplexed, and "mindfully misguided."

Now, however, you can breathe a sigh of relief.

Mindfulness: A Do-It-Yourself Guide to Inner Peace by Bliss Wood is an encouraging, comforting, easy-to-read-and-apply collection of suggestions that will inspire and motivate you to embrace a more centered and balanced life as you choose to create your inner sanctuary of greater serenity.

For over twenty-five years in my own work as a forgiveness coach, spiritual counselor, speaker, ordained minister, composer, and musician, I have had the privilege of working with Bliss as we collaborated, created, and co-facilitated workshops, retreats, special events, and even musical projects.

Long before we began collaborating, our individual healing journeys brought us together in a spirit of mutually supportive friendship, love, and "mindful" accountability as we each faced deeply challenging "dark nights of the soul." Through this process (and lots of time over tea), we both discovered "blessings in the brokenness" that changed us—and the direction of our journeys—forever, enabling us to find the strength, clarity, and courage to redirect our lives and say yes to the greater work to which we are now committed.

I personally have benefited from Bliss' many gifts and talents as I witnessed firsthand her passion for helping others discover how to live a more expansive, centered, and abundant life. Through teaching yoga, meditation, offering mindful coaching, as well as practicing and teaching Reiki as a Reiki Master for over twenty-five years, Bliss has proven time and again that she skillfully lives what she loves.

Her first book, *Empowering Your Life with Yoga* (2004), and her musical project, "Yoga for Deep Relaxation" (2002), have helped countless people on their personal paths of expansion, renewal, and wellness. Sitting in her yoga classes and healing retreats, I have found greater harmony within myself.

In reading her new book, I have been delightfully reminded that peace is possible—simply by selecting from her suggestions to create more mindfulness for myself—and so can you. With "Bliss-full" encouragement and peaceful excitement, I highly recommend treating yourself to *Mindfulness: A Do-It-Yourself Guide to Inner Peace* by Bliss Wood.

Turn to any page and let this unique and practical handbook help you create your own soothing oasis of mindfulness and serenity—without overwhelm—in the midst of our ever-changing world.

Reverend Donna Michael
Ordained Minister, International Forgiveness Coach,
Spiritual Counselor
www.DonnaMichael.com

Preface

The first quarter of the twenty-first century has carried us through a whirlwind of change—at times exhilarating, at times unsettling. We've witnessed global challenges such as Y2K anxieties, climate-related disasters, and the COVID-19 pandemic, right alongside astonishing breakthroughs like cryptocurrencies, 3D printing, and artificial intelligence. In this rapidly evolving world, life can feel loud, crowded, and relentlessly fast. With information expanding faster than we can process it, our inner world can become just as chaotic.

It's in these moments—when life feels disordered or uncertain—that we need to reach deeply into our toolbox of self-care and reclaim steady ground through peaceful awareness.

Do you feel as though something in your life is missing, yet you can't quite name it? Or perhaps you know exactly what you long for but aren't sure how to take the first step.

Would you like more nourishing relationships—with your spouse, your children, your friends, and most importantly, with yourself?

Do you hope for better health, greater peace of mind, and the ability to enjoy your life more fully and more often?

If you answered yes to any of these questions, this book was written for you. It offers a simple, grounded, and practical approach to finding clarity and peace in every corner of your life. Whether you are navigating the busyness of daily routines or facing major life decisions, a mindful approach can strengthen your well-being in extraordinary ways. When you learn to observe your experiences calmly and without judgment, you begin to participate more fully in each moment—and life can unfold in beautiful, unexpected directions.

Mindfulness is the practice of paying attention with gentle awareness. It calls you back from rumination about the past or worries about the future and teaches you to return to the only place life actually happens: the present moment. Through mindfulness, you gain a clearer understanding of your circumstances and a deeper sense of acceptance, both of which are essential for inner peace.

By integrating the practices in this book into your daily life, you can transform ordinary experiences into meaningful moments of clarity, connection, and joy. Mindfulness can also bring coherence and calm to stressful or confusing situations, helping you respond rather than react. Even the most challenging moments become more manageable, more understandable, and more human.

While many books on mindfulness encourage present-moment living—which is invaluable—this guide takes you further. It clearly defines mindfulness and offers simple, everyday techniques that fit naturally into your routines. With consistent practice, peaceful, non-judgmental awareness becomes your default state. Fear loosens its hold. Confusion fades. What remains is a quieter, steadier version of yourself—one who can meet life with clarity and grace.

Drawing on the wisdom of beloved teachers including Thich Nhat Hanh, Jon Kabat-Zinn, Dr. Wayne Dyer, and the Dalai Lama, this book explains how mindfulness strengthens the essential mind–body connection—the very foundation of self-understanding. When your body and mind work in harmony, you perceive the world more clearly and relate to your experiences with greater compassion and ease.

Within these pages you'll find practical guidance for becoming more mindful, along with opportunities to experience the effects of mindfulness firsthand. You'll learn to observe your thoughts without judgment and make conscious, nourishing decisions that support your well-being.

By the time you reach the final page, you will not only understand how awareness can reshape your life—you will have the skills and confidence to begin living the life you choose.

Your journey toward a more peaceful, present, and empowered life begins right here—and you'll be glad you took the first step.

Acknowledgments

Writing a book is no simple task. First, it requires an idea and the inspiration to share it with the world, followed by countless hours of research, writing, and rewriting. Beyond that herculean task, a book would not become a book without knowledgeable, creative, and supportive people who lend their expertise in the areas of editing, formatting, designing, advertising, and especially, moral and financial support.

With that said, I would like to thank some good people who have contributed to the existence of this book.

When it comes to proofreading and editing, **Jon Ims** and **Christopher Budny** are the best! They have helped polish and refine the pages of this work. Thanks to them and their meticulous attention to detail, the "t's are crossed and the i's are dotted" to perfection.

Mikal Belicove my friend and colleague, is responsible for introducing me to **Juli Johnson**, formatter and designer extraordinaire. Without these two, you would not be holding this volume in your hands.

I also wish to thank **Bill Brooks** for "paving the way" with his suggestions and advice on where and how to self-publish. Beyond being a first-rate voice-over coach and teacher, he has guided me around some of the pitfalls on the publishing path. I consider myself lucky to call him "friend."

Karl Hudson, Donna Michael, Cathy Hacker, and **Theda Day**— because of your positive attitudes and regular "check-ins" I have been able to soldier through the writing process, feeling supported and loved.

I would also like to thank those who have financially contributed to the production of this book. **Bill Stevens, John Peed, Doug Fields, Ariane Herring Borgia, Scott Grantham, Jami Grich, Lisa Leman, Michael Bulloch, Alec Caldwell, Mary and Al Koenigsfeld, and Katie**

Fisher, to name a few. Your generosity supports a project that will benefit humanity, one person at a time.

Finally, I wish to thank my family and friends for putting up with me during the long hours it took to complete this book. Your patience and support means the world to me.

Because of the kind and generous people in my world, I am grateful to offer this powerful and mindful guide to your world. Thank you, dear reader, for investing in mindfulness and inner peace.

Introduction

In just a few lines, Thich Nhat Hanh captures the essence of mindfulness: calm awareness, gentle acceptance, and appreciation for the simple beauty of being alive. Mindfulness invites us to stop chasing the past and anticipating the future, and instead, to rest fully in the only time that truly exists—the present moment.

But what is mindfulness, really? And how can it transform your life? At its heart, mindfulness is the art of paying attention—deliberately, without judgment, and with a sense of openness and curiosity. The term originates from the ancient Pali word sati, which means "awareness" or "to remember." It points to a state of consciousness that is both alert and compassionate, allowing us to witness our thoughts, feelings, and experiences as they are, rather than as we wish them to be.

In a world that constantly pulls us in a thousand directions, mindfulness becomes an anchor. It is a return to simplicity—to the rhythm of your breath, the feeling of your feet on the ground, the warmth of sunlight on your skin. Through practice, you begin to see that peace does not depend on external circumstances but is cultivated from within.

When you practice mindfulness, you begin to understand that the present moment is not merely a passage of time—it is life itself. Regret over the past and anxiety about the future dissolve when you give your full attention to now. Every mindful breath, every conscious choice, strengthens your ability to live with clarity, compassion, and intention.

The methods explored in this book are simple, accessible, and deeply transformative. They are not about escaping life, but about engaging with it more fully. As you experiment with the exercises that follow, you will learn how to integrate mindfulness into everyday activities such as eating, walking, speaking, listening, and even doing nothing at all.

You may find that certain techniques resonate with you more than others, and that's perfectly fine. Mindfulness is a personal journey, one that unfolds uniquely for everyone. With patience and practice, the noise of daily life begins to soften, and what emerges is a steady sense of presence and peace.

As Wayne Dyer reminds us, "Stillness is the language of the soul." This stillness—your mindful awareness—is the foundation for a life of joy, purpose, and inner freedom. May these pages guide you home to that place within yourself.

Ways to Accomplish Mindfulness

*"Nothing ever happened in the past that can
prevent you from being present now."*
— ECKHART TOLLE

There is a quiet power in the present moment—a subtle yet profound truth that many of us spend a lifetime chasing. Mindfulness is the art of arriving in this moment, wholly and without judgment. It is not about silencing your thoughts or emptying your mind, but about becoming deeply aware of your experiences as they unfold—your breath, your sensations, your emotions, your surroundings. In this state of conscious awareness, even the most ordinary moments become extraordinary.

Part One of this book is devoted to exploring ways to accomplish mindfulness—a collection of activities and practices that guide you gently back to the present moment. These techniques are not ranked by importance, nor are they meant to be mastered in a particular sequence. Instead, think of them as an open invitation to explore the mindful possibilities that resonate with you the most. Whether you begin with a breathing exercise, a walk in nature, or something as simple as pausing before you speak, each method offers a door into a deeper awareness of yourself and of life.

Mindfulness does not demand grand gestures or complex rituals. It often begins in the most ordinary of places: in the kitchen as you prepare a meal, on a quiet street corner as you wait for the light to change, or while listening to the hum of crickets on a summer night. When you bring your full attention to these moments—when you really taste your food, really hear the sounds around you—you transform routine into ritual, habit into harmony. These small acts of awareness accumulate, gradually reshaping how you perceive and experience the world.

The practices in this section are designed to help you discover your own rhythm of mindfulness. Some may feel instantly natural, while others might challenge you or stir discomfort. Interestingly, it is often the techniques we resist that have the most to teach us. By leaning into that resistance—by asking yourself why a particular exercise feels uncomfortable—you uncover layers of self-understanding that are easy to overlook in daily life. That inquiry itself is mindfulness in motion: curiosity meeting awareness.

You don't need to adopt every technique offered here. In fact, mindfulness thrives on simplicity. Choose one or two methods that speak to you and observe how they shift your internal landscape. Perhaps you'll notice your breathing deepen, your thoughts slow, or your reactions soften. Over time, you may find yourself naturally incorporating more practices, expanding your capacity to stay present even amid life's noisy demands.

Think of the exercises in the following pages as tools in your personal toolbox. Each one serves a purpose, helping you build a foundation of calm awareness and compassion for yourself and others. Whether you explore all of them or focus on just a few, the goal remains the same: to cultivate a conscious, creative, and deeply lived life.

So, begin where you are. Read these pages in order or follow your curiosity wherever it leads. The path to mindfulness is not a straight road but a gentle unfolding. Each step, each breath, each act of awareness, brings you closer to the stillness that has always been within you.

Meditation

---

*"Meditation is not evasion; it is a serene
encounter with reality."*
— THICH NHAT HANH

There is a timeless stillness that lives beneath the noise of our minds. It's not something we create; it's something we uncover by quieting our internal voice long enough to hear it. That, in essence, is meditation.

Across centuries and continents, meditation has been humanity's most intimate practice of looking inward. It began long before science could measure its benefits or before monks wrapped their robes around the idea of mindfulness. It was born from a desire to understand the mind and its mysterious link to the soul.

The Ancient Roots of Stillness

Though meditation's origins are difficult to pinpoint, some of the earliest written records appear in the Vedas, ancient Hindu scriptures composed around 1500 BCE. The Upanishads, a latter part of the Vedic texts, describe meditation as a sacred method for purifying the mind and releasing one's attachment to ego and illusion. The goal was not escape but awakening—seeing reality as it is, rather than through the lens of fear and desire.

Similar practices sprouted independently in other cultures. Buddhist monks in India and Japan sat in silence to observe the impermanence of thought. Taoists in ancient China meditated to harmonize with the natural flow of the universe, while early Jewish mystics and Islamic Sufis used chanting and breath work to draw nearer to the Divine. Even Celts and Druids, known for their deep connection to nature, engaged in meditative trance rituals that linked them to the rhythms of the earth.

Christianity, too, embraced its own contemplative traditions. Catholicism has mentioned meditation since the early Church, and by the fifth century, Eastern Orthodox Christian monks were practicing hesychasm—a form of meditative prayer centered on repeating short phrases, such as the "Jesus Prayer," in rhythm with the breath. The great mystics of the fourteenth century, like Meister Eckhart and St. Teresa of Ávila wrote about stillness as the door through which one meets God.

While these traditions may seem worlds apart, they all point to the same human longing: the need to be present, to transcend distraction, and to rest in awareness itself.

The Western Embrace

Fast forward several millennia. In the 19th and 20th centuries, meditation emerged in the West through a cultural meeting of the minds. Swami Vivekananda was one of the firsts to introduce Indian philosophy to American audiences in 1893 at the Parliament of World Religions in Chicago. His message—that divinity lives within each of us—resonated deeply in a society hungry for spiritual depth.

Then came the wave of modern masters: Maharishi Mahesh Yogi, who popularized Transcendental Meditation (TM); Paramahansa Yogananda, whose Autobiography of a Yogi became a modern classic; and Thich Nhat Hanh, who helped shape Western consciousness by his living example and numerous texts describing present moment awareness.

The Beatles famously espoused TM after visiting the Maharishi in India in 1968, which launched a full-scale revolution in modern spirituality. Meditation suddenly became fashionable. Yet, beyond the pop-culture sparkle, the world began to notice something more profound: people who meditated reported tangible improvements in their health, relationships, and their overall sense of peace.

Besides Eastern philosophical gurus, numerous Christian and secular scholars from the twentieth century have also referenced the practice and benefits of meditation. Thomas Merton, Fr. Richard Rohr,

Jon Kabat-Zinn, and Sharon Salzberg, to name a few, have all contributed to our understanding and use of various meditation techniques and benefits. Because of these and numerous other luminaries, people around the world can experience the healing and life-altering benefits of meditation.

By the late twentieth century, meditation had found its scientific champions. Dr. Dean Ornish, Dr. Deepak Chopra, and Dr. Andrew Weil all recommend meditation for improving physical, mental, and emotional well-being. Dr. Ornish developed a program for reversing heart disease that utilizes meditation. Deepak Chopra created Primordial Sound Meditation™ and has written numerous books promoting the benefits of a regular meditation practice. Dr. Weil is a well-known advocate for integrative treatments, where he combines Western medicine with alternative therapies such as meditation and medicinal plants. Besides the invaluable contributions these three doctors have made in the study and practice of meditation, numerous other masters have also helped to develop a greater understanding of meditation's benefits and why we practice.

Jon Kabat-Zinn founded the Mindfulness-Based Stress Reduction (MBSR) program at the University of Massachusetts, demonstrating through empirical studies that meditation reduces anxiety, improves immune function, and even rewires the brain. Harvard researchers later confirmed these findings: after just eight weeks of regular practice, MRI scans revealed increased gray matter density in areas linked to memory, empathy, and emotional regulation.

Meditation was no longer just a mystical experience; it was medicine for the modern mind.

Many Faces of Meditation

Meditation is not one-size-fits-all. Like art or music, it offers a wide range of expressions—each designed to meet us where we are. Some practices focus on the breath, others on sound, movement, or stillness. What they all share is the cultivation of awareness and the invitation to return, again and again, to the present moment.

Let's explore a few of the most beloved techniques.

- **Mindfulness Meditation:** This is perhaps the simplest form of meditation—and also the heart of mindfulness itself. You simply observe your thoughts, feelings, and sensations as they arise, without judgment or attachment. Imagine sitting on a riverbank, watching thoughts flow by like leaves on the water. You don't jump in the river; you just notice.

- **Breathing Meditation:** Your breath is always with you. It is the most accessible anchor to the present moment. Try the 4-6-8 rhythm; inhale for four counts, hold for six, and exhale for eight. This is one cycle. Repeat this rhythm a few times, and notice the changes: your nervous system begins to settle, your heart rate slows, and your mind starts to quiet. (If this technique is new to you, start with 3-4 cycles and then check in with yourself.) You can increase your practice to thirty minutes or more.

- **Zazen (Zen Meditation):** In the Zen Buddhist tradition, zen means "seated meditation." The practitioner sits upright, spine straight, hands resting gently in the lap, and eyes slightly open. The emphasis is on observing the breath and allowing thoughts to pass without clinging to them. Zen masters often say that meditation is not about becoming calm—it's about becoming real.

- **Walking Meditation:** Sometimes stillness is easier to find in motion. In walking meditation, each step becomes an act of awareness. Feel your foot lift, move, and touch the ground. Notice the rhythm of your breath and the contact of your body with the earth. As Thich Nhat Hanh once said, "Walk as if you are kissing the Earth with your feet."

- **Guided Meditation:** If silence feels intimidating, guided meditations can help. With the soothing voice of a teacher or recording, you are led through imagery and relaxation techniques that engage the imagination and the senses. Many people find this approach especially effective for managing anxiety and insomnia.

- **Yoga Nidra:** Known as "yogic sleep," this is a deeply restorative form of guided meditation practiced lying down. A teacher or recording guides you through a Yoga Nidra script as you rest in complete stillness. Studies show that a thirty-minute Yoga Nidra session can be as rejuvenating as two hours of sleep.

- **Mantra Meditation:** With mantra, repetition becomes the path to stillness. A word or phrase, such as Om (the primordial sound of the universe) or Shanti (peace), is repeated silently or aloud to focus the mind. Over time, the sound dissolves into pure awareness.

- **Transcendental Meditation (TM):** Taught by certified instructors, TM uses a personalized mantra that has no specific meaning and is kept private. Practiced for twenty minutes twice daily, it allows the mind to settle into a state of profound rest while remaining alert. Countless studies have documented its benefits, from lowered blood pressure to increased creativity and emotional resilience.

- **Primordial Sound Meditation (PSM):** Developed by Deepak Chopra, this technique assigns a mantra based on the vibration of the universe at the date, time, and place of your birth. Known as "primordial sounds," the idea is that this "vibration" reconnects you to your original state of harmony. Taught by a certified instructor, it is recommended to practice twice a day, in the morning and late afternoon, for between twenty to thirty minutes to experience the full benefits of the meditation. However, practicing once a day is better than not practicing at all.

- **Loving-Kindness Meditation (Metta):** In this heart-centered practice, popularized by Sharon Salzberg, you silently repeat phrases of goodwill toward yourself and others: May I be happy. May I be healthy. May I live in peace. May I be love. Inspired by ahimsa (avoidance of violence), this meditation focuses on sending compassion and kindness to yourself, then extending the same compassion to loved ones, strangers, and even those who challenge you. Neuroscientists have found that this practice increases empathy and reduces bias by activating the brain's compassion centers.

- **Kriya Yoga:** Popularized by Paramahansa Yogananda, Kriya Yoga combines breath control and meditation, focused on the energy centers (chakras) along the spine to purify the nervous system and accelerate spiritual growth. It emphasizes the importance of devotion and ethical living to deepen one's connection to the Divine.

The Science of Stillness

What makes meditation so powerful? Science suggests it's a workout for the mind that reshapes both brain and body.

Research from Stanford University found that just ten minutes of daily meditation can reduce stress-related activity in the amygdala—a major emotional processing center of the brain—while increasing activation in the prefrontal cortex, responsible for focus and decision-making. Over time, meditation builds emotional resilience, much like physical exercise strengthens muscles.

Physiologically, meditation lowers cortisol (the stress hormone), reduces inflammation, and supports heart health. Dr. Dean Ornish's landmark study demonstrated that meditation and lifestyle changes can actually reverse coronary artery disease. Meanwhile, Dr. Andrew Weil's research in integrative medicine highlights how meditation compliments traditional treatments for anxiety, depression and chronic pain.

Beyond the data, however, lies something more subtle. Meditation changes the quality of your life. It brings color back to dull moments, space to crowded thoughts, and compassion to self-criticism.

A Story from the Cushion

Years ago, I attended a meditation retreat with my best friend at Deer Park Monastery in Escondido, California. Beyond excited to be spending time with Thich Nhat Hanh for a long weekend, she and I found ourselves feeling a bit anxious for the first day or two. Not wanting to "miss out" on anything, and forgetting we were actually at a "mindfulness" retreat, we kept maneuvering to find the best location to see him in the meditation hall.

During a dharma talk, Thay—"teacher," as he is lovingly called—looked out into the sea of faces and motioned for a small group to join him on the platform. My friend and I were included in that group! With nothing more than a soft smile and a quiet "join me" gesture, he invited us into his presence with the warmth of an old friend. As I sat at his feet, I was humbled and grateful to be in the presence of such a profound teacher. In that sacred moment, I experienced the Divine—whatever name one chooses to give It—made manifest through his stillness and compassion.

His teachings that day moved through me with a clarity I had never known. The gentleness of his voice, the spaciousness of his acceptance, and the deep well of nonjudgment that flowed from him struck a chord that changed the course of my life. It was as if he held up a mirror, allowing me to recognize the truth that mindfulness is not merely a practice, but a way of being—a homecoming to the present moment where peace is always waiting.

That's what meditation gives us—perspective.

Finding Your Own Practice

Meditation isn't about escaping life; it's about inhabiting it more fully. You don't need incense, robes, or a Himalayan cave. All you need is a willingness to be with yourself, as you are, right now.

Start small, even if it's only five minutes a day. Sit comfortably, close your eyes if you wish, and follow your breath. When your mind wanders (and it will), gently return to the present moment. Over time, those few minutes will ripple through your entire day, softening your reactions, sharpening your awareness, and deepening your sense of connection.

If one style doesn't resonate, try another. The beauty of meditation lies in its adaptability. Whether you prefer silence or guidance, stillness or movement, every form leads to the same truth: Peace lives within you.

Coming Home

In our age of distraction, meditation is a radical act of remembering—remembering to pause, to breathe, to be. It teaches us that peace isn't something to find; it's something to allow.

From the ancient sages of the Upanishads to the scientists of modern neuroscience, the message remains the same: When we turn inward, we rediscover the wholeness we thought we had lost.

So take a deep breath. Feel it rise, feel it fall. This is where it begins—this quiet revolution of awareness, this do-it-yourself guide to inner peace.

Body Scan

"Take care of your body. It's the only place you have to live."
— JIM ROHN

There is a quiet magic that happens when we turn our attention inward with curiosity, compassion, and stillness. One of my favorite mindfulness techniques is a simple yet profound practice called the body scan, which has the potential to completely change your state of being in a matter of minutes. This method takes a little longer to practice than some of the other selections in this book, however, its benefits are well worth it. If you choose to practice body scanning, give yourself enough undisturbed time alone to complete the scan without interruption.

I first discovered the body scan while living in Nashville. I was attending a Native American journey to find my "spirit animal." Our guide led the group through a body scan to connect us to our bodies before we journeyed to find our spirit guide. As I focused on each body part, I felt something I hadn't experienced in years—a deep, soothing connection to my body. It was as if I had been living slightly outside of myself, and the practice invited me home.

Ancient Roots, Modern Relevance

Body scanning has ancient roots in Buddhist mindfulness and meditation traditions. For centuries, monks and lay practitioners have used this method to cultivate the mind–body connection. It wasn't until the late twentieth century that it found its way into mainstream Western wellness practices, thanks largely to Jon Kabat-Zinn.

Kabat-Zinn, a molecular biologist turned meditation teacher, incorporated body scanning into his Mindfulness-Based Stress Reduction

(MBSR) program. This played a significant role in introducing it to Western model healthcare settings, demystifying its Buddhist foundation and giving it more credence as a wellness technique. His goal was simple but revolutionary: to bring mindfulness out of the monastery and into the hospital. He introduced body scanning as a foundational technique, helping patients manage chronic pain, anxiety, and stress.

Since then, numerous studies have validated what ancient practitioners already knew. Research shows that regular body scan meditation can reduce cortisol levels and improve sleep quality, emotional regulation, and even immune function. In one study published in Psychosomatic Medicine, participants who practiced body scanning for eight weeks experienced measurable decreases in both physical tension and psychological distress. Science, it seems, has caught up with what mindfulness masters have long understood. Awareness heals.

The Practice of Coming Home

Unlike other meditations that focus on the breath or a mantra, body scanning invites you to explore the landscape of your body from the inside out. It's a gentle inward journey, a guided tour of your physical self.

Traditionally, a teacher leads the practice, speaking slowly and calmly as you bring awareness to each part of your body—from the crown of your head to the tips of your toes (or sometimes the reverse). But it can also be practiced alone. All that's required is time and presence.

The instructions are simple: find a quiet space, lie down, and close your eyes. Begin by noticing your breath—its natural rhythm, its rise and fall. Then, direct your attention to your toes. Without judgment, observe any sensations that arise: warmth, tingling, numbness, or nothing at all. Then slowly move upward—feet, ankles, calves, knees—like a gentle wave of awareness washing through you.

The goal isn't to *change* anything. It's to *notice*. To become aware of what *is*, rather than what should be.

With practice, something remarkable begins to happen. You start to uncover subtle layers of tension you didn't even realize you were carrying—a clench in your jaw, tightness in your stomach, a shallow breath. As awareness touches these places, the body softens, the mind quiets, and a deep sense of calm unfolds.

Many people report that after practicing body scans for a few weeks, they begin to sleep better, respond rather than react to stress, and experience more gratitude for their bodies, even with all their imperfections. The key is to approach the practice without expectation. It's a practice that reminds us we are not our thoughts, but we are also not separate from our bodies.

Body scanning teaches us beautiful truths of mindfulness: Peace isn't found by escaping the body or silencing the mind. It's found in coming home to ourselves, moment by moment, sensation by sensation.

Whether you practice for five minutes or fifty, whether guided by a teacher or by your own intuition, the body scan offers a sanctuary within—a space where awareness meets acceptance, and stillness becomes healing.

So, find a quiet corner, close your eyes, and begin. The journey through your body may just lead you back to your soul.

If you'd like to try a body scan, you can find a guided version in Part Three of this book.

Breathing

"I wake up every day and I think,
I'm breathing! It's a good day."
— EVE ENSLER

Everyone breathes—but not everyone breathes mindfully. It's one of life's simplest truths and greatest ironies that our breath sustains us every moment of our lives, yet most of us move through our days without truly noticing it. The breath is both ordinary and sacred, automatic and intentional, ever-changing and ever-present.

I first realized how much my breath reflected my state of mind during a particularly stressful day many years ago when I was attending my first yoga teacher training. I was trying to hold a Tree Pose (Vrksasana) and kept losing my equilibrium. I'd just about find my center and then lose my balance, stepping out of the pose. The more I tried and failed, the more frustrated I became.

As the instructor walked by, he simply said, "Breathe." *Ding, Ding, Ding!* The mindfulness bell rang in my head. Of course, I realized I wasn't breathing! I had been unconsciously holding my breath, suspended between anxiety and anticipation. That single reminder—*breathe*—brought me back to the present moment. My shoulders softened, my mind cleared, and I balanced in *Tree Pose*.

The breath is not just a biological function; it is a barometer of our inner world.

The Breath Mirrors the Mind

Our breathing changes constantly—day to day, hour to hour, even moment to moment. It reflects our inner landscape with astonishing accuracy. Think of how your breath quickens when you're startled, slows when you're calm and relaxed, or catches when you're deep in thought. A single idea can make you hold your breath in tension or anger; another can release you into happiness or a sigh of relief.

When we bring mindfulness to the breath, we begin to see this intimate connection between body, mind, and emotion. Every inhalation and exhalation becomes a message from within, gently guiding us back to the present moment.

Focus on your breath and body for a moment. Without changing anything, simply notice how you are breathing. Is it shallow or deep? Does it reach your belly, or linger only in your chest? Are you breathing freely, or holding tension somewhere along the way? These simple questions open the door to self-awareness.

So often, we hold our breath when concentrating, worrying, or rushing through life. It's a natural but unconscious response to stress. The problem is that holding the breath signals the nervous system to stay alert, even when the danger is long gone. Over time, this pattern can keep the body trapped in a subtle state of fight or flight.

But the good news is, awareness changes everything. Once you notice how you're breathing, you gain the power to shift it, and, in doing so, shift your entire state of being.

Breathing with Awareness

Mindful breathing is a simple yet transformative practice. You don't need a meditation cushion or incense. You just need a few quiet moments and your own attention.

Sit comfortably, close your eyes if you like, and become aware of your *in-breath*. Notice how long it takes for your lungs to fill with air. Feel the expansion in your chest, ribs, and belly. Then turn your attention to your *out-breath*. Observe how the air leaves your body—does it rush out, or flow naturally and gently?

Now, as you breathe in, silently say to yourself, "I'm breathing in." As you exhale, say, "I'm breathing out."

This technique, taught by the beloved Zen master Thich Nhat Hanh, is one of the simplest ways to anchor yourself in the present.

Each phrase is like a handrail on a staircase—it keeps you steady, moment by moment, breath by breath.

Spend a few more cycles with this awareness. Feel the air as it moves through you, the rhythm of your body's natural intelligence. Then pause and notice how you feel. Are your shoulders a little softer, your face more relaxed? Has your mind grown quieter?

The of beauty of mindful breathing is that it works almost instantly. Just one conscious breath can pull you out of distraction and bring you home to the here and now.

Science of Breath

Modern research confirms what ancient traditions have known for centuries: the way we breathe directly affects our body and mind. Deep, steady breathing activates the parasympathetic nervous system—the body's natural "rest and restore" mode. This lowers heart rate, reduces blood pressure, and decreases cortisol, the stress hormone.

Studies from institutions such as Harvard Medical School and Stanford University show that mindful breathing improves emotional regulation, enhances focus, and even boosts immune function. A 2018 peer-reviewed study in the journal *Frontiers in Human Neuroscience* found that participants showed measurable improvement in attention span after one short breath-focused session.

Oxygen is our body's most essential fuel. A deep, mindful breath infuses the bloodstream with oxygen, which in turn nourishes the brain, heart, and muscles. When we breathe fully, every system in the body functions more efficiently. In short, better breathing leads to better living.

Breath as a Bridge

Your breath is always available. It is the one companion that never leaves you. Whether you're stuck in traffic, washing dishes, or walking into a difficult meeting, your breath can be your anchor.

The next time you feel overwhelmed, pause. Take one slow, deliberate inhale. Feel it fill your lungs. Then, exhale fully, letting go of tension with the breath. Notice what shifts. You may find that the situation itself hasn't changed, but *you* have.

Mindful breathing reconnects you to your body, calms the storm of thoughts, and opens space for clarity and peace. It reminds you that calm is not something you have to chase, but is something to return to. Just one mindful breath can bring you back to the present moment. Imagine what a day—a lifetime—of mindful breathing could do for your health and happiness. When you begin to live with awareness of your breath, you begin to live with awareness of each present moment.

Inhale peace.

Exhale presence.

Eating

In the rush of modern life, eating has become an afterthought. Meals are often sandwiched between meetings, consumed in front of screens, or devoured while driving from one obligation to another. We live in a culture that glorifies productivity, but in doing so, we've forgotten one of life's simplest and most profound rituals—mindful eating.

Mindful eating isn't a diet or a set of rules. It's a way of being present with your food, your body, and your senses. It's about slowing down enough to truly *taste* your life.

The Fast-Food Fog

The modern world boasts fast food and twenty-four-hour service, which might seem like a benefit to productivity and a company's bottom line, but it does little to instill wellness in an individual. Eating food on the run, with little nutritional value, is much like holding your breath. It takes you out of present-moment awareness.

Think about the last time you rushed through a meal—maybe grabbing a burger and fries at a drive-thru, eating with one hand while steering with the other. For a few minutes, the salty crunch and quick satisfaction felt good. But what happened afterward? Did you feel energized, focused, and alive—or heavy, sluggish, and slightly guilty? Your body tells you exactly what is happening only if you pay attention to it.

Food is the fuel that allows the body to function. The kind of food and how you consume it decides how well your body functions. Just like high-performance gasoline makes a car run smoothly, high-quality food, eaten with awareness, makes you run smoothly.

When we eat unconsciously, our bodies protest. Because the body takes about twenty minutes to signal the brain that it is full, eating too quickly or without thought can lead to overeating and poor digestion. Eating mindlessly also disconnects us from the act of nourishment, turning food—one of life's great pleasures—into just another task on our to-do list.

Our ancestors ate differently. Meals were often sacred times of gathering and gratitude. They prepared food by hand, aware of where it came from and the energy it offered. In contrast, today's fast-food culture prioritizes convenience over connection. Yet, true nourishment arises not just from what we eat, but *how* we eat.

The Science of Slowing Down

Modern research supports age-old spiritual traditions' ways of mindful eating. It improves both physical and emotional well-being. A 2012 study published in Obesity Reviews found that mindfulness-based eating interventions helped participants reduce binge eating, emotional eating, and body weight. When we eat slowly, savoring each bite, the parasympathetic nervous system (PSNS)—the body's "rest and digest" mode—activates. Digestion improves, blood sugar stabilizes, and our relationship with food softens from control to care.

A Simple Practice

The next time you enjoy a meal, try a little experiment:

1. Pause before you begin. Look at your plate. Notice the colors, textures, and shapes of your food. Take a breath and acknowledge the journey it took to reach you—the farmers, the soil, the sun, the rain.

2. Engage your senses. Inhale the aroma of your meal. Does your mouth water? Do certain smells remind you of home, childhood, or comfort?

3. Take your first bite slowly. Notice the texture. Is it smooth, crisp, chewy, warm, or cold? Pay attention to how the flavors unfold.

4. Chew completely. This not only aids digestion but also gives your brain time to register fullness.

5. Observe your reactions. Are you enjoying this dish? Do certain foods make you feel light or heavy, energized or dull? What emotions arise as you eat—gratitude, guilt, joy, impatience?

6. Give thanks.

By tuning in to these sensations, eating transforms from a mechanical act into a sensory meditation.

Choose Mindfully

Of course, mindfulness also extends to *what* we eat. Whole, unprocessed foods such as fresh fruits, vegetables, grains, and clean proteins naturally support clarity and vitality. These foods are rich in prana, or life force, a concept well understood in Ayurvedic and yogic traditions. In contrast, heavily processed or fast foods often leave the body depleted and the mind clouded.

This doesn't mean you must give up your favorite treats. Rather, it's about awareness and balance. When you eat a slice of cake, truly taste it. Let it be an act of joy, not guilt. When you prepare a salad, notice how your body responds with gratitude. Over time, mindfulness naturally leads you toward foods that make you feel alive, fully experiencing the delight of enjoying your food, one bite at a time.

Food as a Doorway to Gratitude

Mindful eating reconnects us to gratitude—the quiet recognition that we are sustained by the world around us. Each bite represents the interdependence of all life: soil, sunlight, rain, farmers, cooks, and even the person who set the table.

When we remember this, every meal becomes sacred. Eating turns into a conversation with life itself.

So, the next time you sit down to eat, slow down. Put down your phone. Take a breath. Look at the food before you and whisper a silent "thank you."

You might just discover that mindfulness doesn't begin on the meditation cushion—it begins on your plate.

Walking

"When you walk, arrive with every step.
That is walking meditation.
There is nothing else to it."
— THICH NHAT HANH

Do you ever wonder how many steps you walk every day? Wellness experts suggest 5,000–10,000 steps a day is a healthy goal to achieve.

Most of us walk daily without a second thought, never concerned about what life might be like without mobility. We walk to the kitchen for coffee, through hallways at work, down grocery aisles, and across parking lots—each step mechanical, automatic, and unnoticed. Yet within this ordinary act lies a profound opportunity for transformation. Walking mindfully, with full awareness, can become one of the simplest and most powerful ways to cultivate presence, gratitude, and inner peace.

The Forgotten Miracle of Mobility

Movement can be easily taken for granted until something happens to inhibit it. If you've ever injured your leg, broken a foot, or twisted an ankle and needed to rely on crutches, you know the sudden and humbling awareness that comes with losing mobility. What once seemed effortless suddenly becomes an ordeal. However, when healing returns and we take those first pain-free steps, something wonderful happens. Walking feels like freedom.

That moment of renewed movement captures the essence of mindful walking. In our newfound mobility, we can appreciate the gift of each step. Our ability to move through the world is both ordinary and miraculous. Yet in the rush to get somewhere else, we rarely notice the miracle of presence.

Hurry Up and Wait

Modern life moves fast. We rush through airports, stride purposefully in our work, and hustle across parking lots with our eyes glued to our phones. We walk not for the sake of being present, but to get somewhere else. Our bodies move forward, yet our minds sprint even faster—charging to the next task, the next obligation, the next worry waiting just ahead.

In that state, walking becomes a metaphor for the way many of us live: always going somewhere, rarely *arriving.*

Mindful walking invites us to slow down and reconnect our body and mind to the present moment. It's not a practice of speed or distance, but of awareness. Each step is a moving meditation that becomes a gentle reminder to return to the here and now.

Practicing Mindful Walking

Thich Nhat Hanh introduced walking meditation to millions around the world, often beginning his retreats by leading groups in silent, deliberate walks through gardens or along forest paths. "When you walk," he would softly say, "feel each step as a gentle kiss upon the Earth."

To begin your practice of mindful walking, follow these simple steps:

1. Pause before moving. Stand still and take a deep breath. Feel the rise and fall of your chest. Notice the weight of your body standing gently on the ground.

2. Feel your feet. Are you wearing socks and shoes or are you barefoot? Can you sense the texture beneath you— carpet, grass, gravel, earth, or wood? Notice how your feet connect to the earth. Take a moment and feel your feet.

3. Take one conscious step. Once you feel connected to the earth, lift one foot slowly, move it forward, and place

it down with care. Notice how your heel touches first, and how your weight shifts to the ball of your foot.

4. Take the next step...and the next. Can you feel a difference in your body from side to side? How does your back foot lift off the ground? Continue mindfully stepping for a few yards. Notice how you carry your body.

5. Breathe naturally. As you inhale, lift your foot. As you exhale, place it down. Let your breath guide your rhythm.

6. Be aware of your surroundings. Feel the air on your skin, hear the sounds around you, notice the play of light and shadow. Let the world unfold gently, without judgment or analysis.

At first, this may feel awkward or even amusing, feeling as though you've forgotten how to walk, but that awareness is also part of the practice. Adding mindfulness to the act of walking brings your awareness to the "now." You are rediscovering what it truly means to inhabit your body. When your movements initiate from consciousness, you feel more stable and can allow yourself to be flexible with life's changing terrain.

Everyday Pilgrimage

Mindful walking doesn't require a temple, mountain path, or meditation hall. It can happen anywhere—on a quiet morning stroll, a lunchtime break, or even while walking your dog. Each step can become a prayer or offering of gratitude, connecting you to the present moment.

Have you ever run late for a meeting with a friend and found yourself walking fast or almost running to make the appointment? Perhaps you were so engrossed in thought (or your cell phone) while walking down the block that you bumped into someone or completely missed your stop. This is what happens when we're *not* living in the present moment.

Stop, take a breath, put your cell phone in your pocket, and place your awareness back in your feet.

Apple's legendary founder, Steve Jobs, known for his legendary "walking meetings," once remarked that walking helped him think more clearly. Regularly engaging in mindful walking can positively affect your physical, mental, and emotional states of being. With practice, you can enjoy better posture, stronger balance, and most of all, greater mindfulness and inner peace.

Gratitude in Motion

When we walk mindfully, we remember that the Earth supports us with every step. Every movement becomes an expression of gratitude—for our bodies, for the ground beneath us, for the present moment.

As you walk today, practice sensing the subtle joy of being alive. With every step, whisper inwardly: "I have arrived. I am home." In that awareness, you just may find that peace isn't something you must walk *toward.* It is something you've been walking *in* all along

Exercise

When you think of exercise, what comes to mind? Maybe it's the smell of sweat and rubber mats at the gym, the pounding rhythm of sneakers on pavement, or perhaps just the faint dread that accompanies the word "workout." For some, the idea of moving the body sparks excitement and empowerment. For others, it can feel like an obligation—one more task to check off an already full to-do list. Yet exercise, when approached mindfully, becomes far more than a physical pursuit. It transforms into a sacred dialogue between body and mind.

At its core, exercise is any intentional movement that strengthens, stretches, or energizes the body. It can be as structured as yoga or as spontaneous as dancing in your kitchen. It can happen in the quiet of a sunrise meditation or during a friendly soccer match. Gardening, swimming, hiking, walking the dog—each can become a mindful practice when approached with awareness and presence.

The challenge is not in the movement itself but in how we move. In our achievement-driven culture, exercise is often treated as a means to an end: lose weight, gain muscle, run faster, look better. But mindfulness asks something different of us. It invites us to let go of outcome and focus on experience. When we bring awareness to our movement, every breath, stretch, and heartbeat becomes a lesson in being present.

Consider two runners. One is pounding down a forest trail, lost in thought—calculating miles, comparing times, and replaying yesterday's race. His hamstrings feel tight, but he decides to "push through" the discomfort.

The other runner is focused on the rhythmic thud of each footfall, and the cool air expanding her lungs as she breathes. She notices how her heel strikes the ground each time she strides forward, and hears the whisper of leaves underfoot. She is aware of her body and her surroundings.

Which runner is exercising mindfully? I think it is safe to say the second runner is not just exercising her body, she is also exercising her consciousness. In experiencing herself within her environment, she is mindful. Her awareness allows her to monitor bodily sensations and feel a "runner's high." It also attunes her to her surroundings and keeps her safe from obstacles along the path. Mindful movement enhances well-being on every level.

Since ancient times, great thinkers such as Plato and Socrates emphasized the importance of exercise and self-awareness, believing that physical exercise cultivated courage, discipline, and harmony. Although the term "mindfulness" did not exist in Plato's era, he repeatedly stressed self-awareness, self-control, and attention to the present moment, all central to what we now call mindfulness. In *Timaeus*, one of Plato's dialogues written around 360 BC, he describes the body not as an obstacle to the soul's development but as a necessary partner in achieving balance. He wrote, *"The care of the body must precede that of the soul; a sound body gives birth to a sound mind."* He saw exercise as a way to purify the body, preparing it to support a calm and clear mind.

Even professional athletes are turning inward and recognizing the powerful connection of mind and body. NBA legend Michael Jordan famously trained with mindfulness coach George Mumford to improve focus and presence on the court. Jordan once said, *"The game slows down when you're fully there."* That's the essence of mindful exercise—whether you're shooting hoops, cycling, or stretching on your living room floor—the mind quiets, and the body becomes a gateway to peace.

Mindful exercise doesn't require a gym membership or fancy equipment. It begins with awareness of the body in motion. Before your next workout, pause. Feel the air filling your lungs. Notice how your feet make contact with the ground. Ask yourself: *How does my body feel right now? What is it asking of me?* Let that awareness guide your pace and intensity. If your body wants to move slower, honor it. If you feel energy rising, embrace it.

For example, if you're lifting weights, pay attention to the texture of the bar in your hands, the contraction and release of your muscles, the rhythm of your breathing. If you're swimming, tune into the coolness of the water, the resistance against your arms, the feeling of buoyancy as you glide. When cleaning your home, notice the repetitive motion of your hands and the subtle joy in seeing order emerge from chaos. Even the act of stretching before bed can become a meditative ritual when done with awareness.

Mindful exercise is also about listening rather than pushing. Our bodies constantly communicate with us—through fatigue, tightness, lightness, or ease—but we often ignore those signals in the pursuit of progress. When we exercise mindfully, we cultivate a partnership with the body. We begin to recognize when we need rest, when we can challenge ourselves, and when we simply need to breathe.

The rewards go beyond physical fitness. Mindful movement improves not just muscle tone but also mental tone. It strengthens patience, presence, and compassion. It teaches us how to flow through discomfort without judgment, and how to find stillness in motion.

Thich Nhat Hanh would say, *"Feel your steps like kisses upon the Earth."* The same applies to every mindful movement. Each push-up, stretch, or stride can become a kiss of gratitude to the body that carries you through life.

So, the next time you move—whether you're jogging at sunrise or doing gentle yoga before bed—remember, you're not just training your body, you're training your awareness. Let every breath, every heartbeat, every motion remind you that mindfulness isn't something you add to exercise; it is the exercise.

Yoga

*"The practice of yoga teaches us to live fully
in the present moment, with awareness
and compassion for ourselves and others."*
— DONNA FARHI

Yoga has been my *North Star* and is one of the great loves of my life. For more than thirty years, I've had the privilege of guiding thousands of students across North and Central America through this transformative practice of consciousness in motion. Without exaggeration, yoga has changed the entire course of my life.

A Little Girl and a Big Discovery

I was five years old when I first discovered yoga—by accident. It was 1969 and Sesame Street had just begun airing on PBS. It just so happened that, *"Yoga with Lilias"* aired just before my beloved Big Bird and Grover came on. Since I didn't want to miss a single second of counting with Mr. Hooper and *spelling* with Bert and Ernie, I planted myself in front of the television long before my program started.

As I waited for Sesame Street, I watched and was intrigued by this woman with a very long braid and a full-body gold leotard who talked softly and arranged her body in ways I'd never seen before. Lilias Folan changed my life forever. In the half hour her show aired, I attempted to emulate this lovely lady on screen. I stuck my tongue out like a lion, stood like a tree, and even tried to look like a triangle as I followed her instructions as best I could. The postures were fun and new to my brain, but it was her gentle manner and calm presence that affected me the most.

Lying in what she called *savanna* (sha-va-sa-na), during the last few minutes of the class, I knew there was something special about what she was teaching me. I didn't have words for it then, but knew something had changed.

It would take another twenty years before I would find out.

Ancient Roots, Modern Relevance

Yoga is far more than a fitness trend or a series of stretches. Its origins trace back more than 5,000 years to India, where ancient sages—known as *rishis*—developed postures and breathing techniques to help them sit comfortably for long hours of meditation. These early practitioners weren't interested in toned abs or flexibility. Instead, they sought liberation of the soul through mastery of the body.

Texts mentioning yoga date as far back as the Vedic Period (1500–500 BCE), with non-verbal references reaching back into the Pre-Vedic Period (circa 3000–1500 BCE). The *Rig Veda, Upanishads*, and Patanjali's *Yoga Sutras*, written thousands of years ago, are standard sacred texts to this day. Much of what is taught in modern yoga stems from the foundation of these ancient writings.

The Sanskrit word yoga means *to yoke or join*. This union refers to the integration of body, mind, and spirit—a harmony that extends beyond the mat into every aspect of life. When practiced mindfully, yoga becomes a living meditation, a dialogue between movement and awareness, ultimately merging one's human consciousness with that of the Divine.

The Mind–Body Connection

Modern practitioners continue to validate what the ancients knew intuitively: yoga heals. Through the practice of yoga, you can achieve mindful awareness that calms your mental and emotional states. Physiologically, it touches every system in the body—the skeletal and muscular, cardiovascular and respiratory, digestive and endocrine. But perhaps its most profound impact lies in how it teaches us to *feel* again—to listen to the subtle messages of the body and respond with compassion rather than judgment.

When you step onto your mat, your body becomes both a mirror and a messenger. Each pose reveals where you hold tension, fear, or resistance. Each breath becomes a teacher, reminding you to release what no longer serves you.

Paths to Presence

There are many pathways within yoga's vast landscape, each offering a unique route to self-realization. Many of these pathways are encompassed within five main yogic branches. Each branch offers specific ways to reach enlightenment through mindful awareness.

1. **Raja Yoga**, or "royal path," emphasizes meditation and mastery of the mind. It is considered the most introspective branch of yoga and is the heart of Patanjali's *Yoga Sutras*.

2. **Tantra** means "weaving together" and is practiced through sacred ritual, approaching all life with reverence. Tantra yoga invites us to see all of life as sacred, weaving together body, ritual, and energy. Modern examples of Tantra yoga might be the celebration of birthdays and anniversaries as well as the consummation of marriage. While Tantra yoga is most notably identified as sacred sexuality, many schools of tantra encourage celibacy, which creates an esoteric allure and a certain amount of confusion.

3. **Karma Yoga**, embodies the principle that past action creates one's current circumstances. It is considered the path of service, recognizing selfless action as a way to mindful liberation. Examples of Karma yoga would be volunteering at a homeless shelter or regularly checking on your elderly neighbor.

4. **Bhakti Yoga** celebrates devotion and tolerance through prayer, singing, chanting, and dance. It can

be considered the yoga of the heart or emotions, as it provides opportunities to see and celebrate the good in all beings.

5. **Jnana Yoga** follows the path of intellect and wisdom. It requires a disciplined mind, releasing ego identity to become the "observer" of one's life.

6. **Hatha Yoga** is perhaps the most familiar form of yoga in the West. Hatha translates to "force" and relates to the physical, emphasizing physical techniques that channel the body's life force and promote mindfulness.

Each of these branches offers tools for inner peace. While this chapter focuses primarily on Hatha yoga, I encourage you to explore whichever paths resonate most deeply with you.

Hatha Yoga: Mindfulness in Motion

Modern Hatha yoga encompasses many styles such as Ashtanga, Iyengar, Yin, and a host of other forms of practice. Some styles, like Power Yoga or Bikram, challenge the body with intensity; others, like Yin or Restorative, invite stillness and surrender. But beneath the diversity of forms lies the same essence: mindful awareness through movement.

Anyone can practice yoga and reap the benefits of this healing form of mindfulness. You don't need to touch your toes or balance on your hands. You only need a willingness to breathe, move, and listen. The body becomes a bridge between the external world and your inner landscape.

The Heart of Practice

After practicing yoga, some students feel a rush of emotion—tears, laughter, even a sense of profound stillness. This is natural. As you open physical spaces in the body, you also release what's been stored there: memories, emotions, and unspoken truths.

Yoga doesn't just stretch your muscles—it stretches your consciousness. It teaches you to inhabit your life more fully, moment by moment.

For me, yoga has always been less about perfect poses and more about presence. It's about returning—again and again—to the breath, the body, and the beating heart that connects us all.

So roll out your mat, breathe, move, and notice. In every posture, in every pause, lies a doorway to inner peace. All you have to do is step through.

Count to Ten

*"When angry, count to ten before you speak;
if very angry, a hundred."*
— THOMAS JEFFERSON

Life has a way of sweeping us up in its emotional tides, until joy, frustration, love, fear, anger, and a host of other feelings all swirl around, disorienting our sense of stability. Those volatile waves can crash hard as we react before we've had a chance to think, or found ourselves caught in regret after the emotional storm had passed. Most of us can recall a time or two when our emotions got the best of us and we wished we could have taken back the harsh words we blurted out in anger. In those moments, reason seems to vanish, leaving unchecked emotion in full command.

Our emotional outbursts aren't moral failings or personality flaws. They are simply part of how the brain is wired. The limbic system, most notably the amygdala, is to blame for these tantrums and often, regrettable behaviors. Deep within the temporal lobe, just above your ears, lies the amygdala—a small almond-shaped structure that processes emotional reactions and governs your instinctive *"fight, flight, or freeze"* responses. When the brain senses danger, whether it's a honking car, a harsh comment, or a stressful conversation, the amygdala jumps into action.

Its response time is lightning fast—just a fraction of a second quicker than the prefrontal cortex, the part of the brain responsible for logic, reason, and decision-making. That's why, in moments of high emotion, we often react before we think. It's not that we lack discipline, it's that the emotional brain has a head start. Neuroscientist and the author of Emotional Intelligence, Daniel Goleman calls this an *"amygdala hijack"*: when the emotional brain overrides the rational one.

The brain, when in balance, functions beautifully, but things like stress, trauma, PTSD, and exhaustion can throw off that harmony, leaving us vulnerable to overreaction. This is why developing a mindfulness practice is so essential, as it helps restore equilibrium between thought and emotion.

One of the simplest and most effective mindfulness tools is an old piece of advice you've probably heard a thousand times: **count to ten.** It sounds almost too simple, but behind those three words lies profound wisdom that is validated by both experience and modern neuroscience.

When you pause and consciously count, you create just enough space for your emotional surge to subside and for your reasoning mind to catch up. Counting acts as a gentle "cognitive distraction," shifting your attention from the intensity of your emotions to the rhythm of counting your numbers. In essence, it's like pressing a mental "reset" button, allowing your reasoning abilities to catch up with your emotional reactions, giving your nervous system a moment to recalibrate.

The next time you feel your emotions rising, stop what you're doing. Take a slow, deep breath, and as you exhale, count softly from one to ten. Feel the breath move through you. Notice how your heartbeat begins to steady. With each number, you're grounding yourself more firmly in the present moment.

If you want to deepen the practice, **count backward** from ten to one. This requires greater focus and helps pull your attention away from the emotional trigger. You can even add visualization: picture each number dissolving, melting, or fading as you exhale. Others find it powerful to coordinate counting with their breath—inhale on "one," exhale on "two," and so on—until the body and mind move together in rhythm.

These few seconds of awareness may not seem like much, but they open a door to what psychologist and Holocaust survivor Viktor Frankl described in his book, *Man's Search for Meaning*, as "the gap between stimulus and response." Mindfulness lives in that gap.

Within it lies your power to choose how you respond rather than being carried away by instinct.

Frankl wrote, *"Between stimulus and response there is space. In that space lies our power to choose our response. In our response lies our growth and our freedom."* Counting gives us access to that freedom.

Imagine, for a moment, being in a heated conversation. Your pulse quickens, words form on your tongue that you know will sting. But instead of reacting, you pause. You take a breath. You silently count—one ... two ... three ... The person across from you may still be speaking, but something inside you begins to shift. Your body softens. The grip of anger loosens. By the time you reach ten, you're no longer trapped in the emotion—you're observing it.

That is the quiet power of mindfulness. It doesn't erase life's challenges or emotions, but it changes your relationship with them.

Counting to ten might seem small and unsophisticated, but it is a profound act of self-awareness. It reminds us that between feeling and reacting, there is always a choice. Each number you count is a step back toward balance, toward peace, toward the grounded version of yourself that already knows what to do.

The next time you feel frustration bubbling up, anxiety tightening your chest, or anger burning in your throat, pause. Count to ten. Let each number be a breath, a heartbeat, a reminder that you are not your reaction. In that simple act of counting, you're not just calming your emotions—you're reclaiming your peace.

Think Before You Speak

If counting to ten gives us space to pause, then thinking before you speak is how we use that space wisely. Where "counting" cools the emotional storm, "thinking" steers the ship toward calm waters.

We've all been in conversations that teeter on the edge—moments where emotions rise and words hang heavy in the air. Maybe it's a disagreement with your partner, a tense exchange at work, or a political debate at the dinner table. In those moments, the impulse to defend or retaliate can feel irresistible. That's your amygdala at work again—the same emotional command center that triggers fight, flight, or freeze. When it flares, reason retreats, but mindfulness offers a bridge back to balance with a mindful pause that invites thought before speech.

When you consciously pause—even for a breath—you engage the prefrontal cortex, the part of your brain responsible for empathy, reasoning, and self-control. This simple act of awareness slows the cascade of emotional reactions and helps you choose words that align with your true intentions rather than your temporary feelings.

One of my yoga students once described it perfectly. She said, "I used to pride myself on being quick-witted, but I realized my words often cut deeper than I meant. When I started taking a breath before responding, I didn't lose my sharpness—I gained kindness." Her story is a beautiful reminder that mindfulness isn't about suppressing emotion; it's about channeling it with intention.

Thinking before you speak is also a form of compassion. It's not just for your own peace of mind, but for the peace of those around you. When you take that mindful moment, you consider not only *what* you want to say, but *how* your words might land. You begin to listen as much as you speak. You notice tone, body language, and emotion—both yours and theirs. That awareness transforms communication from reaction to connection.

This mindful practice has physiological benefits as well. By pausing to breathe and reflect before speaking, you naturally slow your heart rate and regulate your nervous system. Studies in psychophysiology have shown that conscious breathing activates the parasympathetic nervous system—the body's "rest and digest" mode—helping you stay grounded and present, even in challenging conversations.

Mindful thought creates mindful speech. Mindful speech creates mindful relationships. Mindful relationships, in turn, create peace.

The next time you feel your words rushing forward, pause. Breathe. Notice the sensations in your body, the rhythm of your heart, the tone forming in your mind. Ask yourself, *Does what I'm about to say build a bridge or a wall?*

When you choose to speak from awareness rather than impulse, you don't just avoid regret, you invite understanding. You turn a conversation into a moment of mindfulness, and like counting to ten, that small act of awareness can ripple outward, softening conflict and deepening connection.

In mindfulness, silence is not the absence of communication—it's the birthplace of wisdom.

Deep Listening

*"Deep listening is the kind of listening that can
help relieve the suffering of another person."*
— THICH NHAT HANH

After learning to pause and think before speaking, the next natural step in mindfulness is learning to *listen*—not just with your ears, but with your whole being. Deep listening is mindfulness in motion. It allows us to respond to the world with understanding rather than reaction, compassion rather than control.

Most of us believe we're good listeners. We nod, we make eye contact, we wait for our turn to reply. But often, we're only half present—our minds already racing to what we'll say next, or drifting into our own worries and to-do lists. True listening requires more. It asks us to quiet the internal chatter long enough to hear what's really being said—both by others and by ourselves.

Deep listening goes hand in hand with thinking before you speak. Just as pausing gives space for wisdom to rise, listening allows that wisdom to take root. Whether you're sitting across from a friend, in a tense meeting at work, or facing a major life decision, mindful listening anchors you in the present moment. It connects your inner awareness with the world around you.

Think about a time you faced a decision that could change your life—moving across the country, changing careers, getting married, or starting a family. Those moments often stir anxiety, excitement, or even fear. In times like these, the most valuable voice to listen to is often the quietest one—your intuition.

Your intuition is the whisper beneath the noise, the subtle knowing that lives in both your mind and body. Listening to it is an act of deep mindfulness. It helps you understand your authentic desires and align your choices with your values. Sometimes, your intuition speaks through your body—through a flutter in your chest, a sudden calm, or a wave of tension that signals something isn't quite right.

Maybe you've met someone who instantly felt like an old friend. Before you had time to analyze why, your body leaned in, your face softened, and your heart opened. That was your intuition communicating through sensation. Perhaps, when making a small decision—say, choosing between a hearty vegetarian meal or a juicy burger—you notice your body's cues. Does the idea of fresh vegetables make you feel light and nourished, or does your stomach growl for something heartier, signaling a need for protein? Your body doesn't lie. When you listen closely, it tells you exactly what it needs.

I remember a time when I was planning to have a business lunch with a friend at one of her favorite restaurants. It was a popular Jewish deli that served delicious, but "not so healthy," dishes. I wasn't feeling very focused and energetic that morning, so I wondered what I could eat that would make me feel better during our lunch. Adhering to a vegetarian diet at the time, I was fully planning on having a salad. When I looked at the menu, however, I realized I was craving meat, and chose a patty melt for lunch. That sandwich tasted wonderful and I felt satisfied and energized after eating it. My friend, who always ate meat, decided to have a salad that day, saying she "felt like she needed greens."

As it turned out, my body was craving protein and iron, exactly what red meat could provide. It was asking for support and nudged me to make a healthy choice for that moment. Both my friend and I felt better after listening to the wisdom of our bodies.

Listening to Your Intuition—The Quiet Minute

Your intuition is always whispering, but the world is often too loud to hear it. This simple exercise can help you to tune in.

1. Sit comfortably and take three slow, conscious breaths. With each exhale, release tension and racing thoughts.

2. Ask yourself a meaningful but simple question. *"What feels right for me in this moment?"*

3. Listen with your whole body. Notice sensations—a flutter in your chest, heaviness in your stomach, or a feeling of calm. Let these signals speak.

4. Trust the first whisper that comes to you. Your intuition often speaks before logic intervenes. Listen without judgment.

5. Acknowledge your wisdom with gratitude. Even if clarity doesn't come immediately, appreciate the act of pausing and listening.

This practice reconnects you to your own inner wisdom and helps you move through life with calm awareness.

Your body will never lie to you. Listen to it.

Deep listening extends beyond yourself. It's also about how you hear others. To truly listen to another person is one of the greatest gifts you can give. It means setting aside your inner dialogue—judgments, rebuttals, distractions—and simply being *present*. When you listen without an agenda, you affirm someone's worth. You tell them, "You matter. I see you. I hear you."

Mindful listening builds bridges of understanding. It transforms conversations into opportunities for connection. Sometimes, the most powerful response isn't advice or correction—it's acknowledgment. Simple phrases like "I understand" or "That sounds really hard" can be profoundly healing.

Listening to Others—The Two-Minute Mirror

To listen deeply to another person is to offer presence without conditions. Try this simple yet powerful mindfulness exercise.

1. Set a timer for two minutes. One person speaks freely about something real or important. The other listens without interrupting, fixing, or judging.

2. Switch roles. When the timer ends, trade places and repeat the two-minute exercise in step one.

3. After both have spoken, share what you noticed. How did it feel to be fully heard? How did it feel to listen without interrupting?

When you listen in this way, you begin to understand beyond words. Silence becomes sacred, and connection replaces reaction.

Deep listening, then, is both inward and outward. It invites you to ask yourself gentle questions like, *"What makes me happy?"* or *"What am I feeling right now?"* And it encourages you to ask others, "How can I help?" or "What do you need from me?" Each question roots you deeper in the present moment.

When we listen deeply—to our bodies, our intuition, and to one another, we cultivate peace. We soften the edges of misunderstanding and allow clarity to emerge. Mindful listening doesn't just quiet the noise around us, it brings harmony within us.

Be Forgiving

*"To forgive is to set a prisoner free and
discover that the prisoner was you."*
— LEWIS B. SMEDES

Forgiving yourself is one of the most profound acts of mindfulness—and one of the hardest. We often extend compassion freely to others yet withhold it from ourselves. It's as if there's a quiet critic living in the back of our mind, ready to point out every flaw, every mistake, every *"should have known better."*

You've probably noticed that negative thinking can slip in almost unnoticed, like a slow leak in a tire. Over time, it drains your energy, leaving you feeling flat and unmotivated. Left unchecked, these thoughts can grow into patterns of guilt, shame, or even self-punishment. They might sound like: *"I should've done more."* *"Why did I say that?"* or *"I'll never get it right."* These quiet condemnations don't just affect your mood—they shape how you show up in the world.

But here's the truth: Everyone stumbles. Everyone forgets, lashes out, or falls short sometimes. Mindfulness invites you to meet those moments not with blame, but with understanding. It teaches you that mistakes aren't proof of unworthiness; they're invitations to grow.

How then, do you stop the mind from replaying its harsh soundtrack? The answer lies in gentle awareness. Forgiveness begins when you learn to pause, notice your inner dialogue, and respond with compassion instead of criticism.

Think of your mind like a small puppy learning new habits. You wouldn't scold it for every accident—that wouldn't help either of you. Instead, you'd guide it patiently, offering gentle reminders, consistency, and love. Your thoughts deserve the same kindness. When you catch yourself spiraling into negativity, stop. Take a slow breath in, as you exhale, whisper to yourself, *"I forgive myself."*

At first, it might feel awkward or even unconvincing, but that's okay. You're retraining years—maybe decades—of self-judgment. Each time you choose forgiveness over frustration, you reinforce a new habit: kindness toward yourself. Over time, that inner voice softens. Instead of tearing you down, it starts cheering you on.

Forgiveness doesn't erase what's happened; it simply releases the hold it has on your heart. Psychologist Kristin Neff, a leading researcher on self-compassion, notes that people who practice self-forgiveness report lower levels of anxiety and depression, and higher levels of motivation and resilience. When you forgive yourself, you aren't letting yourself off the hook—you're setting yourself free to move forward.

Try this simple mindfulness practice:

1. When a self-critical thought arises, pause.

2. Take a deep breath, and name the emotion: *"I feel guilt."* Or *"I feel disappointment."*

3. Place a hand over your heart and say, *"I forgive myself."*

4. With each exhale, release a little more tension.

Mindful self-forgiveness doesn't happen overnight. It's a process—a daily decision to treat yourself with the same grace you'd offer a dear friend. The next time you catch that inner critic trying to take the microphone, pause and breathe. Remember, you are learning, evolving, and doing the best you can in this moment. And that, truly, is enough.

Pay Attention

"Attention is the rarest and purest form of generosity."
— SIMONE WEIL

In the words of Deepak Chopra, *"What you pay attention to grows."* Those six words are more than a poetic phrase—they're a roadmap for living with mindfulness. Whatever you dwell upon, you strengthen. Focus on fear, and it multiplies. Focus on gratitude, and it blossoms. Focus on the present moment, and it clarifies. Attention is the quiet architect of your inner world.

Science supports this ancient truth. Your brain processes millions of bits of information every second, constantly sorting, filtering, and connecting data into familiar patterns. Neural pathways—the highways of your brain—grow stronger with repetition. Each time you revisit a thought or behavior, the brain reinforces that pathway, making it easier to return to in the future. Over time, these mental "habits" can define your emotional landscape. That's why paying attention is not just a mental act—it's a creative one. You are literally shaping your brain, one thought at a time.

If you often find yourself worrying or overanalyzing, you're not alone. Modern life is filled with distractions, and our attention is constantly pulled in hundreds of directions. The endless scroll of social media, constant notifications, and multitasking at work can scatter our focus and leave us feeling fragmented. When your attention is split, your energy is too. Mindfulness begins by reclaiming that energy and bringing your awareness back home to the present moment.

Try remembering a time when your attention drifted—perhaps while driving, sitting in a meeting, or listening to someone speak. You might recall that vague feeling of being there but not really there. Your mind wandered to errands, worries, or unfinished conversations. Maybe your breathing became shallow or your body tensed without you even noticing.

Now, take a moment to pause and check in. How does your body feel right now? Are your shoulders relaxed? Is your breath deep or shallow? These small acts of noticing are powerful—they bring your mind and body back into alignment. When you pay attention, you reclaim the present moment, the only place true peace exists.

Attention also has a ripple effect on your emotions. When you consciously notice what is going well—the laughter of a friend, the warmth of sunlight, the taste of your morning tea—you train your mind to seek more of it. Positive psychology calls this *attentional bias*: the more you look for goodness, the more goodness you find. Over time, this mindful focus rewires your brain toward resilience and contentment.

Here's a simple exercise to practice mindful attention:

1. Pause and take a slow, full breath.

2. Choose one thing in your environment—a sound, a scent, a texture.

3. For one minute, place your full attention there. Notice every detail.

4. When your mind wanders, gently return to what you're observing.

This small act of noticing strengthens the muscle of mindfulness. The more you practice, the easier it becomes to redirect your attention toward what truly matters.

When you learn to pay attention—with patience, curiosity, and kindness—you begin to see your life more clearly. You stop moving through it on autopilot and start engaging with it fully. Paying attention is more than awareness—it's a declaration of presence, a quiet promise to live awake.

Observe Before Acting

*"Watch your thoughts, they become your words;
watch your words, they become your actions..."*
— LAO TZU

Paying attention and observing before acting may sound alike, but there's an important difference. *Paying attention* is awareness—it's the art of noticing what's happening within and around you. *Observing before acting* takes that awareness one step further. It's the practice of pausing, reflecting, and choosing a response that aligns with your highest self, rather than reacting from impulse or emotion.

When you pay attention, you awaken to the present moment. But when you observe before acting, you apply that awareness in real time. You become the witness of your own life—the calm eye at the center of the storm. Instead of being swept up by circumstance, you make choices with intention and grace.

Think of observation as the bridge between awareness and wisdom. It allows you to notice your thoughts, feelings, and surroundings, and then ask, *"What is truly needed here?"* That question creates space—space for discernment, kindness, and clarity.

Mindfulness Practice: The Sound of Presence

Try this simple experiment.

The next time your phone "dings"—maybe it's a text, an email, or a social media notification—pause before you reach for it. Don't move right away. Just notice. Observe what's happening in your body. Do your shoulders tense slightly? Does your breath quicken? Is there an anxious urge to *check it now*? That subtle pull—that almost magnetic compulsion—is your habit mind at work.

Now, take one slow, mindful breath. Feel your lungs expand and soften on your exhale. Ask yourself:

What am I feeling right now?

Is this notification truly urgent, or just familiar?

What is my intention if I choose to respond?

Simply observe these questions for a few moments before acting. You might notice that the sense of urgency begins to fade. You might even decide not to pick up your phone at all. This short pause creates a powerful moment of mindfulness. You've moved from automatic reaction to conscious choice.

This small act of observing before reacting gives you space to choose your next step with awareness rather than impulse. You may find that by waiting to respond, you preserve your focus on what really matters, and ultimately respond to the messages with better timing and more clarity and kindness.

This same practice can be applied anywhere: before replying to a heated message, making a big purchase, or speaking in frustration. Each time you pause to observe before acting, you strengthen your ability to stay centered and calm.

Modern life trains us to react instantly. Every ping, buzz, and vibration pulls at our attention, teaching the brain to prioritize speed over presence. But by observing before acting—even in something as ordinary as checking a phone—you interrupt that automatic loop and act with more mindfulness.

Scientific Support for Observation

Neuroscience supports the simple but profound practice of pausing before reacting. When you observe before acting, you engage the prefrontal cortex—the reasoning center of your brain—before the amygdala can take over. In this small but significant space between stimulus and response, mindfulness lives. As Viktor Frankl wisely said, *"In that space lies our power to choose our response. In our response lies our growth and our freedom."*

The more you practice observing before acting, the more natural it becomes. You'll begin to notice subtle shifts like less reactivity, more patience, and deeper understanding. Life begins to feel less like a series of reactions and more like a conscious creation.

When you observe before you act, you align with mindfulness in motion: awareness first, action second, peace always.

Gratitude

*"The miracle of gratitude is that it shifts your
perception to see what is already here."*
— THICH NHAT HANH

Blessings come in all shapes and sizes. Sometimes they arrive like fireworks—brilliant, loud, impossible to miss. Other times, they slip in quietly, disguised as ordinary moments: a stranger's smile, the smell of coffee in the morning, sunlight dancing on the wall. The secret to noticing them lies not in chasing big miracles, but in *recognizing* the small ones that are already here.

That's where mindfulness and gratitude intertwine. Mindfulness helps us slow down enough to see the gifts life continuously offers. Gratitude, in turn, transforms that awareness into appreciation—a softening of the heart that says, "I see this, and I am thankful." Together, they create a powerful loop of presence and peace.

Being grateful is not always easy, of course. When you're racing to meet deadlines, juggling family needs, or managing the constant noise of the world, gratitude can feel like a luxury you don't have time for. Add emotional or physical pain to the mix, and it can seem almost impossible to find anything worth celebrating. Yet it's often during those challenging seasons that gratitude offers the deepest healing.

Gratitude doesn't erase pain or pretend that hardship isn't real—it gently reminds you that life holds beauty *alongside* difficulty. Mindfulness allows you to hold both truths at once. You can acknowledge your struggles and still notice the taste of your tea, the softness of your sheets, or the sound of laughter in another room. These small recognitions become lifelines that pull you back to the richness of the present moment.

The Practice of Noticing

If you'd like to cultivate mindfulness through gratitude, simply start *noticing.* Each day, pause and name three things that make you feel thankful. They don't have to be grand or profound—just real. Maybe it's the way your pet greets you at the door, or how the air smells after rain. Maybe it's the text from a friend that arrived at just the right moment. The point isn't to collect impressive blessings, but to wake up to the ones that already surround you.

To deepen this practice, consider keeping a **gratitude journal.** It doesn't need to be fancy, just dedicate your book to "everything gratitude." A spiral notebook works just fine or you can choose something more special, like a leather-bound diary. What matters most though, is consistency and sincerity. Write three to five things you're grateful for each day. On abundant days, you might fill the page; on harder days, you might struggle to write even one. That's okay. When all else fails, you can always be grateful for your breath, your five senses, and your ability to read—this book included. Some of the most powerful moments of gratitude come when we're willing to look for light in the dark.

As you write, include how these moments make you feel. Does your heart lift when you recall your child's laughter? Do your shoulders relax as you think about your cozy home or a warm meal? Noticing the physical sensations of gratitude—softening, smiling, warmth—anchors you in the present moment. This embodiment is mindfulness in motion. You're not just thinking about gratitude; you're *experiencing* it.

A Moment of Reflection

Try this simple mindfulness exercise in gratitude:

Close your eyes. Take a slow, steady breath in through your nose and exhale gently through your mouth. Bring to mind one thing—just one—that you feel thankful for right now. It might be something as small as the air filling your lungs or the feel of your clothes against your skin. Picture it clearly.

Notice what happens in your body as you focus on that feeling. Does your breath deepen? Do you sense warmth in your chest? Can you feel your facial muscles relax?

Let that gratitude expand for a few breaths, and silently repeat: *Thank you. Thank you. Thank you.*

Open your eyes. You've paused long enough to truly experience appreciation—not as an idea, but as a living, breathing energy. That is mindfulness at work.

Gratitude Ripple

As you continue your gratitude practice, you'll start to notice subtle but profound changes. Colors may seem brighter. Conversations feel richer. You begin to respond to life with more patience and compassion for yourself and others. Gratitude opens the heart and shifts perspective—it reminds you that even in moments of struggle, something good can always be found.

When you end your day by counting blessings instead of burdens, you train your mind to see that everything has a blessing. Keep your gratitude journal by your bedside and let it become a nightly ritual of peace. Let it be a gentle closing to your day, a mindful way to rest your spirit. Because when you live with gratitude, every moment becomes a gift. In that awareness, you'll find the inner peace you've been seeking all along.

Visualization

*"Everything is created twice: first in the
mind and then in reality."*
— ROBIN SHARMA

Have you ever closed your eyes and pictured a peaceful place—a forest glade, a gentle stream, or an open sky? That moment of seeing something in your mind before it exists in the outside world is the essence of visualization. In mindfulness, visualization is more than daydreaming. It's the deliberate act of using your imagination to support your presence, calm, and clarity. It links paying attention to life as it is with shaping the life you choose.

In previous chapters, we practiced paying attention—to body sensations, thoughts, and surroundings—and we learned to observe before acting. Visualization flows naturally from that foundation. First, you notice (pay attention). Then you reflect and respond (observe before acting). With visualization, you create from that space: you use your inner stillness to see possibilities and then carry them into your reality.

Here's how it works: Your brain doesn't always distinguish between what is vividly imagined and what is physically real. Studies in meditation research show that visualization activates many of the same neural pathways as actual experience. When you imagine deeply, your nervous system begins to respond as though you were living that experience. The key is attention: By focusing your mind on a richly detailed, feeling-based visualization, you bring mindfulness into motion.

Consider a personal example: I began offering larger retreats many years ago, and I found myself feeling anxious and wondering if I was good enough to teach so many people. When these worries would come up, I would stop myself and take a few breaths. I'd spend five minutes or so, visualizing my students arriving and settling in. I pictured the room, my greeting, the feel of open minds, wanting to learn. I sensed my effortless breathing, the smiles of my students, the soft light on the windows. What I found was the more I visualized, the more often the actual experience matched what I had seen in my mind. It felt like magic, but it was actually a shift in my nervous system. I had rehearsed calm, presence, and connection in my mind first, so my body followed.

Visualization also becomes a mindful tool when you simply imagine bringing presence into routine tasks. For instance, before meeting someone you know you'll talk to about a difficult subject, you might close your eyes and envision yourself breathing steadily, smiling softly, listening fully. You're not controlling the outcome—you're aligning your state. Then, when the conversation begins, you're already rooted in mindfulness.

Try this simple visualization practice:

- Sit comfortably and close your eyes. Take three
  mindful breaths.

- Visualize a moment of calm in your future (later today,
  this week, or this month). See the environment, sense the
  sensations: how you feel, how you move, how you speak.

- Hold the scene for thirty to sixty seconds. Notice colors,
  sounds, textures, smells. Let it feel real.

- Open your eyes. Ask yourself, *"How can I bring a piece of that
  calm into the next moment I experience?"*

- Finally, take one small action toward that vision right now.
  Smile, take a deep, relaxing breath, or affirm to yourself, in
  the words of Esther Hicks and Abraham, that *"Everything is
  always working out for me."*

By doing this regularly, you build a blueprint in your mind for presence and peace. Your nervous system begins to recognize that blueprint and begins to behave as though you are already living it. This is what turns mindfulness into a habit, and habit into presence.

The next time you sit quietly, close your eyes and let your inner screen light up. Picture the peace you wish to be. See the person you wish to become. Sense the life you long for. Then, with that vision alive inside you, step back into the world feeling grounded with a happy heart and a peaceful mind.

When you can see inner peace clearly, you more easily live it. And that is the art of mindful visualization.

Pet Pets

*"Until one has loved an animal, a part
of one's soul remains unawakened."*
— ANATOLE FRANCE

I f you've ever had a cat curl up in your lap or a dog rest its head on your knee, you already know something profound about mindfulness even though you may not have realized it. The simple act of petting a beloved animal has the power to ground you in the present moment. It soothes not only the animal but also your nervous system. With each gentle stroke, something inside you softens. You become still. You become aware of the present moment.

Petting your pet isn't just a habit or a passing pleasure, it's a shared language of love and trust. The soft fur beneath your fingers, the rhythmic purr of a cat, or the contented sigh of a dog—all of it invites your attention into the now. Science supports what pet lovers have always known instinctively: spending time with animals lowers blood pressure, reduces stress hormones, and increases serotonin and oxytocin—the "feel-good" chemicals that promote bonding and peace.

Beyond the science, however, lies a more subtle truth. When you pause to pet your animal companion with full awareness, you're not only nurturing them, you're nurturing your own spirit. You're giving yourself permission to *just be*.

Imagine this: You're working at your desk, caught up in a flurry of deadlines, when your cat—let's call her Jasmine—leaps into your lap, demanding attention. Your first instinct might be irritation. You're busy. You don't have time for this. But instead of pushing her away, you take a breath. You notice the warmth of her fur, the way she tilts her head into your hand as you rub behind her ears. Within seconds, you hear that gentle purr, steady and deep. Her body relaxes—and so does yours.

Notice what's happening within you. Your breathing slows. The tension in your shoulders eases. The swirl of thoughts in your mind settles into quiet focus. You are fully present—with her, with yourself, with this moment. That is mindfulness in action.

Maybe you're more of a dog lover and Bruno, your loyal basset hound, greets you every evening with a wagging tail and eyes full of devotion. As you kneel to scratch behind his ears, he flops onto his back, exposing his belly in complete trust. In that moment, you realize you're smiling—a genuine, effortless smile. The stresses of your day begin to fade and nothing else matters in that moment except for petting Bruno. This is the healing power of connection.

Even if you don't have a pet of your own, you can still experience this form of mindful connection. Perhaps it's a neighbor's friendly golden retriever who trots over for a pat, or a cat that brushes against your leg as you sit in the garden. These moments, brief as they are, offer a reminder that kindness doesn't have to be grand to be meaningful. Simply being present with another living creature opens the door to compassion—for them, and for yourself.

Next time you find yourself near an animal, treat it as an invitation to practice mindfulness. Before reaching out, take a breath. Notice your surroundings—the air, the sounds, the texture of the animal's fur beneath your hand. Observe how your body responds. Does your chest feel lighter? Does a sense of calm wash over you? Are you smiling? That awareness is your anchor to the present.

Through mindful touch, learn to listen—not with your ears, but with your heart. Notice how animals seem to sense your mood and adjust their behavior to match it. They mirror your energy, teaching you the profound simplicity of being fully present.

Petting pets, then, is far more than an act of affection. It is a shared meditation, a wordless exchange of trust and peace. It is a reminder that mindfulness isn't always found in stillness or solitude—it's often discovered in the quiet companionship of a furry friend, breathing softly beside you, inviting you to return—again and again—to this beautiful, peaceful moment.

Greet a Stranger

*"A simple smile. That's the start of opening your heart
and being compassionate to others."*
— THE DALAI LAMA

Imagine you're walking down the street on a quiet afternoon. The air is crisp, the rhythm of your footsteps steady against the pavement. Up ahead, a woman walks toward you—her arms folded, her gaze fixed on the ground. There's a heaviness about her, as though her thoughts weigh more than the bag on her shoulder. You notice, without judgment, that she seems lost in her own world.

In that small space between you, you make a decision. "Hello," you say, your voice gentle but clear.

She looks up, startled for a moment. Her eyes meet yours, and a smile flickers across her face. "Hi," she replies softly as the two of you pass.

And just like that—something shifts.

You feel a flutter of warmth in your chest, a quickening of the heart that has nothing to do with exertion. It's connection—pure and simple. The kind that doesn't require words or history. It's the exchange of presence between two human beings sharing the same moment. You may never see her again, but for that brief instant, you both existed together in awareness.

That is mindfulness.

Greeting a stranger is more than a polite gesture, it's an exercise in presence and compassion. It's the act of stepping out of your internal monologue and acknowledging another soul in the world. You're saying, "I see you. You exist. You matter." In doing so, you momentarily dissolve the invisible walls that separate us.

The physical sensations that follow such a small interaction can be surprisingly powerful. Maybe you notice a lift in your step or the corners of your mouth lifting into an unplanned smile. Perhaps there's a spark of joy that lingers as you continue down the street. These are your body's ways of reminding you that connection—however brief—is healing.

When you greet someone, you are consciously choosing awareness over autopilot. You're interrupting the momentum of thought, stress, and self-absorption that often clouds the present moment. That small "hello" is a mindful act that grounds you in now—the only place where peace truly exists.

Try this simple experiment:

The next time you're out walking, greet every person you pass. Offer a smile, a nod, or a quiet "good morning." Don't do it for approval or validation—do it for awareness. Notice the energy exchange between you and each person. How does it feel when someone smiles back? What happens when they don't? Do you feel disappointment, pride, amusement, or neutrality?

Observe your thoughts as they arise. Perhaps you notice yourself inventing little stories—assuming why someone didn't respond, or wondering what kind of day they're having. This is an opportunity to practice nonjudgmental observation. The goal isn't to analyze the stranger's behavior, but to become more aware of your own reactions.

When your walk is done, pause for a moment of reflection. Ask yourself three simple questions:

1. What am I thinking right now?

2. How does my body feel?

3. What emotions am I experiencing?

You may wish to jot down your answers in a journal. Writing helps bring clarity and invites a deeper understanding of your experience.

What you'll often discover is that greeting strangers doesn't just brighten their day—it awakens something within you. It softens your perspective, dissolves loneliness, and reminds you that kindness, at its core, is mindful action.

In those fleeting connections—those shared smiles and gentle acknowledgments—meet the present moment face-to-face. Find yourself reflected in others, and others reflected in you. Perhaps, in greeting a stranger, you come home to yourself.

Telephone

It's astonishing how easily we can drift through the day without ever truly being *here*. One moment, we're replaying an awkward conversation from yesterday; the next, we're worrying about tomorrow's to-do list. Before we know it, hours slip away in a haze of thoughts that pull us out of the present moment. The truth is, peace and clarity are always available—but we forget to pause long enough to find them.

That's why mindfulness teachers throughout the ages have used sound as an anchor for awareness. A single bell can pull the mind out of distraction and back into stillness. In our modern world, however, we have our own kind of bell: the telephone.

You might not immediately think of your phone as a mindfulness tool—after all, it's often the very thing that scatters our attention. But what if, instead of reacting automatically to its ring or chime, you used it as a cue to stop, breathe, and return to the present moment?

Imagine this:

You're in the middle of typing an email or thinking about your grocery list when suddenly, *ring!* The sound pierces your concentration and scatters your focus. Normally, you'd grab your phone without thinking, already anticipating the conversation ahead. But instead, today you pause.

You take one slow, conscious breath, feeling the rise and fall of your chest. You notice your body sitting in the chair. You hear the ring as if for the first time—a clear, awakening sound that pulls you right into the now.

This simple act transforms an ordinary interruption into a moment of mindfulness.

If the idea of using your phone feels too tied to stress or urgency, not to worry. Feel free to use any kind of sound as your bell. A gentle sound on your watch, a chime from a mindfulness app, or even the hum of a passing airplane or church bell in the distance will work perfectly. The goal is the same: to create a habit of awareness whenever a certain sound appears.

When you hear your chosen sound, take it as an invitation to "check in" with yourself. Ask gently:

- What am I thinking right now?

- How does my body feel?

- What emotion is guiding me in this moment?

You might notice that your shoulders are tense, or your jaw is tight. Maybe your stomach growls, reminding you it's time to eat. Perhaps you realize your mind has been looping through the same worrisome thought for the past ten minutes. Each of these realizations is a gift— the sound has brought you home to yourself.

Let's say your phone rings again. *Ring!* You stop and breathe. You feel your feet on the floor. You notice your mood. Then, with full awareness, you answer the call. The tone of your voice is calmer and your words are kinder. That single mindful breath before speaking has shifted the energy of the entire conversation.

Mindfulness Bell

Choose a sound from your daily environment to become your "mindfulness bell." It might be your phone's ring, a text notification, the ding of your oven timer, or the distant sound of a train. Each time you hear it, stop whatever you're doing—just for one breath.

Acknowledge the sound. Inhale deeply, exhale slowly, and silently say to yourself, *I am here.* This brief pause brings your mind and body together in the same moment. With every ring, chime, or bell, you can strengthen your connection to presence—and to peace.

Over time, these micro-moments of awareness accumulate. The more you use these auditory cues to bring yourself back to the present, the more naturally mindfulness becomes part of your life. As you begin to respond to challenges instead of reacting to them, you may find yourself calmer, more centered, and more in tune with the world around you.

Soon, you won't need to wait for the phone to ring. The awareness will be internal—arising like a bell from within—calling you back, again and again, to the stillness that has always been there.

The next time you hear that familiar ring, let it remind you:

Breathe.

Smile.

You are here, in this moment.

And that's exactly where peace lives.

Watch Clouds

*"Rest is not idleness, and to lie sometimes on the grass
under the trees on a summer's day, watching the clouds float across
the sky, is by no means a waste of time."*
— JOHN LUBBOCK

When was the last time you let yourself simply *look up?* Not to check the weather or glance at a plane—but to really look—to notice the slow parade of clouds drifting across the sky, forming and dissolving in a rhythm of their own.

You might remember lying in the grass, pointing out shapes to a friend — "That one looks like a dragon!" or "I see a bunny!" Time seemed endless, your mind unburdened.

As a child, this was second nature for me. I would lay in the grass for hours watching those puffy fluff balls float across the sky. I would imagine they formed everything from genie bottles to frogs, and feathers, and everything my imagination could conceive. I watched the clouds continually morph into image after image until they dissipated all together. I was completely present, held in the gentle wonder of the moment. That, in essence, is mindfulness: awareness without effort, attention without agenda.

Cloud watching invites that same quiet wonder back into our lives. It's an effortless meditation that reconnects us to stillness through the beauty of impermanence. Clouds are constantly changing, just like thoughts and emotions. Some float by lightly, others gather and darken—but none stay forever. By observing them without attachment, we begin to understand our own mind more clearly.

Imagine this: You're sitting outside on a warm afternoon. You stretch out, maybe on a patch of soft grass or a bench in the park, and tilt your gaze skyward. Feel the ground beneath you. Take a slow breath. Let your eyes trace the movement of one cloud as it drifts lazily across the blue expanse. Notice how it changes shape, how sunlight and shadow play across its surface.

In that moment, your body softens. The tension in your shoulders releases. Your thoughts, once racing, begin to slow. You realize the cloud doesn't hurry—it simply moves with the wind. It doesn't push nor resist. It just exists. Without effort, like the cloud, you begin to do the same.

I still take the time on a regular basis to look up and observe the clouds dancing in the sky. Especially, when I feel stumped for a creative idea, I give myself permission to go outside and watch the clouds come and go. This relaxing pastime helps me to release frustrating or anxious thoughts for the time being and enjoy the clarity of the here and now. Often, by giving myself a few moments to change my focus, I am able to return to my tasks with a broader perspective and calmer viewpoint.

Watching clouds teaches us to let go, to understand that life, like the sky, is always shifting. Worries pass. Emotions change form. Nothing is permanent except for that eternal peace within us all.

The next time you feel weighed down, look up. Give yourself a few minutes to be with the sky. Watch clouds. Breathe deeply. Remind yourself: I, too, can let go. I, too, can flow.

Feel the Breeze on Your Skin

As a child, I believed the wind had moods. Growing up in the ever-breezy state of New Mexico, I got to know its many temperaments intimately. When the branches began to sway and the air danced across my face, I'd close my eyes and try to guess what kind of day the wind was having.

On soft days, the breeze would make me feel loved and lull me into a peaceful stupor. On fierce days, when the wind was strong and cold, I would turn my head to sidestep its punishing blows. In those moments, it felt as if I was defending myself against a bully!

I much preferred the softer breezes to the ferocious gales, but in each experience of the wind, I was present, feeling the tangible effects of Mother Nature. I didn't know it at the time, but those moments were lessons in mindfulness. I was learning how to notice what is, rather than wishing it were different.

The wind is a perfect teacher because, though invisible, it cannot be ignored. You can't see it, but you can *feel* it—on your skin, in your hair, in the way it moves through the trees or ripples across water. Whether a gentle zephyr or a roaring gust, it demands attention. That attention—the act of feeling and responding consciously—is mindfulness.

Mindfulness begins with awareness, and few experiences anchor us more firmly in the body than the sensation of touch. Feeling the wind on our skin draws us out of our head and back into our physical presence. It's impossible to dwell on yesterday's worries or tomorrow's to-do list when our senses are alive to the air brushing against us in the present moment.

The next time you're outside, take a mindful pause. Stop walking, close your eyes if you can, and let the wind find you. Notice how it greets you. Is it warm and inviting or brisk and invigorating? Does it make you lean into it or turn away? Observe without judgment and let your body respond naturally—adjusting your stance, deepening your breath, relaxing your shoulders.

Even a few seconds of awareness can reset your entire nervous system. No longer lost in thought, be in the world, breathing with it and feeling its energy move through you.

When the next breeze touches your skin, let it remind you that you're alive, grounded, and connected to something far larger than yourself.

Listen to Crickets

> *"Listen to the crickets and you will hear the rhythm of your own soul."*
> — HENRY DAVID THOREAU

Every summer I look forward to the warm, balmy evenings and the sounds of the crickets. Many nights find me sitting on the porch, taking in the evening air and listening to the cricket choruses chirping from somewhere out in the darkness. Especially after a full day of business and distractions, this evening opportunity to sit in mindful contemplation is a gift. Listening to the crickets helps me to let go of the day's activities and experience the present moment with comfort and awareness. In these moments, I have time to visit with myself and process the thoughts and feelings I've accumulated from the day. Listening to these musical creatures is a perfect opportunity for me to acknowledge my own needs and desires.

Crickets are nature's metronomes, keeping time for the world when everything else quiets down. Their chirping, often overlooked as background noise, becomes something magical when you truly listen. Each note, each pause, carries an invitation: *Be still. Pay attention. Listen.*

When I close my eyes and focus on their song, I notice how my breathing begins to synchronize with the rhythm. My body relaxes, my thoughts slow, and a quiet awareness emerges. I become fully present—no longer tangled in the conversations, tasks, or worries of the day. The crickets remind me that peace is always available; I just have to tune in.

If crickets aren't part of your local symphony, you can practice this same mindful listening with any ambient sound. The hum of your refrigerator, the ticking of a clock, the distant murmur of traffic—all can become mindfulness bells if you allow them. The goal isn't to judge or label what you hear, but simply to listen *deeply.*

Try this simple exercise:

Wherever you are, pause for a moment. Close your eyes and take a few slow breaths. Let your awareness expand outward, catching every sound around you. Perhaps you hear the soft whoosh of air through a vent, the faint buzz of electricity, or the shuffle of your own breath. Now, choose one sound that stands out. Follow it with your full attention. Notice its rhythm, tone, and texture. Does it remain steady or change with time? How does your body respond to it?

After a minute or two, open your eyes and stay with the same sound. Does it feel different now that you've identified it? What shifted in your perception—or in you?

This small act of mindful listening helps to strengthen one of the most essential aspects of mindfulness: awareness without judgment. As you become more attuned to the sounds in your outer world, you also begin to recognize the internal, quiet hum of your thoughts, emotions, and intuitions. You may notice which inner "voices" are restless and which are calm, which are loving and which are critical.

Listening to crickets—or to any sound in the stillness—becomes a metaphor for listening to your inner life. It teaches patience, presence, and acceptance. In the same way that the crickets' chorus rises and falls, your thoughts will come and go. You don't have to chase or silence them. You only need to listen.

So, when the evening settles and the world grows quiet, step outside and listen to the crickets sing. Let their simple symphony remind you that peace is not something you have to create. It's already here—chirping softly in the background, waiting for you to notice.

Befriend Nature

*"Look deep into nature, and then you will
understand everything better."*
— ALBERT EINSTEIN

I love spending time in nature. Whether I'm hiking though the misty Highlands of Scotland, walking along the white sand shores of the Gulf Coast, floating in the bluest waters of the Mediterranean, or gardening in my own backyard, the healing touch of the earth grounds and rejuvenates me. Within minutes after stepping outside, the rhythm of the natural world steadies my breath, clears my mind, and brings me back to the peace of the present moment.

The beauty of the outdoors lies in its simplicity. We don't need to travel far or plan anything elaborate to connect with it—we just have to notice it. The warmth of the sun, the scent of freshly cut grass, the sight of a hummingbird darting toward a blossom, or the way a dove coos softly at sunrise—all of these small, sensory moments invite us into mindfulness. Each sound, texture, and scent gently draws our attention away from worry or distraction and back toward awareness.

At its core, mindfulness is the practice of being fully present and open to what is happening in the moment. Nature's quiet brilliance, gives us endless opportunities to do exactly that. When we listen closely to birdsong, trace the veins of a leaf, or feel the bark of a tree beneath our fingertips, we are practicing presence. These experiences require nothing more than attention—no judgment, no agenda—just the willingness to be aware of what is before us.

Science confirms what humans instinctively know. Nature has the power to heal and restore. From our ancient ancestors using herbs and plants as remedies, to modern research showing that spending even small amounts of time outdoors—especially in green or blue spaces—can reduce stress, ease loneliness, and lift one's mood. Being in nature also sharpens focus and creativity, improves memory, and even increases feelings of connection and compassion. In essence, the calm, balanced state that mindfulness creates within us is mirrored in the natural world around us.

There are countless ways to befriend nature and practice mindfulness. You might find it while skiing down a mountain, feeling the cold air brush your cheeks and hearing the whoosh of snow beneath your skis. Maybe it comes from kneeling in your garden, hands deep in the soil as you plant new seeds. One activity is filled with motion, the other with stillness, but both are alive with awareness. In those moments, your senses awaken, your mind quiets, and you become part of something larger than yourself.

Let Nature Find You

This simple exercise can be done several times a day:

Step outside—or open a window—and pause. Don't look for anything in particular; let something in nature catch your attention. Maybe it's birdsong, a drifting leaf, or the warmth of sunlight on your hand.

Give it your full attention for one minute. Notice its color, motion, texture, sound. Check in with your breath. Does it naturally fall into rhythm with what you're observing?

Ask yourself: *What is this moment teaching me about being alive?* Then let it go and smile. The lesson is already within you.

Nature also reminds us that change is natural and necessary. Trees shed their leaves without resistance. Flowers bloom and fade without regret. Rivers shift and flow, finding new paths when obstacles appear. Observing these rhythms teaches us to do the same—to accept life's seasons with grace and to trust that renewal always follows loss.

When we befriend nature, we enter into a quiet partnership with the living world. Each mindful step we take outdoors becomes an act of respect, each deep breath a silent thank-you. As we listen to the wind through the trees or feel the soil beneath our hands, we begin to remember that we are not separate from the Earth—we are part of its rhythm, its pulse, its unfolding life. Mindfulness helps us see this truth clearly. It softens our habits of taking and replaces them with gratitude and care. When we walk lightly, consume thoughtfully, and honor the beauty around us, we give back to the planet that gives us everything. In this exchange—simple, sincere, and ongoing—we rediscover balance, belonging, and peace.

Journal

"Writing is the painting of the voice."
— VOLTAIRE

Before we dive deeper into this chapter, let's clarify something simple but important: a *journal* and a *diary* are not all that different. While a diary might capture daily events and a journal leans more toward reflection and insight, both are sacred spaces where our inner world meets the page. Here, I'll use the words interchangeably, because whether you call it journaling or diary writing, the essence is the same—it's a conversation with yourself.

"Are You There God? It's Me, Margaret" by Judy Blume is one of the most beloved coming-of-age novels highlighting a young girl's use of her diary to help her make sense of the rapid changes occurring in her young life. In the novel, Margaret writes messages to God in her diary, hoping to make sense of the confusion growing up caused her.

Just like Margaret, I was one of those little girls who filled numerous diaries (as I called them then), writing pages and pages of my hopes, dreams, fears, ideas, and even questions about the nature of life. There were certain things I couldn't share with my parents or friends, so I wrote them in my diary. If I had embarrassing questions, they went in my diary. When boys entered the picture, they too, were placed in my diary. Channelling all those words onto paper was cathartic. It was a safe space, a friend who never judged and always listened. Writing in it helped me untangle my thoughts and see them more clearly, almost like holding up a mirror to my own heart.

As adults, journaling still offers that same refuge. It's a mindful practice that helps us pause, reflect, and make sense of our inner landscape. When we write, we slow down. We shift from reacting to observing—from getting lost in thought to becoming aware of it. Whether you're processing a difficult emotion, expressing gratitude, or simply recording a fleeting idea, journaling invites you into the present moment.

Writing also helps lighten emotional weight. Thoughts that loop endlessly in your mind often lose their grip once they're on paper. Seeing your words laid out before you allows for distance and perspective—you're no longer *inside* the chaos; you're witnessing it. From this mindful distance, understanding begins to unfold.

Your journal can take any form that feels right. Some people write daily reflections, others jot notes of gratitude or letters to their future selves. Some use it to explore dreams, others to pray or connect with a higher power. There are no rules here—just honesty. Your journal is your space to explore without editing and without apology.

Can you recall a time when you were overwhelmed with emotion—so elated, angry, or heartbroken that you had to write just to make sense of it all? As your pen moved, did you notice your body relax and your breath deepen? Mindfulness is forming through writing. You were not just *thinking* about your feelings—you were *being with* them, acknowledging them without judgment.

Each time you journal, you cultivate awareness. Revisiting the past through the lens of the present, you are able to see how far you've come, what still lingers, and what you're ready to release. Journaling helps you learn to witness your thoughts without becoming entangled in them. In this way, it transforms from mere writing into a mindful dialogue—a bridge between who you were, who you are, and who you're becoming.

The page never interrupts, never rushes you, never turns away. It simply holds space. That alone can be deeply mindful. When you write regularly, patterns begin to emerge such as habits of thought, recurring fears, or quiet longings. You start to recognize yourself more fully, and with recognition comes compassion.

Mindful journaling isn't about perfect sentences or profound revelations. It's about showing up with curiosity, honesty, and presence. It's a chance to listen deeply to your own inner voice, to understand what stirs within you, and to respond with awareness rather than reaction.

In a world that moves quickly, your journal becomes a sanctuary—a still point where you can breathe, reflect, and return to yourself. Each word written brings you closer to clarity and peace. Through journaling, mindfulness moves from a concept to a lived experience, one line at a time.

Repeat Mantras

When you hear the word *mantra*, you might imagine monks chanting in temples, their voices rising and falling like waves. Or maybe you think of someone sitting cross-legged, eyes closed, whispering a word like Om over and over again. But the truth is, mantra is for everyone. You don't have to be spiritual, religious, or even experienced in meditation to reap the benefits of mantra. All that is needed is a willingness to listen to your breath, your words, and the subtle vibration of your own mind.

Mantras have been used for thousands of years, first appearing in the Hindu *Vedas*, dating back approximately 1500–1200 BCE. One of the oldest sacred written works in existence, the *Rigveda* is the foundational text of hymns from which mantras originated. The ancient rishis—sages—believed these sounds were not mere words, but living vibrations that could connect the human mind to divine consciousness. Over time, Buddhist monks, Christian mystics, and modern seekers alike have used mantra as a doorway to stillness and inner peace. Specific traditions may differ, but the essence is universal: Words carry energy, and that energy shapes our awareness.

In its simplest form, a mantra is a word, phrase, or sound that focuses the mind, soothes the nervous system, and calms inner chatter. When repeated with awareness—silently or aloud—it becomes a rhythm that steadies your breath and gathers your attention. Over time, the mantra begins to do its quiet work. It softens the edges of restless thinking, loosens the grip of anxiety, and draws you back into the here and now.

If you've ever tried to meditate, you know how the mind resists stillness. You sit down with the best intentions, close your eyes—and suddenly you're replaying yesterday's argument, planning tomorrow's dinner, or wondering if you remembered to feed the dog. The mind, by nature, is a wanderer.

This is where a mantra becomes your anchor. It gives the mind something steady to rest upon, a single point of focus amid the constant tide of thoughts. With regular practice, this simple repetition begins to train the brain to relax into presence. Thoughts still come, but instead of getting swept away, you can watch them drift by, unbothered.

Mantra as Mindfulness

Mantra is a vehicle for mindfulness because it draws your awareness back to the present moment. When you repeat a mantra, you're not escaping your thoughts, you're observing them through a clearer lens. The sound or phrase you repeat becomes a gentle reminder: *I am here. I am present.*

It also helps you listen beneath the surface noise of the mind. You begin to notice patterns—the doubts, the fears, the old stories you tell yourself. When you bring these subconscious habits into the light, you have the power to release them.

For example, imagine someone who has carried a lifelong feeling of unworthiness. This subtle belief shows up in their relationships, their work, and even in their self-talk. If this person begins to use the mantra "I am enough," and repeats it daily, they begin to plant new seeds in their consciousness. At first, it may feel untrue or awkward, but with practice, the vibration of those words starts to dissolve the old mental script. Eventually, the mantra becomes not just a phrase, but a lived truth.

Science Behind Sound

Modern neuroscience supports the ancient wisdom of repetition changing the brain. Each time you repeat a mantra, you strengthen new neural pathways. Studies show that rhythmic sound repetition can reduce heart rate, lower stress hormones, and even improve focus and emotional regulation.

There is also a physical dimension to mantra. The act of humming, chanting, or even silently repeating a sound activates the vagus nerve, affectionately known as the superhighway of the body. The vagus nerve is responsible for numerous involuntary and life-sustaining activities in the body. Also a major component of the parasympathetic nervous system (PSNS), it plays a major role in calming the nervous system. In other words, mantras not only shift the mind; they also soothe the body.

Mantra Practice

Let's make this practical.

Give yourself about five minutes of uninterrupted time. Close your office door, step away from your computer and phone, or take a walk.

Find a quiet place where you won't be disturbed. Take a few slow breaths, in and out through your nose. Feel your shoulders, face, and jaw soften.

On your next exhalation, make the sound "Eeee" for as long as you are breathing out. On the following inhale, sustain "Eeee" silently.

With your next exhalation, make the sound "Eeee" again. Repeat this mantra for three more cycles; inhaling, silently saying "Eeee," and exhaling, verbally repeating "Eeee."

If your mind wanders (and it will), simply return to your mantra without judgment. The mantra is not meant to suppress thought, but is a way of returning back to the present moment each time you drift away.

Now, as you breathe regularly, *silently* sustain "Eeee" on both your inhale and your exhale. Repeat this mantra for three more breath cycles.

Now, release the mantra and let it fade.

Notice your state of mind and how your body is feeling. Do you feel lighter or sense more stillness? Maybe you feel a little more spaciousness between thoughts? That subtle shift is mindfulness.

The sound "Eeee" naturally lifts the corners of your mouth into a smile, creating a subtle shift in your mood and energy. Whether spoken aloud or repeated silently, it echoes the tone of laughter and joy.

Because the sound carries no meaning, the mind feels rather than analyzes—allowing emotion to guide awareness. This direct connection to feeling fosters calm, clarity, and the quiet presence of mindfulness.

Meaningful or Sound-Based Mantras

Some mantras carry specific meanings—like "I am grateful," "I am safe," or "Let go." These affirmations can be powerful when you're working through emotional blocks or trying to cultivate a new mindset.

Other mantras are sound-based, without literal meaning. Sanskrit mantras like *Om, So Hum* ("I am that"), or *Om Shanti* ("Peace") work on a vibrational level, bypassing conscious thought and resonating with your deeper awareness. Even if you don't understand the words, your body and mind respond to their energy.

Experiment with both. Try repeating "I am at peace" for one week and then *Om Shanti* the next. Notice how each affects your mood, your energy, and your focus. The right mantra feels natural and draws you into effortless stillness.

Mantra as Emotional Medicine

Think of mantras as medicine for the mind. Each one carries a certain frequency that can help balance the emotional body. When you feel anxious, try repeating "Calm." When you're restless, repeat "Still." When you're tired or uninspired, whisper "Light." The repetition doesn't have to be perfect however, practicing with sincerity increases the effectiveness. Over time, you may find numerous mantras to support your mindfulness journey.

You might even create your own personal mantra. Make it simple, honest, and meaningful to you—like "I choose peace" or "I am guided." When chosen with awareness and repeated with heart, your mantra becomes a companion—a steady friend who reminds you of who you truly are when life pulls you off center.

Repetition

The more you practice, the more your mantra seeps into everyday life. You may find yourself silently repeating it in traffic, before a difficult conversation, or when you wake in the middle of the night.

Eventually, it becomes part of your inner rhythm—a background hum of calm that anchors you, no matter what's happening around you.

The purpose of repeating mantras is not to escape reality, but to meet it with a steady, peaceful mind. With regular use, the repetition reveals something deeper than words: a quiet presence behind all thought. That is where mindfulness lives—not in effort, but in awareness.

Mantra, more than a practice, is a relationship with your own inner stillness. Each repetition is like dropping a pebble into a still pond, creating small ripples expanding outward, reshaping your inner world. Through the vibration of sound and the constancy of attention, you begin to remember your natural state: calm, clear, connected, and whole.

When the mind grows noisy, return to your mantra. When doubt or fear arises, return to your mantra. When joy surprises you, return to your mantra.

Because the mantra doesn't just calm the mind—it awakens the heart.

Smile

"You're never fully dressed without a smile."
— LUCILLE BALL

I don't know about you, but just thinking about a smile makes my eyes twinkle and turns the corners of my mouth up into a grin. A smile seems like such a simple thing, yet it has the power to change everything from your mood and body chemistry to how you relate to the world around you. In fact, "smile" could easily be considered a mantra in itself: a single word that opens the heart and quiets the mind. (Refer to the previous chapter.)

Smiling is one of the most natural human expressions. Long before we learned to speak, we smiled. Babies smile in their sleep before they ever say their first words. It's an instinctive gesture of safety, connection, and joy. And yet, as adults, we often forget how healing it can be. We save smiles for moments that "deserve" them, not realizing that smiling first can actually create the joy we are waiting for.

Studies have shown that smiling positively affects the nervous system. When you lift the corners of your mouth and let your eyes soften, your brain releases a cascade of neurotransmitters—endorphins, dopamine, serotonin, and oxytocin. These "feel good" chemicals are your body's natural trigger for happiness, calm, and connection. They help slow the heart rate, lower blood pressure, and relax your muscles. Smiling, quite literally, tells your nervous system that it's safe to rest.

These "feel-good" chemicals belong to the parasympathetic nervous system (PSNS)—the part of your body responsible for relaxation and restoration. This is the same system that counterbalances your *fight-or-flight* response. When life feels chaotic, stressful, or overwhelming, smiling acts as a switch that turns off the internal alarm—reducing blood pressure and heart rate—and invites you back into calm awareness. Even when your smile feels a little forced, your brain doesn't know the difference. The muscles still send the same signals, and your body still responds with relaxation.

You might think of smiling as mindfulness made visible. It draws your attention to the present moment, connecting your body and mind in calm awareness. When you smile with intention, you're quietly acknowledging, *"I'm here, and this moment is enough."*

Smiling doesn't mean denying pain or pretending that everything is perfect. It's not about covering up sadness or forcing positivity. Instead, it's an invitation to soften. To open. To remember that beneath every challenge, there's a steady current of peace that never leaves you. A smile helps you touch that current. It's a bridge between your inner stillness and the outer world.

Think about the last time someone smiled at you—really smiled, with warmth and sincerity. Didn't it shift something inside you? Even a brief smile can communicate compassion and presence without a single word. When you share a smile, you're offering the world a moment of connection, and that exchange amplifies mindfulness—for both of you.

Try this simple practice the next time you feel anxious or tense:

Breathe normally and turn your lips into a gentle smile. Feel the subtle changes in your face. Notice if your shoulders relax, or if your breath deepens. Let that feeling spread through your body. You don't need to think your way into calmness—the smile will do the work for you.

Let's take this smiling practice a step further. Look into a mirror and smile at yourself. It may feel silly at first—good. Stay with it. Keep smiling. Notice not only the physical sensations, but any shifts in your mood or mindset. Do you feel a little lighter and a bit more open and playful?

Smiling can interrupt negative spirals and soften the tension around difficult moments. It's a simple gesture with real power. And bonus: smiling could just help you make a new friend, and that friend could be you.

So, the next time you catch yourself tightening your jaw or furrowing your brow, pause. Take a slow, deep breath and smile, not because everything is perfect, but because you're choosing to meet the moment with awareness. You are here. That alone is something to smile about.

Random Acts
of Kindness

"Kindness is my religion."
— THE DALAI LAMA

Random acts of kindness may seem like a modern trend, but the movement has deep roots. In 1982, Author and Activist Anne Herbert scribbled a simple line on a restaurant placemat: *"Practice random acts of kindness and acts of senseless beauty."* That small spark ignited a global shift in how we think about generosity, eventually inspiring her 1993 book and later the Random Acts of Kindness Foundation in 1995. What began as a simple invitation— to be kind without needing a reason—has grown into a worldwide reminder that the smallest gestures can have the greatest impact.

Beyond the obvious social and emotional benefits, however, random acts of kindness offer something many people overlook: they are powerful pathways to mindfulness.

Mindfulness is, at its core, the practice of being fully present— awake to our thoughts, aware of our emotions, and engaged with our surroundings in real time. Kindness naturally supports this state, because every act of genuine goodwill requires awareness. We have to notice someone's need, observe the moment, and respond consciously rather than drifting through life on autopilot. Kindness wakes us up.

Think of the last time you held the door for a parent juggling a toddler and groceries, or paid for the person behind you in line. Even before the action, there was a flicker of recognition—*I can help here.* That moment of noticing is mindfulness. And once the act is

"

complete, something inside you shifts. Your chest feels lighter. Your breath deepens. You walk away feeling more connected to the world around you.

Random Acts of Kindness and Biology

Kindness isn't just anecdotal—it's biological. Research from the University of British Columbia shows that performing acts of kindness boosts levels of serotonin, the neurotransmitter responsible for feelings of well-being and satisfaction. Another found that people who engaged in daily acts of kindness reported reduced stress and improved mood (Amit Kumar, 2022). Kindness activates the parasympathetic nervous system—your body's "rest and digest" mode—encouraging emotional balance and mental clarity. In other words, kindness physically brings you into a more mindful state.

Here's something even more remarkable: Kindness is contagious. Scientists at the University of California, San Diego, discovered that generosity can spread through social networks up to three degrees of separation (James Fowler & Nicholas Christakis, 2010). If you hold the door for one person, that person is more likely to help someone else—and so on. Even observers who witness kindness, without participating in it, experience what researchers call the *"moral elevation effect,"* a warm, inspired feeling that increases their likelihood of acting kindly too. Your mindfulness can awaken mindfulness in others.

There are endless ways to bring kindness into your daily life. Here are just a few to inspire you:

- Compliment someone—genuinely.
- Let another driver merge without hesitation.
- Send a text to someone who's been on your mind.
- Pick up litter during your walk.
- Welcome a new co-worker or neighbor.
- Call your parents and/or grandparents to tell them you love them.
- Pay for the person behind you at the café.
- Leave a positive note on a colleague's desk.

- Donate to a charity or to someone down on their luck.
- Offer to pick up groceries for an elderly neighbor.
- Smile at a stranger.
- Share a joke to lighten someone's day.
- Help a stray dog or cat find a forever home.
- Say "thank you."

Each one, no matter how small, shifts your attention outward in a meaningful way. You pause, you notice, you act—and in doing so, you align yourself with the present moment. Kindness doesn't require money, time, or a grand gesture. It simply asks you to look up from your own concerns long enough to recognize that you are part of a shared human experience.

Try offering one small act of kindness today. Feel the way your body responds. Notice the openness it creates. Let it pull you gently into mindfulness and remember: every time you choose kindness, you make the world—and yourself—a little more peaceful.

Loving-Kindness Practice

Loving-kindness, otherwise known as Metta, is the simple yet radical practice of directing goodwill toward yourself and others. In Buddhist tradition, it is described as a boundless, unconditional warmth, extended without expectation. In modern mindfulness, it has become one of the most accessible tools for transforming how we relate to our own inner experience and to the world around us.

The practice seems gentle, but don't mistake gentleness for weakness. Loving-kindness is one of the most powerful forms of mental training available. Studies from researchers like Barbara Fredrickson at the University of North Carolina have shown that cultivating positive emotions through practices like Metta can increase resilience, strengthen social connection, and even improve physical well-being (Fredrickson, 2008). In other words, kindness literally reshapes the mind toward flourishing.

In her book, *Lovingkindness: The Revolutionary Art of Happiness*, Sharon Salzberg describes the journey of Metta as unfolding in stages, each one gradually widening the circle of compassion. Begin with the person you are most likely to forget: yourself.

Stage One: Offering Kindness Within

May I be happy.
May I be peaceful.
May I be healthy.

It may feel awkward at first to offer these statements to yourself. Many of us are accustomed to pushing ourselves, judging ourselves, or rushing past our own needs. Speaking to yourself with love may feel unfamiliar, but stay with it. As you repeat these phrases, you are planting seeds that soften self-criticism and strengthen awareness.

Stage Two: Widening to Someone You Love

Next, call to your mind someone dear to you—a friend, partner, family member. Picture their face and feel their presence. Offer the same phrases, inserting their name:

May _____ be happy. May _____ be peaceful. May _____ be healthy.

This step feels more natural for many people. Love tends to flow easily toward those who support us. Practice holding that love intentionally, with attention and warmth.

Stage Three: Extending to a Neutral Person

Now, bring to mind a casual acquaintance—your mail carrier, your barista, the neighbor you wave to but rarely speak with. You may not know their name, but you know who they are to you. For example, you might say something like *"may my mail carrier be happy,"* or *"may my neighbor be peaceful."* The point is to offer the same words of goodwill. This stage expands your awareness beyond the usual boundaries of your emotional world.

Stage Four: The Challenging One

This is where Metta becomes transformative. Think of someone who triggers irritation or discomfort. Using the same three or four loving statements you have previously used, even if it feels strained, send compassion to those who challenge your mental and emotional equilibrium. There's no need to choose the "hardest" person—start small if you like. This stage may require extra practice before you can direct your love and compassion toward that person, but don't give up. If it is difficult in the beginning, challenge yourself to find, even a small amount of caring for that person.

You are not excusing their behavior, you are simply freeing yourself from the grip of resentment. Even one minute of practice can loosen knots you may have carried for years.

Stage Five: All Beings Everywhere

Finally, widen your heart as far as it can go. Offer loving-kindness to everyone—people, animals, forests, cities, even places of conflict. Your intention becomes a quiet blessing released into the world. And especially during this time in history, cities and countries of the world would do well with receiving loving-kindness intentions.

Practicing loving-kindness makes mindfulness easier because it softens the noise of judgment and strengthens your capacity to stay present with whatever arises. Compassion steadies the mind. Kindness opens it.

May you be happy. May you be healthy. May you experience love. May you live in peace.

Think Less

"A quiet mind is all you need."
— HUANG PO

If you've ever lain awake replaying a conversation, worrying about tomorrow, or inventing scenarios that may never happen, you already know how exhausting the thinking mind can be. Huang Po, the influential Zen Master of the ninth century, taught that enlightenment isn't something you earn through effort—it's what you uncover when the mind finally stops grasping at every thought that appears. He believed that our suffering comes from clinging—clinging to opinions, to stories, to worries, to the constant hum of mental commentary.

Most of us fear the idea of a quiet mind. We've been conditioned to believe that constant thinking equals control, safety, or productivity. But as Huang Po points out, this is the illusion of the ego. The deeper part of you—your wiser, higher awareness—already knows that clarity doesn't come from thinking more; it comes from thinking *less*.

Thich Nhat Hanh often reminded his students that peace is always available in the space between thoughts. The moment you catch yourself spinning a story—replaying what happened, predicting what will happen, or assuming what someone else meant—you've already stepped out of the present moment. But the instant you simply notice the thought without following it, you return to yourself. That small pause is mindfulness.

This practice is not about suppressing thoughts or forcing silence. It's about recognizing when you've wandered and gently coming back to the present moment. I once heard someone describe overthinking as "mental popcorn"—thoughts exploding in every direction. Like popcorn, when the heat is turned up, thoughts fly everywhere. It's when the heat is turned off that everything begins to settle. Awareness is like turning down the heat.

The next time you catch yourself ruminating about a mistake or a conversation that didn't go the way you hoped, take a breath. Say to yourself, *"This is only a story."* That simple reminder loosens the mind's grip. You might even smile at how quickly your imagination tried to run away with you.

In that small, spacious moment, you're not thinking—you're simply present. Once you realize you have been telling yourself tall tales, you just might smile and drop into the present moment of no-thought.

Relax Your Face

"Let your face relax and the mind will follow."
— THICH NHAT HANH

If you've ever caught yourself clenching your jaw during a difficult conversation or furrowing your brow while reading an email, you already know how closely the face mirrors the mind. Our facial muscles respond instantly to stress, concentration, and emotion—often long before we consciously register what we're feeling. The good news is, this connection works both ways. When we relax the face, we signal to the entire nervous system that it's safe to settle, breathe, and return to the present moment.

Just as smiling activates "feel-good" chemistry in the brain, softening the muscles of the face can lower levels of stress hormones and increase the release of endorphins, dopamine, and oxytocin. These biochemical shifts aren't imagined—they've been demonstrated in research exploring facial feedback and emotional regulation, where even slight changes in facial tension influence mood and physiological stress responses (Kraft & Pressman, 2012). In other words, when you relax your face, your body listens.

Many of us walk around tightening our jaw, squinting our eyes, or pinching our eyebrows together without ever noticing. Worry creates its own weather system upon the face. We've all felt it: the jaw locks, the tongue presses upward, and our forehead becomes a battlefield of micro-contractions. It's no wonder we feel mentally tight when our facial muscles are working overtime. Relaxing the face offers a doorway out of mental tension and into mindful awareness.

Try this simple exercise:

Close your eyes for a moment. Bring your attention to the top of your head, as though you were placing a warm hand on your crown. With your next breath, imagine the skin of your scalp and the tiny muscles underneath softening. As you continue to breathe, feel the back of your head and neck melt into stillness.

Now, picture your brain and give it permission to relax. Focus two or three breaths into your skull, bathing your brain in tranquility.

Shift your awareness to your forehead and eyes. Let your breath sweep across your brow like a gentle tide, smoothing the tension you didn't know you were holding. Feel your eyes settle back into their sockets, heavy and relaxed.

Moving your awareness to your ears, soften the outer lobes and feel relaxation trickle to the tiny muscles deep inside the canals. Feel your breath moving from ear to ear, bringing clarity and balance.

Feeling calmer, focus your awareness on your nose and upper lip. Sense the rush of breath through your nostrils as you breathe in and out, softening the bridge of your nose and your upper lip.

Bring your awareness to your mouth and tongue. Soften your jaw. Release the tension of your tongue, letting it float in the space of your mouth. Relax your mouth, tongue and jaw.

Finally, guide your awareness to your chin and neck. With each breath, feel tension melting away, flowing down your shoulders and into the ground. Rest here for a few moments, simply feeling yourself unwind.

When you open your eyes, notice what has changed. Is there a sense of spaciousness behind your forehead? Do your jaw and neck feel lighter? Does your mind feel quieter, less urgent?

Relaxing your face is a small practice with profound impact. It draws you out of worry, into your body, and back to the present moment. Soften your face, and the world softens with you.

PART TWO

What Mindfulness Can Do for You

"Nature does not hurry, yet everything is accomplished."
— LAO TZU

As you begin integrating the practices from Part One into your daily life, you may already sense subtle, positive shifts. Perhaps your body feels less tense, your thoughts feel a bit more spacious, and you're able to pause before reacting to stressful situations. These small changes are meaningful. They signal that your efforts to cultivate mindfulness are beginning to influence the way you experience yourself and the world around you.

Mindfulness rarely announces itself with dramatic transformation. Instead, it emerges in steady and subtle ways. Over time, you may notice greater clarity in your thinking, deeper emotional awareness, and an increased ability to stay present rather than being swept away by habit or worry. You may find yourself breathing more fully, listening more attentively, and feeling more grounded during moments that once overwhelmed you.

Part Two explores the practical benefits of a mindfulness practice. Its impact is both concrete and measurable. Research has shown that a regular mindfulness practice can improve attention, reduce stress, support immune function, and enhance emotional regulation. Beyond these physiological and psychological effects, mindfulness also enriches everyday life by strengthening relationships, sharpening decision-making, and encouraging a sense of calm in the midst of complexity.

As you read through the chapters ahead, some of these benefits may already be apparent. I invite you to observe how mindfulness is already influencing your life. What patterns are becoming clearer? Where do you feel more ease or spaciousness?

It may be helpful to make a personal list of the benefits you've already noticed, even if they seem modest. The shifts you are making are not insignificant, they are signs of deeper change unfolding.

Mindfulness affects each of us uniquely, but its essence is universal. When we bring awareness to our experiences, we reclaim the ability to meet life with greater steadiness, compassion, and authenticity. Part Two guides us through the many ways mindfulness can enrich and transform everyday living. Inner peace, here we come!

Stress Reduction

"It's not stress that kills us—it's our reaction to it."
— HANS SELYE

Who hasn't longed for a moment of peace in the midst of today's relentless pace? Everywhere we turn, there seems to be a constant barrage from the news media reporting on wars, political takeovers, and people suffering around the world. Our nervous systems absorb more now than they were ever designed to handle. Add the daily flood of flashing advertising ads on cellphones, computers, billboards, and screens of every size, and it's no wonder so many people report record levels of anxiety, depression, and burnout.

The world has become noisy, and that noise follows us everywhere unless we learn how to step back from it and take a pause. Without intentional boundaries, these interruptions begin to erode our mental clarity and emotional steadiness. They pull us away from the people we love, keep us scattered, and drain our energy before we realize what has happened. Stress becomes less of an occasional visitor and more of a constant (unwelcome) companion.

Yet, even in this age of overwhelm, there is hope, and it begins with something surprisingly simple: mindfulness. Finding equilibrium through a mindfulness practice is one of the best sources for stress reduction.

Mindfulness offers one of the most effective and accessible paths to stress relief. Countless studies have proven time and again, that intention, attention, and attitude—components of mindfulness—can lead to stress reduction through a change in perception of circumstances. In fact, mindfulness meditation has been proven to positively affect brain chemistry. One influential meta-analysis on Mindfulness-Based

Stress Reduction (MBSR) found significant improvements in anxiety, stress, and overall well-being among participants (Grossman et al., 2004). In other words, mindfulness doesn't merely make you *feel* calmer, it changes the way your brain responds to stress.

Often, these shifts begin with the smallest actions. Relaxing your facial muscles, softening your jaw, or offering a genuine smile to a stranger can trigger the body's relaxation response. Stress hormones such as cortisol begin to decline, while calming chemicals—including endorphins and oxytocin—rise. Something as ordinary as a smile can lift your mood, brighten someone else's day, and momentarily interrupt the stress cycle for both of you.

Mindfulness works because it interrupts your mental "autopilot." When stressful feelings start to build—shallow breathing, swirling thoughts, tense muscles—you have the power to pause. A single conscious breath can anchor you back into the present moment. That pause might last only a few seconds, but it creates space—to choose, to soften, to respond rather than react.

With continued practice, stress becomes less overpowering. Your body learns to return to equilibrium more quickly. Your mind becomes clearer. Your emotional resilience strengthens. And perhaps most importantly, you begin to remember that calm is not something you chase—it's something you cultivate.

Mindfulness doesn't erase the pressures of life. Instead, it equips you with the inner steadiness to meet them with clarity and compassion. When you can manage your stress, you reclaim authority over your well-being—and with that, you reclaim your life.

Self-Control

"Self-control is strength; calmness is mastery."
— JAMES ALLEN

Self-control is often misunderstood as sheer willpower—a gritted-teeth effort to hold yourself together. But in mindfulness, self-control has a different quality. It isn't forceful; it's spacious. It arises from calm awareness rather than tension. When you practice mindfulness, you begin to discover that self-control is found in the mindful awareness of the present moment. This strength doesn't come from tightening your grip, but from relaxing into clarity. When you can stay present with your thoughts and emotions instead of being swept away by them, you create the inner stability that allows you to choose your next step wisely. This mindful self-control can transform every part of your life.

Imagine you have been waiting to get a big promotion at work, which would finally bring recognition for your efforts and a paycheck that could ease the financial strain you've been juggling. Your boss has been hinting for weeks that the position is practically yours. Daring to hope, your anticipation for the big day has been growing. You can picture yourself stepping into a new chapter of your life with pride and relief.

The decision has finally been made. The job was given—not to you—but to the new girl across the hall. Your mind floods with disbelief, disappointment, and the sting of betrayal. The news seems to short-circuit your ability to think clearly. The rest of the afternoon passes in a haze, as if you're watching someone else live your life. By the time you pull into your driveway, you hardly remember how you got home.

Inside, the house is quiet. Dropping your keys on the kitchen table, you head for the refrigerator to drown your sorrows in a quart of double chocolate fudge brownie ice cream. Your hand automatically reaches into the freezer.

You are at a crossroads.

Will you succumb to that chocolatey temptation to numb what's left of your feelings, or will you summon every ounce of your self-control and consciously experience this disappointing moment for what it is?

The choice is yours. Double chocolate fudge brownie ice cream isn't a bad thing. In fact, heartache and ice cream make an easy match. No one would blame you for wallowing in the pain of such a huge disappointment by swimming in a tub of chocolate soft serve. However, because you have been practicing mindfulness meditation for some time now, you can sense—however faintly—that there is another option. You have developed enough awareness to pause in this painful moment rather than be swept away by it.

Mindfulness doesn't eliminate disappointment. It does, however, illuminate choice. You understand that you cannot control your boss's decision, but you can choose how to meet your own suffering. Having the courage to acknowledge your pain and step out of self-pity for a moment, it is possible for you to clearly see the different outcomes of the choices you are faced with.

You could eat the ice cream, enjoying the taste for the first few bites, then mindlessly devouring the rest of the container to divert your awareness from your pain. What follows would be a self-induced sugar coma that gives you a headache and makes you feel as bloated as the United States deficit, and bonus, you still feel the sting of your boss's betrayal!

Or...

You could allow yourself a few moments of alligator tears and pillow punching, then take a few conscious, deep breaths and actually feel the disappointment rather than running from it. Mindfully experiencing your emotions—anger, loss, and disappointment—without analyzing them or drowning in them, helps them soften.

As the shock from losing the promotion begins to lessen, you recognize that your boss's decision doesn't reflect on you as a person.

You can be proud of yourself for your strong work ethic and leadership qualities, which he couldn't see. In this clarity, a new idea emerges—a spark of ambition you didn't expect. Maybe this setback isn't a dead end after all. Maybe it's pointing you toward something bigger, to the dream of starting your own company.

Being aware of your circumstances and staying present with whatever you're feeling gives you options. When you meet your emotions with attention rather than avoidance, you create a moment of choice. Mindfulness sharpens your clarity in the moment, helping you see the situation as it is, not as your stress or disappointment might distort it. From this grounded place, you can respond intentionally instead of reacting impulsively. Self-control is one of the most empowering and motivating benefits of a mindfulness practice

Better Relationships

According to the dictionary, a *relationship* is how two or more people or objects relate and connect. That definition barely scratches the surface of how deeply connection shapes our lives. Although romantic relationships often capture the spotlight, human experience is far more expansive. We form bonds with friends, mentors, colleagues, neighbors, pets, places, memories—even the houseplant on the windowsill. Every connection, large or small, influences our sense of belonging, purpose, and emotional well-being.

The most important relationship, however, is the one you have with yourself. Without mindful awareness and quiet contemplation, it would be difficult to understand what motivates you—emotionally, mentally, spiritually. You can go years living on autopilot, reacting rather than responding, never pausing long enough to notice how certain moments affect you. However, when you practice mindfulness, something remarkable happens: You gain the ability to recognize what you're feeling while you're feeling it. This awareness becomes the foundation for every healthy relationship you will ever build.

If you're honest, you can probably remember a time when you were so triggered by an event or someone's tone of voice that you said or did something you regretted later. I know I can. I've had more than a few times when I snapped at someone I cared about, only to regret it long after the moment passed. Those instances, uncomfortable as they were, became humbling teachers. They showed me that when I'm not grounded in the present moment, I lose sight of my values and my compassion. Mindfulness has repeatedly helped me reclaim that clarity.

Think of a time when you were triggered. Maybe you had just received difficult news from your boss when your partner casually asked you what you'd like for dinner. You flipped out—not because of their question, but because your emotional cup was already overflowing. In truth, your reaction had nothing to do with your partner. It was an unconscious discharge of stress. Mindfulness would not have erased the difficult news, but it could have changed your response. A single slow breath, a brief pause, or even silently counting to ten could have shifted the moment from conflict to understanding. These tiny practices are so simple, but can be the difference between connection and misunderstanding.

The power of mindfulness in relationships gives space. Space to notice your emotions before they hijack your behavior. Space to listen more deeply. Space to speak with clarity instead of defensiveness. Space to choose patience over reactivity.

Let's explore the wide variety of relationships people experience. While romantic partnerships and family ties matter greatly, so do quieter connections. The bond with a long-time friend, the comfort you receive from your adoring dog, support from acquaintances at church, the trust you have with your next-door neighbor, or the warmth you feel toward the barista who remembers your order are all meaningful connections and have value. Even the relationship you have with your plants is important.

In order to care for these connections, you must be aware of not only your needs, but the needs of others. Mindfulness invites us to pay attention to what's happening inside of us, as well as pay attention to those in front of us. Ultimately, relationship thrives on presence. Everyone involved in every relationship gives and receives benefit from being connected.

Consider some of your own relationships. Do you communicate clearly with your partner about finances or household responsibilities? Can you relate to your teenage daughter, who spends all her time and allowance at the mall? How do you feel about that woman at church who sings loud and off-key during the hymns? Do you water your plants because it brings you joy, or because you feel guilty when you forget? These examples may seem unrelated, but they reveal something about the way you experience relationship.

If you're unhappy with the quality of certain relationships, mindfulness invites you to look inward, not outward. The better relationship you have with yourself, the better your relationships will be with others.

Take the example of a tidy spouse living with a partner who is naturally more clutter-prone. Without mindfulness, this mismatch can become a battleground of resentment. But with mindful awareness, you can recognize that your partner's habits aren't personal—they're simply patterns learned over time. From that understanding, you can approach the situation calmly, expressing your need for an orderly space without shaming or blaming. Maybe you both agree on small changes that honor each other's comfort. That single shift—from reacting to responding—can save a relationship from unnecessary conflict.

Mindfulness also improves your ability to listen—truly listen. That means hearing not only the words someone says, but the emotions behind them. It means letting go of the urge to interrupt, fix, or defend. It means being curious instead of critical. When you show up with presence, openness, and awareness, you become a safe place for others. In turn, you begin to feel safe to trust in relationships.

As you've learned throughout this book, mindfulness is awareness in action. It is the clarity that helps you understand yourself and others in far more depth. When you know what you feel and need in the present moment, you can communicate honestly and compassionately. Better communication leads to healthier relationships, and healthier relationships lead to a more grounded, peaceful, and enjoyable life.

Mindfulness doesn't just help you connect with others—it helps you connect with yourself. And that is the foundation of every meaningful relationship you will ever have.

Lower Blood Pressure

"Mindfulness isn't difficult; we just need to remember to do it."
— SHARON SALZBERG

If you're someone who believes mindfulness is strictly a mental exercise, here's some heart-healthy news: Your body disagrees—quite enthusiastically. Over the past decade, research has shown again and again that mindfulness doesn't just calm your mind; it can calm your cardiovascular system as well. A 2019 study from Brown University, for instance, found that mindfulness practice helps regulate emotions, improve attention control, and increase awareness of healthy habits—all of which contribute to lower blood pressure. Another long-term study published in *PLOS One* followed forty-three participants with hypertension for more than a year. By the end, every participant's blood pressure had dropped below their baseline, some by as much as fifteen points, and many reported adopting healthier habits as a natural extension of their mindfulness practice.

To appreciate why this matters, it helps to understand what blood pressure actually is. Each time your heart beats, it sends blood pulsing through your arteries with enough force to nourish every cell in your body. That force—your blood pressure—is measured using two numbers. The first, systolic pressure, reflects the force when your heart contracts. The second, diastolic pressure, measures the pressure when your heart relaxes between beats. A healthy reading typically falls between 90/60 mmHg and 120/80 mmHg (millimeters of mercury). Anything consistently above that range can place you at risk for heart disease, stroke, or other serious medical complications.

Because high blood pressure is a serious health risk, and is prevalent in the modern world, it is wise to know your numbers. Whether you are prone to high blood pressure or not, monitoring your stress levels and opting for regular enjoyable and calming activities is an important way to stay healthy.

Most people don't realize how often their blood pressure fluctuates throughout the day. A stressful email, a tense conversation, even heavy traffic can cause a temporary spike. Modern life provides no shortage of these triggers. That's why awareness—mindful awareness—is essential. Without it, stress can accumulate quietly, tightening the body before the mind even realizes what's happening.

This is where mindfulness becomes more than a self-care practice; it becomes a physiological ally. Something as simple as a few slow, intentional breaths can activate your parasympathetic nervous system—"rest and digest." When this system turns on, your heart rate slows, your blood vessels soften, and your entire cardiovascular system begins to settle. Over time and with regular practice, these micro-moments of calm add up, training your body to recover more quickly from stress and lowering your baseline level of tension.

People often ask whether mindfulness alone can make a measurable difference. The answer, quite simply, is yes. But don't take my word for it—try the following experiment yourself.

For two weeks, take your blood pressure at roughly the same time each day. Then choose one or two mindfulness practices from Part One: deep breathing, journaling, a walking meditation, or even a few minutes of mindful stillness. After finishing your mindfulness activity, recheck your blood pressure. Make a note of both sets of numbers. You might want to keep a simple log. At the end of the two weeks, compare the numbers. You might be surprised by the shift—not only in your readings, but in how you feel moving through your day.

If you would like to monitor the benefits of a long-term mindfulness practice, consider purchasing a home blood pressure cuff. They're inexpensive, easy to use, and provide concrete feedback—useful when you want to see the tangible effects of an intangible practice.

Mindfulness is not a magic wand, but it is a powerful tool. With consistency and curiosity, it can support your heart as surely as it supports your mind. When you bring your awareness back to the present moment you are literally giving your heart a moment of rest.

Greater Self-Awareness

"Knowing yourself is the beginning of all wisdom."
— ARISTOTLE

Aristotle, perhaps one of the greatest ancient philosophers to influence modern times, understood that self-awareness is more than being conscious of your body in time and space. He taught that knowing yourself is foundational for a good life.

Self-awareness is the art of turning inward—noticing your thoughts, emotions, and impulses—while simultaneously understanding how your words and actions land in the world around you. It is a dual awareness of knowing what is happening within you and how you are experienced by others. Mindfulness strengthens both sides of this awareness, giving you the ability to see yourself with more honesty, understanding, and compassion.

Deepak Chopra describes this capacity as becoming "the watcher of the watched." In mindfulness terms, the "watched" is your everyday conscious self: the part of you that feels irritated in traffic, excited about good news, or anxious before a difficult conversation. The "watcher" is the quiet, stable awareness that notices all of this without becoming tangled in it. It observes your reactions, your patterns, and even the way you respond to other people's perceptions of you. When you access this watcher, you gain a wider view of your life—one that isn't clouded by momentary emotion or old conditioning.

This observer perspective is what allows you to step out of self-centeredness and into relational awareness. You begin to sense how your tone, energy, or body language might be interpreted by someone else. You start to recognize when your words uplift or when they unintentionally close someone down. This isn't about pleasing others, but about becoming conscious of the impact you have on the people and environments you move through. With self-awareness, you can understand that your inner world and the outer world are in constant dialogue.

Mindfulness deepens this awareness by anchoring you in the present moment. Through simple practices—such as conscious breathing, body scans, or quiet reflection—you learn to steady your mind long enough to observe yourself without judgment. That stability allows you to see patterns you might otherwise miss, like the stories you tell yourself, the emotional habits you default to, or the assumptions that discolor your interactions. As you cultivate this clarity, your confidence grows. You begin to trust your inner wisdom, understand your motivations, and make choices that align with who you truly are.

This clarity also extends to how you understand your place in the larger picture. When you're present, you recognize your connection to others and to the world around you. You can see that your reactions are not isolated. They ripple outward into your relationships, your work, and your daily life. With self-awareness, you can meet each moment with intention rather than reactivity.

To build this awareness, take time to inquire within. The age-old philosophical question, *"Who am I,"* may sound cliché, but it gives stark permission to explore your true identity. Rather than defining your job title or family standing, this question helps to uncover your purpose for being. Journaling can be a powerful companion to your mindfulness practice, helping you uncover deeper layers of truth as they arise. Contemplate questions such as:

"What are my values and beliefs?"

"How do others experience me?"

"What patterns keep showing up in my life?"

"What do I truly want to experience or contribute?"

There are no right or wrong answers—only revealing ones. Like peeling back layers of an onion, each reflection brings you closer to the authentic self beneath your roles, routines, and expectations. Take your time contemplating each question and write down what comes to mind. As your self-awareness expands, so does your capacity to shape the quality of your life with clarity, intention, and grace.

Patience

The old English poet William Langland reminded us in his medieval poem, "patience is a virtue." You've probably heard this in childhood from a parent or teacher. I certainly did. But the meaning didn't land until years later, when yoga and meditation quieted my mind for the message to finally be understood. Through those practices, I learned to accept my own quirks, soften my resistance, and trust the unpredictable rhythm of life. That trust, slowly built, became my foundation of patience.

When I think of patience today, I often return to the classic arc of the Hero's Journey. Whether it's Moses wandering the desert, Luke Skywalker wrestling with self-doubt, or modern leaders like Nelson Mandela and Volodymyr Zelenskyy enduring hardship with resolve, every hero must learn to wait, endure, and move forward without losing heart. Their stories remind us that patience is not passive. It is an active, courageous choice to stay present even when the outcome is unclear.

What about your story? How would you describe your relationship with patience? Were you born with it, or has life—through traffic jams, personal setbacks, long healing processes, or wildly unpredictable circumstances—trained you in it? Patience, at its core, is the capacity to meet delay, difficulty, or discomfort without collapsing into frustration. It is the willingness to let yourself and others be imperfect. It is the skill of staying aware of your internal weather while observing what's happening around you with steady eyes.

Our struggle with patience is ancient. Sacred texts across cultures describe humans wrestling with impulsiveness and restlessness. Eve grew impatient with God's instructions in the Garden of Eden. The Israelites lost faith in Moses' return from Mount Sinai. In Buddhist tradition, Siddhartha's impatience with his confined palace life propelled him into a journey that ultimately awakened him as Gautama Buddha. These stories underline an enduring human truth: Impatience is easy, patience is transformational.

Now, in the age of instant everything—instant answers from AI, instant meals, instant communication—patience is more endangered than ever. We rarely linger. We scroll, swipe, click, and consume at a pace that leaves little room for savoring and curiosity. The joy of researching something deeply or preparing a thoughtful meal has been overshadowed by quick fixes. But patience asks something radical of us: *Slow down enough to actually live your life.* This is where mindfulness enters and eloquently completes the picture.

Mindfulness requires patience, and patience grows through mindfulness. They form a reciprocal loop, strengthening one another with each conscious breath and awareness. You may wonder, "How do I cultivate mindfulness if I'm not naturally patient?" The answer is, gently, gradually, and with compassion. Every time you pause before reacting, every time you take one deep breath instead of erupting in frustration, every time you choose to listen fully to the person in front of you—you are practicing mindfulness. With each practice, your patience reservoir grows.

A Father's Patience

One of my earliest lessons in patience came when I was in the third grade. It happened on the sidewalk outside our house, where my purple banana-seat bicycle—complete with sparkly streamers— wobbled under my uncertain grip. My dad worked with me regularly, teaching me to ride without training wheels. Each time I leaned too far to one side and bent the little wheels out of shape, he never sighed, never scolded. He simply crouched down, tools in hand, and repaired them so I could try again. His patience felt infinite.

Then came *the* day. He removed the training wheels from my

bike, loaded it into the back of his pickup, and drove us to my grade-school playground—a flat dirt expanse of possibility. The afternoon was warm and the dusty lot seemed insurmountable. My stomach fluttered with equal parts excitement and dread.

He set the bike down, tapped the seat, and said, "Hop on."

I did, trusting that he wouldn't let anything happen to me.

"I'm going to hold the back of the seat," he said, resting one strong hand behind me, "and we'll walk together while you learn to balance."

So we did. Over and over, pedal after pedal, he walked beside me, supporting the bike, steadying my shaky confidence. When I tipped over, he would catch me or lift me up from the ground, brushing the dust off me.

"You're getting there," he'd say every time, as though progress was inevitable, as though falling was just part of the journey—not a failure, but a step.

And because he believed that, I believed it too.

Finally, I climbed onto the bike again, found my center, and began to pedal. Slowly at first, thinking of nothing but balance—the feel of the handlebars in my hands, the crunch of the wheels on hard dirt. Then I pedaled faster. And faster. Suddenly, the world opened up, and I was flying.

It felt like freedom. It felt like magic.

But something was off—my dad couldn't possibly be running that fast, could he?

I dared to glance back.

There he was, standing a good ten yards behind me, hands lifted, waving proudly. A huge smile spread across his face—the kind a parent wears when they know they've just witnessed a moment that will shape their child's life forever.

He had let go. And I hadn't even noticed.

In that moment, the world felt bigger, brighter, and entirely possible. My dad's patience had become my courage—steady, invisible, and absolutely essential. Even now, whenever I feel myself wobbling in life, I remember that feeling of freedom my dad gave to me. He patiently encouraged me to "try again" and "keep going" until I succeeded. Never underestimate the power of patience.

Exercising Patience

Try this simple exercise the next time you're stuck in traffic and notice the frustration rising. Acknowledge it without judgment. Then take a slow breath in and offer yourself peace. As you exhale, imagine sending patience and goodwill to every driver around you. Continue as long as the traffic lasts. When movement begins again, observe how your energy has shifted. This moment of mindful patience can transform the entire experience.

As patience develops within you, expectations soften too. You become less rigid, more intuitive, more able to reflect and respond rather than react impulsively. Mindfulness teaches you to become the observer of your life, watching thoughts and emotions come and go without clinging to any of them. Patience teaches you to trust the timing of your inner unfolding. Together, they create a steadiness that allows you to meet life with grace.

Patience is not simply a virtue. It is a quiet strength that arises from mindful living.

Better Sleep

Of all the gifts we give ourselves, sleep is one of the most underestimated. Most people don't appreciate its power until they lose it—tossing and turning at 2:00 a.m., rehearsing old conversations, worrying about tomorrow's obligations, or scrolling mindlessly through their phones in the dark. Yet, as the Dalai Lama reminds us, sleep is one of the body's most natural and profound states of renewal. When paired with mindfulness, sleep becomes not only deeper and more restorative, but also easier to access.

Science continues to confirm that healthy sleep is essential for a healthy life. Matthew Walker, PhD, author of *Why We Sleep*, reveals that insufficient sleep weakens the immune system, disrupts emotional regulation, and increases the risk of numerous diseases—including Alzheimer's. Ayurveda emphasizes sleep as one of the three pillars of well-being, alongside diet and exercise. Consistent, quality rest supports memory, focus, mood regulation, and even appetite. Sleep is both the foundation and the fuel for a balanced, mindful life.

But before you can transform your sleep, you must understand your relationship with it.

Is sleep a necessary inconvenience that interrupts your productivity? Do you listen to your body when it whispers, *please stop?*

Can you fall asleep easily, or is bedtime a nightly struggle?

Simply asking these questions is a mindfulness practice. It invites you to be aware of your habits, beliefs, and patterns. Some are helpful and others are not. The more clearly you see those patterns, the more empowered you become to change them.

When Distraction Steals Sleep

One of the biggest obstacles to healthy sleep is distraction. Not just the kind that comes from glowing screens, but the deeper distractions of worry, fear, overstimulation, and emotional overload. We live in a world buzzing with uncertainty. Economic unrest, political tension, global conflict, and constant digital noise create subtle unease in the body. Even if you try to turn off your mind at night, your nervous system may still be running laps.

The good news? Mindfulness is one of the most effective ways to interrupt that cycle.

Mindfulness teaches the brain to recognize what is real and present versus what is imagined or anticipated. It helps regulate the nervous system, slow down racing thoughts, and return the body to a state of calm—conditions the brain associates with sleep. Just as you would dim the lights before bedtime, mindfulness dims the mind's internal "brightness," making it easier to slip into deep, nourishing rest.

How Sleep Works—and Why Mindfulness Supports It

To understand how mindfulness enhances sleep, it helps to know what happens when you fall asleep. Sleep is not a single event, but is a cycle of distinct stages, each offering unique benefits.

Light Sleep. This is the transition between wakefulness and sleep, when muscles soften, breathing slows, and the brain begins releasing its grip on conscious thoughts. Ideally, it should take you between ten to twenty minutes to fall asleep. If you've had a stressful day, your mind may resist shutting down, keeping you stuck in this doorway longer than necessary.

Mindfulness—especially practices like slow breathing or a simple body scan—helps quiet the mental static that delays sleep. By relaxing the body and regulating the nervous system, mindful awareness makes the doorway of light sleep easier to walk through.

REM Sleep. REM (Rapid Eye Movement) is the dream stage. Your brain becomes almost as active as it is when awake, processing emotions, solving problems, and consolidating memories. In this stage, your body is temporarily paralyzed—nature's way of protecting you from acting out your dreams.

Mindfulness supports REM sleep by reducing emotional reactivity during the day. The more you process feelings in real time, the less unresolved material your brain must sort through at night.

Deep Sleep. This is the most restorative stage of sleep. The body repairs tissues, strengthens the immune system, and resets physiological processes. Brain waves slow to their most peaceful rhythm. Many people rarely get enough deep sleep, especially as they age.

Deep sleep is more accessible when the mind is calm, the body relaxed, and the nervous system grounded. Mindfulness cultivates exactly these conditions.

In essence, mindfulness creates the internal environment sleep needs to flourish.

Your Mind Before Bed: Friend or Foe?

Think of your pre-bedtime thoughts as the "warm-up act" before sleep. If you spend the final hour before bed worrying, scrolling, rushing, or replaying the day's mistakes, your brain won't magically switch into relaxation mode the moment the lights go off.

Mindfulness gives you a kinder transition. A few minutes of slow breathing, gentle stretching, body scanning, or gratitude reflection signals to your brain: *It's safe to rest now.* Even asking simple mindful questions like *"What do I need right now," "How does my body feel,"* and *"What can I release from today"* can ease you into a more peaceful state.

A Personal Story About Mindfulness and Sleep

When I first began practicing mindfulness, I expected improvements in my focus, clarity, and mood, but I didn't expect such a dramatic impact on my sleep.

I used to lie in bed for hours, thinking through every conversation I'd had that day, planning tomorrow's schedule, and mentally solving problems that weren't even mine to solve. I had acquired the bad habit of taking my day to bed with me.

One night, exhausted and frustrated, I tried a simple mindfulness technique. I placed my hands on my belly and counted my breaths from one to ten, then back down to one. I didn't try to stop thinking. I didn't fight my emotions. I simply stayed with my breath.

By the second breath, my body had softened.

By breath five or six, my mind was relaxing.

By the second round, I was asleep.

Mindfulness Tools for Better Sleep

Choose one or two of these techniques and practice them nightly for at least two weeks:

- **Body Scan:** Start at your toes and slowly move your awareness upward, releasing tension.

- **Breath Counting:** Inhale through your nose for a slow count of four, exhale slowly for six.

- **Gratitude Reflection:** Think of three things that went well today.

- **Mindful Stretching:** Gentle movements to release your muscles and settle the breath.

- **Sensory Awareness:** Notice the weight of the blankets, the temperature of the room, the sensation of your body resting.

Consistency is key. The more regularly you practice, the more quickly your body will associate these techniques with relaxation and sleep. As mindfulness settles your mind, the body naturally follows. You can fall asleep faster, stay asleep longer, and wake feeling more restored. Over time, your sleep becomes not just longer, but better.

When you sleep better, your mindfulness practice deepens. It becomes easier to stay present. Easier to regulate emotions. Easier to meet each moment as it comes.

Mindfulness supports sleep.

Sleep supports mindfulness.

Together, they nurture inner peace.

Mental Focus

"The mind is everything. What you think you become."
— BUDDHA

What does it really mean to have mental focus? At its simplest, focus is your ability to direct your attention—and keep it there—long enough for something meaningful to happen. It is the quiet but powerful skill of choosing where your mind rests, even when the world (or your own internal chatter) tries to pull you in every direction at once. In many ways, mental focus is the heart of mindfulness. As Buddhist teacher Thich Nhat Hanh once wrote, *"The present moment is filled with joy and happiness. If you are attentive, you will see it."* Attentiveness—steady, intentional focus—is both the doorway to mindfulness and one of its greatest rewards.

Think about the mental precision of an Olympic ice skater preparing for a gold-medal performance. As he steps onto the ice, he must skillfully shut out the roar of the crowd, the fear of making a mistake, and the temptation to second-guess months of practice. He brings his attention to one thing—the next movement. That is focus in action: the discipline to stay rooted in the present moment long enough for excellence to emerge.

Or picture a high school senior sitting down to take her final algebra exam. This one test determines whether she graduates with honors. Anxiety could easily steal her clarity, but she directs her mental energy toward each equation, one careful step at a time. She trusts her preparation and stays connected to the only moment she can influence—the one she's in right now.

You may not be skating in the Olympics or taking an exam, but your daily life is full of moments that require the same ability to concentrate. Yet focus can feel frustratingly out of reach. Economic uncertainty, global tension, family pressures, endless multitasking, and constant digital stimulation all compete for your attention. Your thoughts may jump from worry to planning and from distraction to fatigue. Then there are the internal distractions of self-doubt, criticism, and worry, which can be even louder than the outside world. With so many forces tugging at your attention, it's completely understandable to feel unfocused and overwhelmed.

The good news is that mental focus is not a fixed trait—it is a skill. And like any skill, it strengthens with practice.

Mindfulness is one of the most effective ways to train your mind to concentrate. When you sit quietly and observe your breath, when you bring awareness to the feeling of your clothes against your skin, or when you pause simply to witness your thoughts without being swept away, you are sharpening your attention. Every moment you return to your point of focus—even if you have to return a hundred times—is a moment of mental strength training.

Mindfulness works so well because it teaches you to recognize distraction without falling into it. You learn to gather your awareness, gently but firmly, and place it exactly where you want it to be.

As your practice deepens, you may notice subtle but life-changing shifts. You listen more fully. Your thoughts feel more organized. Decisions become clearer. You are less reactive and more patient. You begin to trust your inner guidance. And perhaps most importantly, you become more present to the people you love. Mindfulness strengthens your internal focus so that your external life becomes smoother, more intentional, and more connected.

Remember, your mind will wander—that's what minds do. The magic is in returning to the present moment. Each time you refocus, you are training your brain to live in the now with greater steadiness and clarity.

Little by little, focus becomes not just something you do, but something you are cultivating within yourself: a grounded presence, a clearer mind, and a stronger ability to direct your life from the inside out.

Emotional Intelligence

"In a very real sense we have two minds,
one that thinks and one that feels."
— DANIEL GOLEMAN

Emotional Intelligence (EI) is a term that was introduced in 1990 by Psychologists Peter Salovey and John D. Mayer. They described it as our ability to understand and manage our emotions, as well as recognize and skillfully respond to the emotions of others. In practical terms, it means learning to steer your emotions instead of letting them steer you.

For much of human history, emotions were viewed as noisy, unreliable, and irrational troublemakers. They were considered a human weakness due to their dramatic displays and lack of logical reasoning. It was considered best to keep them out of decision-making. However, as positive psychology emerged in the late twentieth century, emotions began receiving a long-overdue reevaluation. Scientists discovered that all emotions have a biological function that carries useful information. Anxiety accelerates the heart so the body is ready to respond. Joy softens the facial muscles and signals connection. Anger sharpens focus and compels us to address something important. In other words, emotions aren't the problem. The problem is responding automatically, without awareness.

The foundation of emotional intelligence is the shift from reacting unconsciously to responding with awareness. It begins with noticing the ways your emotions influence your behavior. Do you lash out when you're caught off guard? Do you shut down when you feel overwhelmed? Do your reactions uplift or unsettle the people around you? Asking these questions opens the door to emotional intelligence, which rests on three core skills: self-awareness, empathy, and discipline.

Self-awareness is the ability to notice the internal weather patterns within you. Empathy is the capacity to sense and care about how your behavior affects others. Discipline is the mindful restraint that allows you to respond rather than react.

A manager under pressure of a tight deadline at work who threatens his employees' jobs if they don't stay late to complete the task is someone who exhibits a lower emotional intelligence (EI). This person could not control his stress under pressure. On the other hand, you and your best friend are having difficulty seeing eye-to-eye on a subject. Rather than continue the disagreement, you both agree to disagree and you acknowledge each other for your points of view and respect your friendship. This is an example of higher emotional intelligence. Both you and your bestie recognize your relationship is more important than being right.

Daniel Goleman, who later popularized EI in his bestselling book *Emotional Intelligence*, argued that EQ might matter even more than IQ when it comes to navigating everyday life. IQ may measure reasoning abilities, but EQ reflects how effectively we relate, empathize, communicate, and problem-solve with others. He suggests emotional intelligence is not fixed at birth. It can be shaped by childhood experiences. It can also be nurtured (or damaged) throughout adulthood. Higher emotional intelligence has numerous benefits, such as enhanced communication skills, reduced stress, better social skills, and increased tolerance.

Science suggests that emotions precede the thought process. When you are on high alert, emotions can alter brain function and diminish cognitive skills and your ability to make good decisions. This is where mindfulness becomes transformative.

Mindfulness creates a pause—a sacred split second—between emotion and reaction. Practices like walking meditation, yoga, counting to ten, smiling, or any of the other techniques in this book, can actually raise your emotional intelligence (EI). A 2011 Harvard study found that mindfulness reduces amygdala activation and enhances emotion regulation (Hölzel et al., 2011). In everyday terms, this means mindfulness helps you stay steady in the moments you are most likely to lose yourself.

David Caruso, a leading EI researcher, once said that emotional intelligence is not about heart versus head, but about the "unique intersection of both." Mindfulness is the training ground where heart and head learn to work together. It helps you to recognize your emotions without being swept away by them. It strengthens empathy by attuning you to the emotional currents of others, and it cultivates discipline by allowing you to choose your response instead of reacting impulsively.

Higher emotional intelligence offers the benefits of better communication, healthier collaboration, improved conflict resolution, more motivation, and stronger feelings of safety within personal and work environments. When you become more self-aware, you become more emotionally intelligent. When you become more emotionally intelligent, you become more peaceful.

Ultimately, mindfulness enhances emotional intelligence because it strengthens your relationship with the present moment. You learn to witness your emotions instead of wrestling with them. You learn to breathe through discomfort rather than explode or retreat. In doing so, you give yourself—and everyone around you—the gift of your presence.

Emotional intelligence doesn't make life easier, but it does make life clearer. Clarity, paired with compassion, is one of the greatest forms of inner peace you can cultivate.

Critical Thinking

What is critical thinking and why is it such an important part of being human? I admit, the word *critical* doesn't sound supportive. It feels sharp, harsh, and judgmental, as if finding fault rather than uncovering the truth. When you look deeper, however, critical thinking is far from hostile. It is a skill, an inner compass of sorts. When paired with mindfulness, it can be a powerful ally on your path to inner peace.

The Oxford English Dictionary defines critical thinking as "the objective, systematic, and rational analysis and evaluation of factual evidence in order to form a judgment on a subject, issue, etc." In more understandable terms, critical thinking is your ability to explore a situation, idea, or experience without being clouded by bias or emotional reactivity. It is the willingness to pause, look closely, and evaluate your reality with clarity rather than assumption.

Critical thinking is an important trait to possess when it comes to making decisions and evaluating the world around you. It enables you to look beyond the surface of a story, a headline, or even a conversation with a friend, and ask: *Is this true? Is this accurate? What else might be happening here?* Without it, you may find yourself making quick, emotionally charged decisions that do not reflect your values.

Critical thinking without mindfulness can be equally problematic. It can turn into cold skepticism—an overly intellectual approach that forgets compassion and human nuance.

Mindfulness brings warmth into critical thinking, giving it balance. On the surface, they may seem like opposites—one rooted in thoughtful analysis, the other in sensing and presence. But they are deeply connected. Critical thinking requires curiosity and openness to different viewpoints, and mindfulness strengthens that openness by creating space between stimulus and response. While critical thinking sharpens the mind, mindfulness softens the heart. Together, they create what author Jon Kabat-Zinn describes as "full catastrophe living"—meeting life with both clarity and compassion.

Mindfulness is a foundation for effective critical thinking. When you are mindful, you are less likely to react impulsively or cling to old beliefs out of habit. Instead, you approach your experiences—internal and external—with steady awareness. Mindfulness activates the parasympathetic nervous system, calming the body and lowering reactivity. This physiological shift creates coherence between your emotions and your reasoning, allowing you to see more clearly. As mindfulness teacher Amit Ray says, "If you want to understand the universe, look deep within your own mind."

Consider this example:

You're watching a news clip about a controversial topic. Before the report even ends, your mind is already forming an opinion—pulling from past experiences, social conditioning, and personal beliefs. But were you aware of those influences as they arose? Did you notice the tightening in your chest or the rush of agreement (or disagreement) before all the information was presented? Did you consider perspectives other than your own, or research the story before sharing it with someone else?

This internal process happens in seconds, and without mindfulness, it happens automatically. But when you bring mindful awareness into the moment, you can pause long enough to ask yourself: *Is my reaction based on facts or assumptions? Is this perspective balanced? What might I be overlooking?* That small pause is the birthplace of critical thinking.

Research shows that emotional arousal—especially fear, anger, or stress—reduces activity in the prefrontal cortex, the part of the brain responsible for reasoning and decision-making (LeDoux, 1996). In other words, when emotions run high, the thinking brain goes offline. Mindfulness, however, helps regulate those emotions so that reasoning and decision-making can return to balance. When you are calm, grounded, and present, you are better equipped to think clearly and evaluate information objectively.

Think back to a moment of emotional overwhelm—perhaps the end of a relationship or the sudden loss of a pet. In the intensity of the moment, clear thinking becomes difficult. You might imagine worst-case scenarios, jump to conclusions, or behave in ways you later regret. But with mindfulness, even in painful situations, you learn to breathe, acknowledge the moment, and gently return to yourself. You may still feel sad, frightened, or confused, but mindfulness gives you enough clarity to respond rather than react.

That clarity is what supports critical thinking. When your emotions are regulated, you can examine your circumstances more logically. You become aware of your own assumptions, able to recognize where bias might be creeping in. You remain open-minded, willing to see multiple perspectives rather than clinging to the first one that arises.

A mindful approach to critical thinking enhances nearly every aspect of your life. It improves your decision-making process whether you're writing a thesis, choosing a new career path, deciding how to vote, or navigating a difficult conversation. Mindfulness brings you back to the present—where truth resides—while critical thinking gives you the tools to understand that truth with fairness and depth.

In the words of the Buddha, "The mind is everything. What you think you become."

Critical thinking shapes *how* you *think*; mindfulness shapes what you become as a result. This powerful combination empowers you to live with wisdom, clarity, and compassionate discernment, creating space for inner peace.

Job Satisfaction

Many people wake up each morning wishing they didn't have to go to work because they feel overwhelmed by stress, disconnected from purpose, or exhausted from poor work–life balance. Long commutes, toxic workplaces, and unclear expectations can also create a sense of dread before the day even begins. Resistance can also come from a lack of internal awareness of our needs. When a job no longer fits a person's values and desires, it ceases to be supportive. Mindfulness helps clarify what we need from life—and our jobs— by fostering awareness, resilience, and grounded decision-making.

Do you like your job? Not the polite, automatic "It's fine" answer you give at social gatherings, but the real, internal one. Does your work energize you, stretch you, or give you a sense of meaning, or do you find yourself glancing at the clock every hour, waiting for the day to end and the weekend to begin? Whether you run your own business, report to a supervisor, or are exploring what comes next, job satisfaction plays a powerful role in overall well-being.

Mindfulness is one of the most reliable tools to improve that satisfaction—not by magically transforming your job into your dream career, but by transforming the way you experience the work you do. When you practice presence, you become attuned to your own needs, values, and emotional patterns. You begin to see clearly what supports you and what drains you, what inspires you and what you tolerate out of habit. When you know what you want, you know what you don't want, and you make better choices about ... everything.

People who already enjoy their jobs often find that mindfulness deepens that satisfaction. New ideas arise more easily because the mind feels less burdened. Communication improves because you become more aware of your emotions and the needs of others. Work relationships tend to feel lighter and more meaningful because presence fosters connection. A mindful employee or leader becomes more resilient, more creative, more engaged, and ultimately, they become more peaceful within themselves.

People who feel frustrated or drained at work benefit from mindfulness in a different way. A mindful pause creates space to reflect on what is truly happening beneath the surface. Sometimes the dissatisfaction comes from stress, unmet needs, or blurred boundaries rather than from the job itself. Other times mindfulness reveals a deeper truth: The work no longer aligns with your growth, your passion, or your well-being. Once clarity emerges, choices become more intentional. You either discover new ways to appreciate your current role or you begin directing your energy toward positive change. Both paths are valid and lead toward greater fulfillment.

The growing interest in workplace mindfulness shows that this connection is not just philosophical. Organizations throughout the world have implemented trainings to help their employees cope with stress. Companies such as Apple, Google, LinkedIn, the Mayo Clinic, and the US Army, to name a few, have incorporated mindfulness practices such as meditation and breath work into their wellness programs. A 2015 study published in *Journal of Management* found that workplace mindfulness programs significantly reduced employee stress and improved job satisfaction and performance (Brown et al., 2015). Companies recognize that calmer employees communicate better, make wiser decisions, and contribute more sustainably to team goals.

Stress remains one of the most common barriers to job satisfaction and has negative effects on employees' mental and emotional health. Studies show that productivity declines when employees are unhappy, especially if that unhappiness is generated in their work environment. High expectations, tight deadlines, and constant digital communication often keep the nervous system in a state of alert. Mindfulness interrupts that cycle.

Mindfulness practices such as body scanning, brief meditation breaks, or visualization can also reset your mood during a busy workday. When leaders practice these techniques, they demonstrate more patience, flexibility, and empathy toward their teams. When employees engage in mindfulness, they report clearer thinking, stronger motivation, and fewer interpersonal conflicts. This emotional steadiness strengthens ethical awareness as well. People become less likely to cut corners, exaggerate, or act impulsively when they feel grounded and aware of themselves.

Everyone benefits when mindfulness shapes the workplace. Productivity grows naturally because people feel calm enough to think clearly. Communication becomes more honest and respectful because individuals feel less defensive or overwhelmed. Creativity increases because the mind has room to wander thoughtfully rather than anxiously. Job satisfaction becomes less dependent on perfect circumstances and more connected to a sense of inner steadiness.

A fulfilling work life is never limited to traditional employment. Job satisfaction arises whenever you commit your energy to something meaningful—raising a family, volunteering in your community, creating art, building a home, caring for loved ones, or managing your own personal projects. Mindfulness encourages pride in effort, clarity in intention, and appreciation for each moment of contribution.

A mindful approach to work invites you to bring presence to whatever task lies in front of you. Whether you spend your days teaching, building, analyzing, caregiving, writing, or healing, your work becomes a place to practice awareness, compassion, and balance. The more connected you become to yourself, the more connected you become to what you do. Through mindfulness, job satisfaction transforms from something you chase into something you cultivate— one breath, one choice, and one day at a time.

Courage

*"I learned that courage was not the absence of fear,
but the triumph over it. The brave man is not he who does not
feel afraid, but he who conquers that fear."*
— NELSON MANDELA

Courage often hides in plain sight. Many people imagine bravery as something dramatic—a firefighter running into a burning building, a soldier stepping onto a battlefield, or a stranger jumping into a river to save someone. These moments deserve recognition, yet they represent only one side of courage. The deeper truth is that courage shows up long before the spotlight ever does. It can be found in a person who finally schedules a medical appointment they've been avoiding, a teenager who gets behind the wheel for the first time, or an employee who speaks up when something at work doesn't feel right. Courage is the steady breath taken before walking into an uncomfortable conversation, or the willingness to show up for yourself when fear insists you stay small. Courage isn't the absence of fear, but is feeling fear and moving forward anyway.

Mindfulness is central to this process. Fear is not a sign of weakness, but is a sign that you are alive. Your mind is doing exactly what it was designed to do—protect you. When fear arises, the difference between reacting impulsively and responding courageously lies in the small space between stimulus and response. Mindfulness expands that space. A mindful pause slows the automatic reactions driven by fear and gives you the clarity needed to choose your next step with intention. This is what allows real courage to emerge. Soldiers still feel fear in battle and firefighters still understand the danger in front of them, however, their courage comes from acting with purpose despite feeling fear. The same applies to the rest of us in far more ordinary situations.

Understanding courage becomes easier when we explore how our mind and body respond to danger. Researchers often describe the experience of courage as the interaction of three influences: *biology, psychology, and sociology.* These elements shape the way we interpret the world and respond to fear, which is why no two people express courage the same way. Someone may freeze during a challenge you would rush toward, while you might hesitate where someone else acts decisively. Mindfulness allows us to approach these differences with curiosity rather than judgment, making room for growth.

Biology plays a powerful role in the relationship between fear and courage in part, through the amygdala and neurotransmitters of the brain. The amygdala detects fear and controls aggression. Once triggered, it releases adrenaline and cortisol into your system, causing familiar sensations like shaky hands, a racing heart, or a surge of energy. These reactions are part of the nervous system's *fight/flight/ freeze* response, designed to keep you safe. The amygdala activates before the conscious mind even registers a threat, which means your body often reacts before you have time to think. Courage begins when your awareness catches up with your biology.

Dopamine and serotonin, considered *feel-good* hormones, also affect your level of bravery. Dopamine is linked to motivation and calculated risk-taking, while serotonin helps regulate mood and the perception of threat. Biologically speaking, courage is a combination of neurotransmitters that affect the structures of your brain to produce the motivations of fight, flight, or freeze.

Psychology shapes courage through your reasoning and emotional regulation. The prefrontal cortex, responsible for decision-making, squares off with your instinct-driven amygdala, helping you to make conscious decisions in any given situation. When functioning effectively, it helps you separate real threats from perceived ones. Mindfulness strengthens this system.

Psychologists have found that mindfulness meditation changes our brain and biology in positive ways, improving mental and physical health (Creswell et al., 2019). This means mindfulness literally gives your brain more capacity to handle fear in a grounded, intentional way.

Social and cultural influences also impact how courage develops. Families, communities, and cultures each define what bravery looks like. A child raised in an environment where curiosity is encouraged and mistakes are treated as learning opportunities tends to develop confidence and resilience. Such children learn that taking risks is part of growing. On the other hand, a child who grows up with constant warnings, criticism, or punishment may learn to associate risk with danger rather than opportunity. These early messages form unconscious patterns that influence behavior throughout adulthood.

Mindfulness helps soften these long-standing patterns. Through mindful awareness, you begin to recognize when your fear is based on real danger and when it stems from old conditioning. This recognition alone begins to shift behavior. Many adults discover courage only after life forces them into challenging situations—starting therapy, going through a divorce, moving to a new city, or accepting a promotion that feels bigger than their confidence. Mindfulness supports courage in these moments by keeping your attention on the present step, not the magnitude of the entire situation. When you breathe, name what you're feeling, and focus on what you can control right now, fear becomes more manageable and courage becomes more accessible.

Retraining the mind after years of avoidance requires patience. Mindfulness offers practical tools that make this process gentler. Mindful breathing reduces the body's stress response, allowing clearer thinking. Observing your inner dialogue helps you catch unhelpful thoughts—like "I can't handle this"—and replace them with more supportive ones. Naming your emotions out loud has been shown to reduce amygdala activity and calm the nervous system (Lieberman et al., 2007). These simple practices create space between feeling fear and acting on it, strengthening your ability to move through challenges intentionally.

Mistakes are another important part of courage. It takes bravery to admit when you're wrong, apologize, or take responsibility for your actions. These moments can feel uncomfortable because they expose you to vulnerability—regret, embarrassment, or fear of being judged. Mindfulness helps regulate those emotions so that you can stay grounded long enough to make amends rather than avoid them. Each time you acknowledge a mistake openly and work to correct it, you reinforce your integrity and strengthen your sense of inner courage.

Forgiveness—whether for others or for yourself—is one of the quietest yet most powerful forms of bravery. Holding onto resentment may feel protective, but it drains energy and keeps you anchored to the past. Mindfulness helps you observe these emotional burdens without being consumed by them. When you choose to let go, you are not excusing someone else's behavior; you are releasing yourself from the weight of it. That release is an act of courage.

Courage grows when you consistently step outside your comfort zone. You don't need to take enormous leaps—small actions count. Signing up for a class, trying a new hobby, speaking up in a meeting, or initiating a conversation can all stretch your boundaries in healthy ways. Each time you willingly enter unfamiliar territory, you teach your brain that discomfort does not equal danger. Over time, this builds resilience and confidence.

My favorite, and perhaps, the best training for increasing courage, is gratitude. Gratitude strengthens courage. When you intentionally focus on what's working rather than everything that could go wrong, your perception shifts. A grateful mindset helps reframe challenges, making them feel more manageable. In my own life, asking the simple question *"What's good about this?"* has helped me to approach fear with a sense of possibility rather than defeat. It doesn't erase difficulties, but it gives me courage to move forward and take meaningful risks that open new paths in my life.

Ultimately, courage is not something reserved for a rare group of heroic individuals. It is a practice, a choice, and a way of relating to fear with awareness and compassion. Mindfulness helps you slow down long enough to recognize fear without letting it control your behavior. It teaches you to stay present with discomfort, trust your inner wisdom, and move forward with intention.

Every day offers countless opportunities to practice courage— speaking honestly, setting a boundary, learning something new, asking for help, forgiving someone, or trying again after a setback. Mindfulness illuminates these moments and reminds you that courage is already within you, waiting for your attention.

Courage isn't the absence of fear, but the mindful embrace of it. When you meet fear with presence, patience, and self-kindness, courage becomes less of a rare event and more of a daily companion guiding you toward a grounded, resilient, and peaceful life.

Strengthen Intuition

Intuition often gets mistaken for something mystical or exclusive—a gift reserved for psychics or gurus. In reality, intuition is something you use far more often than you realize. It shows up in subtle nudges, quick signals, and moments where you "just know." You might feel it as a sudden urge to call a friend, or a sense that you should take a different route home. Sometimes it shows up as an unmistakable inner yes—or just as importantly, a firm, no.

These moments aren't random. Intuition is the natural expression of a mind that is paying attention. When the noise of worry and distraction softens, your inner guidance system starts to speak more clearly. Mindfulness, at its core, sharpens that signal. A scattered mind confuses intuition with anxiety and a clear mind can tell the difference.

The Oxford Dictionary defines intuition as *"the ability to understand something immediately, without the need for conscious reasoning."* That simplicity is part of what makes intuition so remarkable. It bypasses your thinking mind and draws instead from the vast storehouse of your experiences—every conversation you've had, every pattern you've recognized, every emotion your body has memorized, even when you weren't consciously paying attention.

Intuition often feels instantaneous because your brain is constantly sorting, comparing, matching, and evaluating information behind the scenes. Neuroscientists describe this as a quick, non-conscious process of pattern recognition and subconscious processing. Spiritual teachers describe it as the voice of the soul, or the whisper of higher consciousness. Both descriptions point toward the same thing—intuition is a bridge between what you consciously know and what you deeply understand.

The Everyday Nature of Inner Knowing

Most people underestimate how often intuition guides them. Think about the moment you met a stranger and instantly felt comfortable, sensing they would become important in your life. Do you remember the morning you postponed a trip without understanding why, only to discover later that something unexpected had unfolded on the route you normally would have taken? We have all had similar experiences, yet often dismiss them as coincidences.

Human intuition has typically been a survival skill. Long before advanced reasoning evolved, early humans relied on subtle cues to stay alive—the rustle of leaves, the tone of another tribe member's voice, a shift in the environment. Our bodies and brains learned to interpret signals long before language existed. While our modern world has changed dramatically, this intuitive capability hasn't disappeared. It simply gets buried under the noise of social pressure, anxiety, multitasking, and habitual distraction.

Mindfulness cuts through that noise.

When you slow down and reconnect with the present moment, your intuitive signals stop blending into the background. You begin noticing things that were always there—changes in energy, subtle emotional cues from others, bodily sensations that communicate valuable information. Intuition becomes not only more accessible but more trustworthy.

Intuition Has Many Languages

People encounter intuition differently, through the physical sensations of their five senses and sometimes through mental impressions. Can you remember a moment of insight that didn't come from logical analysis, or a time when your body reacted before your mind knew what it was reacting to? The following terms are used to describe different modes of intuitive perception. Can you recognize any of these experiences in your own life?

Claircognizance (clear knowing). Clear knowing often appears as a strong inner certainty without any logical explanation. You may suddenly understand the answer to a problem or sense whether someone is trustworthy. A common everyday example is sensing who is calling before you look at your phone. People often dismiss claircognizance as coincidence, but the more you pay attention, the more clearly you recognize its presence.

Clairvoyance (clear seeing). Clairvoyance isn't about dramatic visions like you would see in the movies. More often, it shows up as mental images or symbolic pictures that offer insight.

My grandfather used to tell a childhood story of playing in an old abandoned house with his dog and his friends on the South Dakota prairie in the early 1900s. The house was considered haunted and the boys would test their courage by exploring the interior. One afternoon, they climbed the dilapidated staircase to prove their bravery.

As they reached the top, they encountered a battered old trunk sitting in the middle of the landing. The dog started barking uncontrollably and lunged toward the wispy, shadowed figure they saw rising from the decrepit chest. The nebulous creature declared, "Ray, you killed me" just as the dog sailed through the phantom apparition.

Without thinking twice, they turned and all bounded down the stairs, two and three at a time, to get away from the ghostly threat. Once outside and safely away from the building, trying to catch their breath, my grandfather saw the figure standing at the upstairs window. While the boys had difficulty making sense of their spooky encounter, they each felt uneasy and cautious with what they saw.

As it turned out, the old house had been a gangster hideaway where many had suffered and perished at the hands of *hit men* and criminals. My grandfather's experience illustrates how intuitive sight (and knowing) can protect us, even if it feels frightening at times. It ultimately impressed upon my grandfather and his friends, the dangers of playing in a condemned and haunted building.

Clairaudience (clear hearing). Clear hearing may involve hearing a voice or tone that communicates a message when no external sound is present. Science lacks empirical evidence that clairaudience exists, however, ask anyone who has experienced hearing a loud command in their head to "STOP" before backing their car into unexpected oncoming traffic, and they will tell you of the validity of clairaudience. A sudden ringing in your ears, music, or voices followed by guidance or memories can all be signs of clairaudience. If you have ever had the experience of clearly hearing a loved one's voice who is either deceased or living far away from you, you have most likely experienced clairaudience.

Clairsentience (clear sensing). Clear sensing is the ability to feel energy or emotions through the body without the other person saying a word. Facial expressions, tone of voice, body language and energy all offer cues. Think of a time when you walked into a room and felt the residue of an earlier argument or "just knew" your child was struggling—across the county.

While living in Tennessee, I provided reiki for an unconscious patient whose family was hopeful that it would help their dad. Entering the hospital room, I could see that William (let's call him) was uncomfortable. Lips pursed in his unconscious state, deep lines of stress were set into his forehead. Gently resting my hands on his head, I heard a man's voice in my head tell me he was in pain. I continued the session, gently moving my hands to his shoulders. While resting my hands there, I noticed my own shoulders starting to ache.

Placing my hands on William's spine, I was immediately overcome with panic and severe back pain to the point where I almost doubled over and stopped the session. Breathing through the excruciating pain a moment longer, I heard the man's voice speak again, telling me his body had not been exercised while he had been in a coma. As I registered what he said, the pain in my body subsided and his face noticeably relaxed.

I relayed the information I received to his son, who contacted the attending nurse. She confirmed that William had not been exercised since being brought to the hospital. I saw him once again, after he received passive physical therapy, and even though he was still in a coma, his countenance and energy felt calmer and I didn't experience any discomfort during our second reiki session.

Although I can't logically explain, I was clearly sensing in my body what William was trying to communicate.

Clairalience (intuitive smell) and **Clairgustance** (intuitive taste). These less common intuitive senses appear as smells or tastes not present in the physical environment. For many years after my grandmother passed away, I would smell the sudden aroma of Dove soap out of the blue. It brought a feeling of connection and comfort, as though she were visiting in spirit. Can you remember a time when you smelled or tasted something that wasn't in your current environment? Do you remember how it made you feel?

Intuition as an Energetic Experience

From an energetic perspective, intuition can be understood as communication between your consciousness and the larger field of energy that surrounds you. Everything—thoughts, emotions, physical matter—vibrates. Sensitive individuals often perceive these subtle vibrations more easily, especially when they are emotionally regulated and grounded in the present moment.

Energy healers, empaths, and spiritual practitioners describe intuition as a form of resonance. When your mind is quiet, you pick up what harmonizes—or clashes—with your own energy. This explains why intuition often communicates through the body. Your nervous system responds to information faster than your rational mind can interpret it.

This perspective doesn't reject science; it expands upon it. Neuroscience can explain pattern recognition, emotional recall, and unconscious processing. Energy work describes how intuition also connects you to fields of information beyond your personal memory—sometimes through symbolic imagery, sensory messages, or bodily sensations.

Both perspectives reveal that intuition is a natural human ability that grows stronger through awareness.

Intuition Leads the Way

During my years as a Reiki master, numerous intuitive experiences have unfolded while working with my clients. One example occurred when working with a man at a holistic retreat center in southern Tennessee. I had never met him before, and had no prior knowledge of his medical history, yet the moment I met him, a clear vision of a frail, grayish skeleton appeared in my mind's eye.

I instructed him to lie down on the massage table and he rested peacefully with his eyes closed. As I began to work, a single word—*cancer*—echoed through my awareness. After a few moments, I heard the words *"New England"* and saw a man whom I didn't recognize, holding a telephone receiver.

The remainder of the session was quiet and comforting. As I worked, my hands tingled and felt hot, which was typical. I noticed my client breathing more deeply as he visibly relaxed. As I ended the session, a surge of energy moved through my fingertips and expanded outward, like blowing into a balloon. The image of the skeleton returned to my mind, only this time, it had a whiter hue.

When my client and I recapped his session, he admitted to me that he was in remission from bone cancer and my vision of a man in New England holding a telephone receiver was an old college friend from Maine whom he had been thinking about.

Intuition often works this way—offering just enough information at the right moment to guide healing, clarity, and connection.

How Mindfulness Strengthens Intuition

Intuition is always functioning in the background, yet mindfulness determines how well we recognize it. To access intuitive insight, we need the ability to hear our own mental, physical, and emotional cues without distortion. Mindfulness supports this by slowing us down, helping us observe the present moment rather than reacting to it.

A quieter mind makes intuition easier to detect. When you're grounded in the present moment, internal chatter fades, giving rise to subtle impressions. Intuition rarely shouts, but speaks through gentle nudges and instant knowing.

The body often senses truth before the mind does and mindfulness increases awareness of these early signals. You may notice sensations that offer valuable clues about what feels aligned or off. These cues often reflect intuitive wisdom.

Mindfulness improves emotional clarity. Strong emotions can

disguise themselves as intuition, but mindfulness separates emotional reactivity from deeper knowing.

Over time, mindfulness enhances your ability to recognize patterns in your thoughts, behaviors, and surroundings, thus helping you make connections you might otherwise overlook.

Most people talk themselves out of intuitive insights because they doubt themselves. Mindfulness builds self-trust by cultivating present moment awareness, teaching you to trust your inner voice.

Strengthening intuition rarely requires force or strain; it only asks for presence. As your awareness sharpens, the subtle cues that once slipped past your attention begin to stand out with surprising clarity. You may feel a sudden shift in your body, or an unmistakable spark of recognition when you enter a new situation. Sometimes the message arrives as a simple inner yes or no, a subtle sense of leaning toward something or gently pulling away. Other times, it comes as an image, a phrase, or a memory that surfaces out of nowhere and somehow feels relevant.

Mindfulness turns these moments from passing curiosities into meaningful information. When you pair awareness with practice, you strengthen the ability to discern what's true intuition and what's simply fear, habit, or old conditioning repeating itself. The more you practice, the easier it becomes to recognize the difference. True intuition is quiet, direct, and neutral. It doesn't panic, push, or overwhelm. Fear, on the other hand, tends to shout. It feels urgent, dramatic, or catastrophic. Habit feels predictable and familiar. Projection feels emotional and reactive.

As you continue to tune in, sense the distinctions in your body as naturally as you sense temperature or hunger. Your inner signals refine themselves. Your instincts become clearer. The more present you are, the more fluent you become in your own intuitive language, the one you've been speaking all along, even if you didn't realize you were listening.

Creativity

*"Mindfulness opens the door to creativity by teaching us
to see the world with fresh eyes."*
— JON KABAT-ZINN

Creativity is one of those experiences you recognize instantly, even if you can't quite define it. Britannica describes it as "having or showing an ability to make new things or think of new ideas," but anyone who has ever solved a tricky math problem, improvised a meal that somehow tasted amazing, or finally finished a song lyric that had been dancing around in their head knows creativity feels like much more than a new idea. Creativity is a spark—an internal lift—that announces, *This is new ... and it's mine.*

If you think back, you probably remember a moment when an idea arrived so suddenly it almost startled you. Maybe it happened while you were driving, taking a shower, or staring at the ceiling waiting for sleep. It might have felt like a gentle nudge, or like the universe tapped you on the shoulder and dropped an insight right in front of your face. It is something that is more easily felt than defined. When these moments come into my life, I feel a lightness in my body and tingling down my arms. Sometimes I lose track of time when I get caught up in the process of moving the creation from my mind into the physical world. Hours of exhilaration and excitement pass as if they were minutes.

This is the quiet magic of creativity—an experience built from curiosity, observation, openness, and intuition. Interestingly, these qualities are also fundamental aspects of mindfulness. When we learn to pay attention to our inner and outer world with more presence and less judgment, creativity becomes easier to access. It rises naturally, like cream floats to the surface of farm-fresh milk.

Think about what happens when your mind is cluttered. Stress, deadlines, and rapid-fire thoughts leave little room for inspiration to take shape. Many people assume they "lost" their creativity somewhere between childhood and adulthood, when in reality it has simply been buried under noise. Mindfulness clears that space. Research has shown that allowing the mind to wander intentionally—especially after mindfulness practice—enhances creative idea generation because the brain is more relaxed and focused. When the mind quiets, ideas have room to land and expand.

This is why a mindfulness practice doesn't just calm you—it unlocks your imagination. A few minutes of breathing, a short walk without your phone, or simply observing the sky can shift your mental state enough to reveal connections you didn't notice before. Creativity thrives in spaciousness, not pressure.

Consider the creative process of a professional songwriter. I have a friend who has built a successful career writing songs for well-known artists, and even performing a few of his own. Whenever I ask him how he comes up with such original melodies, he never describes a rigid formula or a forced stroke of genius. Instead, he talks about what he calls "noodling" on the guitar.

To an outsider, it might look like he's simply absentmindedly strumming. Yet when he explains it, "noodling" is his version of entering a mindful state. He settles into his body, breathes, and allows his fingers to move across the strings without pressure or expectation. As the busy thoughts in his mind quiet down, his awareness drops into the sound, the vibration, and the subtle emotional tones that rise with each chord.

In that relaxed, open space—somewhere between focus and daydream—new melodies begin to emerge. Sometimes it happens quickly; sometimes it takes days. Either way, he isn't "trying" to be creative. He's listening and allowing. He's paying attention to the faint spark of intuition that whispers. This gentle, mindful wandering is what helps him catch ideas that would never show up through effort alone. He often says the best songs come when he trusts whatever wants to come through.

That is creativity strengthened by mindfulness: a quiet mind, an open channel, and the willingness to follow intuitive threads as they appear.

Creativity belongs to everyone. It shows up in problem-solving, parenting, gardening, negotiating, cooking, and countless everyday moments. Mindfulness simply reminds us to slow down enough to notice the ideas already forming beneath the surface.

If you haven't yet begun a mindfulness practice, start small. Pay attention to one breath, one tree, one quiet moment in your day. Let your awareness soften. You might be surprised to discover how creative you already are.

Deepen Your Connection
to Source

"The quieter you become, the more you are able to hear."
— RUMI

Every person has their own understanding of Spirit, but almost everyone feels some inner pull toward something greater—something wiser, more compassionate, more expansive than the thinking mind. Before exploring how mindfulness strengthens this connection, it helps to understand what we mean by *spirit, Spirit, and spirituality.*

The common dictionary definition of *spirit* describes it as the non-physical essence of a person—the part of you that gives life and character. Many spiritual traditions describe spirit as the vital energy or consciousness that animates all living beings. When Spirit is spelled with a capital "S," it often refers to the Divine in a more religious context, such as Christianity's Holy Spirit. In more metaphysical traditions, Spirit is understood as the creative intelligence of God, the Universe, Source, or Universal Mind. These names vary, but the idea remains consistent: Spirit is the life force behind all things, the presence that continues even when the physical body stops.

Spirituality, however, stretches far wider than religious doctrine. Some people feel deeply spiritual without belonging to any religion. Others find that spirituality simply means living with awareness, kindness, and respect for the interconnectedness of all life. Spirituality invites you to look beneath the ordinary rush of life and wonder, *What is my life really about?* It encourages you to consider the values you live by, the meaning you make from your experiences, and the unseen thread that seems to connect you to others.

For me, spirituality is the recognition that I am part of a Higher Consciousness—a vast, creative intelligence that flows through every living being. It reminds me to treat myself and others with gentleness. It softens the edges of judgment and replaces them with curiosity. It gives me the sense that my life is happening with me, not to me, and that every moment carries both meaning and mystery.

You have your own interpretation, and that's important. Knowing what Spirit and spirituality mean to you gives shape to the deeper work of self-awareness. You might ask yourself: *What do I believe about Spirit?*

Do I feel connected to something larger than myself? How does that connection—or lack of it—show up in my daily life?

Write these questions down. Sit with them without trying to find the *"right"* answer. Whatever comes up—clarity, confusion, curiosity—is welcome. The act of asking begins the journey.

Understanding your relationship with Spirit often brings comfort, especially during life's harder seasons. It offers the reassurance that you are not isolated in your struggles or your joys. Many people describe spirituality as a sense of belonging to themselves and to a larger whole.

So, where does mindfulness fit into this?

Mindfulness is, at its heart, the practice of being present—of observing your thoughts, emotions, and sensations without immediately clinging to them or pushing them away. This simple practice of awareness becomes a powerful doorway to Spirit. When you are fully present, you step out of the relentless chatter of the mind. You stop rehearsing old stories, worrying about outcomes, or replaying mistakes. The noise quiets and the static clears. In that spaciousness, you feel something that was there all along but often overlooked: connection.

A mindfulness practice doesn't ask you to adopt a belief system or change your worldview. It simply opens you to the possibility that Spirit is easiest to feel when you are not distracted. When your mind is present, you begin to sense the life pulsing through everything.

You notice synchronicities. You feel intuitive nudges more clearly. You recognize a deeper wisdom beneath your everyday thoughts.

Research supports this, though it may use different language. Studies from Harvard-affiliated neuroscientist Sara Lazar show that mindfulness can reduce activity in the brain's default mode network, the system responsible for rumination and self-centered thinking (Lazar et al., 2014). When this network quiets, people often report feeling more connected, compassionate, and grounded—experiences that many would call *spiritual.*

Mindfulness helps you become aware of who you are and, just as importantly, who you are not. You are not the running commentary inside your mind that produces fear and anxiety. As you learn to detach from these internal habits, you create room for a presence to emerge. That presence is your spirit—your connection to Source.

Connection to Spirit often shows up in the simplest of moments. It may appear as a wave of gratitude when you step outside and notice the way sunlight hits the ground. It may arrive during a quiet morning breath, the kind where you feel your whole body exhale. It may slip in while journaling or reflecting, when your mind settles just long enough for clarity to surface.

Try incorporating mindfulness into small moments throughout your day. Sit with your breath for a minute before picking up your phone. Pause before speaking during a tense conversation. Take a few mindful steps as you walk to your car or your kitchen. These tiny practices open the door to Spirit again and again. Over time, they build a reliable, peaceful pathway back to your own deeper knowing.

When your awareness rests in the present moment, you reconnect not only with yourself but with the greater field of consciousness that holds all beings. In that space, separation softens. Fear loosens. Gratitude expands. The presence you feel is the unmistakable whisper of Spirit reminding you that you are already connected, already guided, already whole.

Forgiveness

Forgiveness is often spoken of as a virtue, a moral ideal, or a spiritual directive. Rarely is it used as a practical path to inner peace. Yet forgiveness is one of the most liberating skills you can cultivate, and mindfulness is one of the most effective tools for developing it. When you understand forgiveness as a conscious, present-moment practice rather than a one-time emotional event, it becomes far more accessible, grounded, and transformative.

One of the best definitions of forgiveness I have heard comes from author and forgiveness expert, Fred Luskin. He states forgiveness is the ability to make peace with the word "no." Think about that for a moment. Living through a loss means your life, in some way, has said "no" to you. You haven't gotten what you wanted.

The loss can be as minor as your husband eating the last piece of pie you were saving, or as grave and far-reaching as the ending of a relationship due to infidelity. Not getting to eat your piece of pie is a loss. It is a "no" to your anticipation of a tasty delight. Likewise, the loss of your relationship is a "no" that ends your hopes and dreams for a particular future, signifying a loss of trust in yourself and your partner. Not getting to eat your pie is a much smaller "no" than the loss of a committed relationship, however, while the grievances vary in severity, the action of forgiveness is the same.

At its essence, forgiveness is the process of releasing resentment, judgment, or hostility toward yourself or someone else. It does **not** require forgetting, condoning harmful behavior, or pretending that something painful was acceptable. Rather, forgiveness is about loosening the grip the past has on your mind. It allows you to reclaim the emotional energy you have invested in old hurt, anger, or disappointment. This shift—from holding on to letting go—is precisely where mindfulness becomes essential.

Mindfulness teaches you to witness thoughts and emotions without collapsing into them. When hurt arises, the untrained mind tends to repeat the same narrative: *They were wrong. I was wronged. I'm still angry.* These thoughts become familiar, almost comfortable, even as they keep you bound to suffering. Mindfulness interrupts this cycle. Through conscious awareness of the present moment, you begin to see resentment not as a fixed truth but as a mental event passing through your awareness. You can feel its weight without allowing it to define you.

Consider a friend of mine who was engaged in a bitter dispute with her ex-husband for nearly a decade over the custody of their children. Each time she spoke about him, her jaw tightened, her breath shortened, and her voice rose slightly—all physiological signs of relived stress.

On one unsuspecting afternoon, she received results from a routine mammogram that determined she had stage IV breast cancer. She was stunned and heartbroken to realize how unfair her life seemed. Fear for her life, worry for her children, and resentment for her ex-husband flooded her senses, before she could think clearly. When she finally gathered her thoughts, she realized years of negative emotions had contributed to her now, life-threatening situation. It was a huge spiritual wake-up call that changed her approach to life.

Instead of fighting her ex-husband, she allowed her children to spend more time with him. She changed her diet and lifestyle to be more supportive of her healing. Most importantly, she realized the power and importance of forgiving: her ex-husband **and** herself.

Through several weeks of practice, she noticed negative reactions as they emerged. Instead of fueling them with more storylines, she simply observed: tightness ... heat ... anger. As her awareness sharpened, she discovered a softer layer beneath the anger—sadness and regret. Beneath that, longing. Beneath that, love.

Nothing about the past changed, but her relationship to the memories did. Through mindfulness, she recognized that forgiveness was not an event waiting for her ex-husband's apology; it was an internal shift waiting for her presence.

She passed away seven years after her diagnosis, having forgiven her ex-husband and living her new life to the fullest, embracing herself and forgiveness.

Forgiveness requires courage because it asks you to face pain directly. The unexamined mind prefers avoidance, distraction, or rumination—all of which intensify suffering. The mindful mind stays with the experience long enough to understand it. You can only release what you are willing to feel. By anchoring yourself in breath and body, you create a safe internal space where difficult emotions can rise and fall without overwhelming you. Mindfulness makes forgiveness possible by stabilizing you long enough to open your heart.

The relationship between forgiveness and inner peace becomes clear when you reflect on how much energy resentment consumes. Anger taxes the nervous system, elevates stress hormones, and interrupts sleep. Rumination keeps the mind looping through imaginary arguments that replay long after the event has ended. Resentment is like carrying a backpack filled with stones—you may be able to walk with it, but it weighs you down and shapes every step.

Forgiveness is not about absolving someone else; it is about putting down the backpack.

Equally important is the role of self-forgiveness. Many people turn harsh judgment inward, replaying mistakes from the past as if punishing themselves will somehow prevent future missteps, but self-criticism rarely breeds growth. It keeps you stuck in shame, limiting your capacity for change. Mindfulness disrupts this pattern by teaching you to observe self-judgment without believing it. You begin to see the inner critic as a collection of old messages—fear, insecurity, perfectionism—not as a reliable narrator. With practice, you can replace self-condemnation with self-compassion, allowing space for healing, responsibility, and renewal.

One of the most surprising elements of forgiveness is how ordinary the doorway can be. It often begins not with a profound revelation, but with a single breath. When you sit quietly and bring your attention to the present moment, you disrupt the habitual chain of resentment. You introduce softness into a hardened narrative. A few minutes of mindful breathing each day can gradually unwind patterns of emotional rigidity. Over time, you may find that forgiveness emerges less as a forced choice and more as a natural consequence of inner clarity.

Practical mindfulness techniques can support this process. You might begin with a brief body scan, noticing areas of tension associated with old hurts and simply softening around them. You might try mindful journaling, writing not about the story of what happened but about the sensations and emotions arising in the present moment. Even mindful walking can help release emotional tightness; the rhythm of movement has a way of loosening mental knots.

Another useful practice is silently offering phrases of goodwill—first to yourself, then to the person who hurt you, even if you do not feel ready to forgive them. You do not have to force emotion. Simply offering the intention of goodwill plants the seeds of forgiveness. Over time, intention becomes capacity.

Forgiveness is not linear. Some days you may feel spacious and openhearted; other days the old wounds may feel fresh again. This is not failure. It is the nature of healing. Mindfulness supports this ebb and flow by allowing each moment to be exactly as it is—without pushing yourself to "hurry up and heal." When forgiveness becomes a mindful practice rather than a demand, it unfolds with more authenticity and depth.

Ultimately, forgiveness invites you into a more peaceful relationship with yourself and the world. It frees you from mental bondage and reconnects you with the present moment, where life is actually happening. When you commit to mindfulness, you cultivate the clarity and compassion needed to release what no longer serves you. And when you release the past, even partially, you create space for inner peace to take root.

Forgiveness does not mean you forget the past. It means you refuse to let the past determine your peace.

It is one of the greatest gifts you can give yourself.

Pain Relief

"Pain is inevitable. Suffering is optional."
— HARUKI MURAKAMI

Pain is one of the few experiences every human understands. At some point, you've stubbed a toe, pulled a muscle, grieved a heartbreak, or endured the long, dull echo of something that felt like it might never end. Most forms of pain appear suddenly and fade quickly as the body heals. Chronic pain, however, has a very different rhythm. It lingers for months or even years, reshaping daily life and challenging the spirit. Globally, more than 10% of people live with chronic pain, with women experiencing it at higher rates than men (CDC, 2023).

The rise in chronic pain is not surprising when you look at modern life. Longevity brings many gifts, but it also increases exposure to the wear and tear of aging—arthritis, joint degeneration, disc issues, and balance or cognitive changes. At the same time, technology has quietly rewritten how bodies move and rest. Many of us spend hours hunched over keyboards, tablets, or phones, unaware of how little we blink or how long we go without shifting our posture. Neck pain, back pain, stiff shoulders, aching wrists, and eye strain are now woven into the daily fabric of work and school. Over time, this sedentary lifestyle amplifies discomfort, and in some cases, teaches the brain to expect pain even when no physical injury is present.

Stress, anxiety, and depression also play significant roles in pain. When your nervous system senses a threat—anything from financial worry to an argument—it activates the sympathetic *"fight/flight/ freeze"* response. Heart rate rises. Breathing quickens. Hormones such as adrenaline and cortisol surge through the bloodstream.

These changes help you react quickly, but they also create inflammation. In today's world, where threats feel constant and rarely physical, the body can remain in this heightened state far longer than it was designed to. The result is a cycle in which inflammation intensifies pain, pain increases fear, and fear keeps the nervous system stuck in overdrive.

The cycle continues until something interrupts it. That "something" is **mindfulness**, our conscious and powerful ally. Mindfulness does not claim to cure disease or eliminate physical injury, but what it can do is transform your relationship with pain and reduce its intensity by changing how you perceive and respond to it. When you observe discomfort through a lens of curiosity rather than fear, you shift from reacting to responding. That shift helps calm the nervous system, quiet emotional reactivity, and create enough space for healing to begin.

Harvard researchers reported in 2015 that mindful practices such as meditation, deep breathing, yoga, tai chi, and guided imagery can significantly reduce pain by altering the brain's perception of it. Because pain involves both the body and the mind, integrating these approaches often creates meaningful relief. For example, two people with similar injuries may experience very different levels of suffering depending on their stress level, emotional history, and thought patterns. Mindfulness helps regulate all three.

Think of mindfulness as a gentle spotlight. It illuminates your internal landscape—your physical sensations, your thoughts, your emotional responses—without judgment. Instead of tightening around pain or mentally fighting it, you learn to observe it. Observation creates clarity. Clarity reduces fear. Reduced fear lowers stress. Lower stress reduces inflammation. Behold, less inflammation often eases pain.

For those who experience chronic discomfort, this internal shift is invaluable. Repeated pain can actually retrain the brain to anticipate suffering, even when no active stimulus is present. Neural pathways become overly sensitive, like a fire alarm that sounds because someone made toast. Mindfulness helps retrain the alarm system. You learn to recognize sensations for what they are, not what you fear they might become.

Two effective mindfulness techniques for pain relief are **deep breathing** and the **body scan**. These tools are simple and effective because they redirect attention away from catastrophic thinking and toward immediate sensory experience.

Begin by sitting quietly and noticing your body from head to toe.

You might discover tension in a place you hadn't noticed. Maybe you feel nothing at all. Both experiences are valid. If discomfort is present, approach it the way you would approach a frightened child—with curiosity and compassion.

Ask yourself:

- *Where exactly is the pain?*
- *What shape does it take—sharp, dull, throbbing, hot, tingling?*
- *Is it steady or intermittent?*
- *Does it change when I breathe?*
- *What emotions seem attached to it? Fear? Anger? Sadness? Fatigue?*

Instead of recoiling, breathe into that area. With each inhalation, soften around the discomfort. With each exhalation, imagine releasing tension, even if only a fraction. Repeat this several times. People often report that simply giving the pain attention—not resistance—reduces its intensity. The goal is not to "make it disappear," but to change how you relate to it.

Mindfulness encourages us to become a compassionate witness to our own experience. When we observe a sensation without judgment, the mind quiets. Fear loosens. Space opens. That open space is where relief begins.

Mindfulness meditation is a powerful tool for transforming pain. Research shows that meditation decreases activation in brain regions associated with emotional evaluation of pain, while increasing activation in areas associated with sensory processing. In simple terms, meditation helps us feel the pain without attaching fear, frustration, or storylines to it. Pain becomes information rather than identity.

Many people living with chronic pain describe a shift from *"This is happening TO me"* to *"This is something happening FOR me."* That shift increases resilience and reduces suffering.

If meditation feels intimidating, movement-based practices offer an alternative. Numerous studies show that exercise—whether walking, swimming, stretching, or strength training—can reduce chronic pain by releasing endorphins, improving circulation, strengthening supportive muscles, and decreasing inflammation. Movement also reduces stress, which indirectly reduces pain. The key is to move mindfully, at a pace that respects your body's limits rather than challenges them.

Understanding the mind–body connection is essential to lasting relief. Emotional distress often shows up as physical pain—a tight jaw, clenched stomach, or aching back. Conversely, physical pain creates emotional strain. A calm mind contributes to a calm body. When you experience pain of any kind—physical or emotional—it signals an imbalance. Mindfulness helps you listen for the message beneath the sensation. Maybe it's asking for rest, boundaries, nourishment, or emotional release. When you approach pain as communication rather than punishment, something shifts inside you. You feel more empowered, less frightened, and more connected to yourself.

Mindfulness is not the elimination of discomfort, but is the cultivation of peace within discomfort. The practice teaches you to stay grounded even when your body or heart feels tender. Through gentle awareness, pain becomes not only something you manage, but something you learn from.

With consistent practice, mindfulness allows you to see opportunities for healing that were once obscured by fear or resistance. You gain the capacity to soften around pain rather than brace against it. You become more present, more patient, more resilient. Pain may still arise, but your relationship to it becomes wiser, and that wisdom—born from acceptance, and mindful presence—creates the inner peace this book is all about.

Better Decision-Making

Life is created from a continual collection of choices and outcomes that shape the story of who we become. Every decision, whether made with intention or made on autopilot, is a thread woven into the fabric of our experience. Some choices arrive lightly, without much consequence, while others are heavy, emotional, and require careful consideration. Then there are the impulsive decisions, made in a split-second, without conscious thought. Regardless of the form they take, our choices profoundly influence the quality of our inner and outer world. Every choice we make affects the quality of our life.

Mindfulness does not promise that every decision will lead to a perfect outcome. What it does offer is the ability to see more clearly, choose with greater awareness, and continually refine our actions in ways that serve our well-being. When we bring presence to the decision-making process, we create space—to breathe, to reflect, to listen, and to act with intention rather than habit.

Many Layers of Decision-Making

Human decisions occur on several levels. Some are practical and require strategic thought like buying a home, comparing schools, planning a career change. Others carry emotional weight, such as choosing whether to marry, start a family, or end a relationship. Split-second decisions, such as swerving to avoid danger or pulling your hand away from a hot surface, happen without conscious thought at all.

Mindfulness improves each type of decision, not by slowing you down, but by making you more aware—of your emotions, your internal patterns, your environment, and your deeper values. When your mind is calmer and more attuned to the present, your choices become clearer and more aligned with the life you hope to create.

Mindfulness Enhances Decision-Making

Scientific research has been exploring the measurable benefits of mindfulness since the early 1970s, largely inspired by Jon Kabat-Zinn, founder of Mindfulness-Based Stress Reduction (MBSR). His work helped establish mindfulness as a respected tool for reducing stress, increasing resilience, and strengthening emotional intelligence.

Today we know far more about how mindfulness affects the brain. Regular practice—especially meditation—has been shown to reduce the size and reactivity of the amygdala, the brain region responsible for fear and impulsive responses. This physiological shift promotes steadiness, clearer thinking, and greater impulse control. The prefrontal cortex, which supports reasoning and decision-making, becomes more active and efficient.

Simply put, mindfulness calms the noise so you can hear your wisdom. When we're less reactive, decisions become less tangled in fear, projection, or emotional overload. We're able to evaluate our choices more thoughtfully, with a grounded perspective. Mindfulness also increases self-awareness, helping to distinguish between old patterns and genuine intuition. Over time, decisions become less about avoiding discomfort and more about aligning with our deeper goals, values, and well-being.

Mindfulness in Action

The benefits of mindfulness are not theoretical. They show up in daily life, from home environments to the workplace, and in schools, hospitals, athletic arenas, and beyond. Mindfulness affects every relationship in every area of life.

Professionals in high-stress environments consistently report improvements in focus, clarity, creativity, and problem-solving when they incorporate mindfulness into their routines. Organizations such as Google, Intel, and General Mills have introduced mindfulness programs with powerful results: clearer thinking in meetings, more strategic decision-making, and improved communication. Leaders describe feeling less reactive and more balanced, even when faced with demanding situations.

Elite athletes like Michael Phelps and LeBron James openly discuss their use of visualization and breath work as part of their training. These techniques help them remain calm, centered, and capable of making quick, accurate decisions under intense pressure. Their mindfulness practice enhances present-moment awareness—the very quality that helps any of us think more clearly when faced with challenge.

Teachers who practice mindfulness through meditation, breathing techniques, gratitude exercises, or journaling report being more patient, empathetic, and attuned to the needs of their students. They make decisions about classroom management, student behavior, and lesson planning with greater clarity and compassion. Mindfulness also helps reduce burnout, making space for more intuitive and effective teaching.

An article in *Forbes* highlighted how mindfulness helps healthcare providers manage overwhelming stress, avoid burnout, and think more clearly when making life-impacting choices. Physicians and nurses noted that mindfulness improved their ability to listen deeply, communicate effectively, and deliver compassionate care. Their decisions—often made under intense time pressure—became more grounded and precise.

Perhaps the most profound benefits of mindfulness appear in everyday living. Individuals who integrate simple practices such as breathing exercises, visualization, yoga, or meditation often notice that they communicate more clearly, react less impulsively, and make choices that reflect their true values. Their relationships deepen, their confidence increases, and they feel a sense of inner steadiness that supports wise, thoughtful decision-making.

These examples demonstrate how mindfulness can help anyone make better-informed and thoughtful decisions. Presence is the gateway to better choices—everywhere, every time.

Wouldn't it be a good decision to practice mindfulness?

One Unplanned Decision Changed Everything

When I was finishing my bachelor's degree in the early 1990s, I discovered at the last minute that I needed one more physical education credit to graduate. Already overloaded—working full-time and attending school full-time—I panicked. I skimmed the course list, ruling out sports I had no interest in, and finally landed on the "Y" section—Yoga. It was as if a forgotten door in my memory swung open. I remembered watching it on TV when I was a kid. Barely reading the course description, I signed up for an *Intro to Yoga* class because it fit my schedule.

It was not a mindful decision.

I assumed it would be easy—stretch a little, lie around on a mat. How hard could it be?

That thought lasted about five minutes into the first class. Yoga was far more demanding physically and mentally than I expected. The poses challenged my every muscle, and the philosophy stretched my mind just as much. I was overwhelmed by the unfamiliar terminology, the breathing techniques, and the sheer intensity of the practice.

The first day of the first week of class I wondered what I had gotten myself into. This was not the same peaceful experience I had as a five-year-old watching Lilias before Sesame Street.

The second week felt a little more familiar and easier. I even found myself interested in the philosophy. By midterms, I noticed subtle, positive changes in my sleep and eating habits. My anxiety softened and I felt clearer and more grounded. Not only was I doing better in yoga, all my other classes were easier too. By the end of the semester, I not only felt stronger but more connected to myself than I had in years.

That single, rushed decision—made in a moment of stress—ended up shaping the rest of my life. Yoga became a cornerstone of my personal growth, eventually leading me to study and write about it, logging thousands of hours of training, practicing, and teaching, and later to write *Empowering Your Life with Yoga*. It opened the door to mindfulness and expanded my understanding of how presence can transform one's choices—my choices.

The real lesson of this story is not about luck or fate—it's about awareness and more mindful decision-making. When you live "by the seat of your pants," you increase your chances of stress, confusion, and regret. It just so happened that grace turned my hasty decision into a mindful way of being. When you live mindfully, you increase your chances of wisdom, clarity, and freedom.

The Heart of Wise Decision-Making

Consider a decision you've been avoiding or one that feels emotionally charged. Is it something you fear? How does the responsibility of the decision make you feel?

Take a full and focused breath to bring your awareness into your body. Notice any physical sensations—tightness, heaviness, fluttering, warmth. Observe your thoughts without judging them. Give yourself a few moments to contemplate your answer.

Take another deep breath, letting your exhale carry some tension out of your body. Now, imagine how you will feel once the decision is made. What emotions arise—relief, pride, freedom, fear? What steps will move you closer to your decision? How does it feel to bring consciousness to your decision-making process?

You may want to journal your observations. Writing often reveals insights that are easily missed in the mind's rush.

Mindfulness does not force a decision. It *clarifies* it. It returns you back to your needs, your values, and your truth.

There is no universal "right" or "wrong" way to make decisions—there is only choosing with awareness or choosing on autopilot. The invitation is simply to notice how you make your choices. Are you satisfied with the results they create? If so, trust that confidence. But if you sense that your decisions could be more intentional or aligned with the life you want, mindfulness offers a powerful way forward. By bringing presence to your thoughts, emotions, and motivations, you begin making choices from clarity rather than habit or impulse. Mindfulness steadies your emotions, sharpens your insight, and adds wisdom to every decision you make.

Alleviate Arguments

"Peace begins with a pause."
—THICH NHAT HANH

Conflict is a hot topic these days. Across the globe, countries and communities grapple with long-standing tensions, political disagreements, cultural divides, and struggles for safety and dignity. Even within our own countries, conflict shows up in public institutions, workplaces, neighborhoods, and families. We can't overlook the harsh words, rigid opinions, and escalating emotions that spill into everyday conversation—especially in the digital spaces where many of us now interact.

On the global stage, conflict feels overwhelming. On a personal level, it feels exhausting. Disagreements between partners, co-workers, neighbors, and friends arise daily. Human beings collide—not because we are broken or cruel, but because we each carry our own histories, fears, assumptions, and values. With more than eight billion people on the planet, disagreement is unavoidable.

However, disagreement doesn't *have* to become conflict. Differences don't have to ignite arguments, hostility, or emotional harm. This is where mindfulness becomes one of the most powerful tools we have. One conscious pause can soften tension and reverse the momentum of an argument. Mindfulness cannot erase opposing viewpoints, but it can change the way we relate to them—and to one another.

To grasp how this works, we must understand what happens inside our bodies and minds during conflict.

When Arguments Hijack the Body

The human brain is fundamentally wired to prioritize safety over pleasure to ensure the survival of our species. From cavemen, looking out for saber tooth tigers, to the modern-day company executive worried about a bottom line, our brains have always focused on safety first and comfort last.

Imagine you're in the middle of a conversation that suddenly takes a turn. A tone shifts. A phrase lands wrong. Someone misunderstands your intention—or you misunderstand theirs. In a single moment, your heart begins to beat faster, your chest tightens, and your jaw subtly tenses. You feel heat rise. Your breath shortens without your permission.

This is not your "bad habit." This is your nervous system.

Deep inside the brain sits the amygdala—an almond-shaped structure that acts like a tiny internal alarm. It exists for the primordial purpose of keeping you alive. When the amygdala senses threat—physical or emotional—it signals the sympathetic nervous system (SNS) to prepare for action. Adrenaline spikes. Muscles brace. The mind descends into survival mode and the "fight or flight" response is activated.

The moment the amygdala perceives danger, the brain temporarily downshifts away from empathy, reasoning, compassion, and curiosity. These functions live in the prefrontal cortex—the seat of thoughtful communication—and when we're stressed, access to them decreases.

This is how arguments escalate before we even realize we're in them.

It's not personal. It's biology.

Fortunately, we aren't prisoners of our impulses. The parasympathetic nervous system (PSNS)—the "rest and digest" system—can turn the alarm off. The most reliable way to activate the PSNS is through mindfulness practices such as slowing breath, relaxing the body, grounding attention in awareness, and choosing presence over reactivity.

This is where the argument begins to dissolve.

Why We Argue in the First Place

There are over eight billion people on the planet, with over eight billion unique viewpoints. This makes for an interesting mix of perspectives that don't always agree.

Our brains use this limited information to form opinions and judgments to make sense of life. Unfortunately, this internal perception can sometimes form bias toward other people and their ideas. Most arguments aren't really about the topic at hand. They're about the meaning we attach to them. People rarely fight about the dishes; they fight about feeling unappreciated. They rarely fight about the schedule; they fight about feeling unheard. They rarely fight about the facts; they fight about the emotions underneath.

Arguments occur when two people try—consciously or not—to defend their view of the world. Every person carries a private universe of opinions, memories, fears, hopes, biases, and interpretations shaped by countless life experiences. And when someone challenges our viewpoint, it can feel like they are challenging us.

However, difference is not the problem. The problem is the lack of mindful space around those differences.

Without mindfulness, our ego leaps in to protect itself. We interrupt. We defend. We raise our voice. We retreat. We accuse. We negotiate like warriors rather than collaborators. In this state, we don't listen to understand; we listen to react.

Mindfulness, however, changes the inner environment so completely that even the same disagreement unfolds in a different way.

Mindfulness: The Antidote to Conflict

Mindfulness softens arguments because it changes what we're paying attention to. Instead of focusing on being right, we begin noticing our physical sensations, our breath, our tone, our emotional waves, our thought patterns, and even the nervous system of the person in front of us. We become less aggressive and more attuned—less reactive and more receptive.

Even a few seconds of silent counting or deep breathing during an argument can disrupt the emotional cascade. This mindful "reset" engages the parasympathetic nervous system (PSNS), which lowers blood pressure and neutralizes stress hormones. In other words, breath gives the brain back its ability to think before reacting.

Mindfulness also enhances active listening. When we are fully present, we notice not only words but facial expressions, body language, tension, hesitation, and the subtle cues that help us understand what the other person truly needs. Arguments cool when understanding rises.

Most importantly, mindfulness helps us separate the moment from the story. Instead of reacting to all the times we've felt hurt, we respond to this moment alone. This allows compassion to emerge where defensiveness once stood.

One Breath Changed Everything

Some time ago, I found myself in the middle of a tense conversation with my good friend. We were both tired, overwhelmed, and convinced the other person was "not getting it." The more we talked, the more we misunderstood each other. A familiar heat rose in my chest—a signal that I was about to say something I would regret.

Something in me paused.

I closed my eyes briefly and inhaled slowly, feeling the air stretch my ribs. As I exhaled, the tension softened just enough for clarity to return. In the few seconds of that mindful pause, I could suddenly hear the hurt beneath my friend's words. The defensiveness left my voice, and my whole body relaxed.

"Let me hear you again," I said gently.

Her expression changed instantly. She softened too. Within minutes, the argument dissolved—not because we agreed, but because we remembered that we cared about each other more than winning.

Presence healed what reactivity had damaged.

The quiet power of mindfulness interrupts the momentum of conflict and replaces it with understanding.

How Arguments Begin and How Mindfulness Stops Them

Arguments generally start in one of three ways. We default to either the "fight," "flight," or "freeze" response.

Once the stress response is engaged, the argument can spiral out of control with raised voices, name-calling, unfair accusations, and a host of other antagonistic behaviors. This would be considered the "fight" part of the stress response.

On the other hand, you might be someone who doesn't like conflict, and will do anything to avoid it, including agreeing with your opponent even if you feel they are wrong. This "flight" response causes anger and emotional withdrawal because your thoughts and emotions don't have a safe place to be expressed. The argument is still present, but there is no outlet for resolution, leaving you feeling drained and frustrated.

Freezing in an argument can cause panic and feel quite overwhelming. It may feel as if your mind is short-circuiting which stops you from communicating effectively.

Mindfulness disrupts each of these patterns.

If you tend to "fight," presence helps you notice your rising anger before it spills over.

If you tend to "flee," mindfulness grounds you so you can stay in the conversation without abandoning yourself.

If you tend to "freeze." awareness reconnects you with your breath and thoughts so you can express your needs.

Mindfulness doesn't eliminate conflict, but merely transforms the way we move through it.

Communication With or Without Mindfulness

The next time you have a disagreement with someone, check to see if mindfulness is present. This difference of opinion has an opportunity for growth. With mindfulness, you can quickly come to an understanding and this can be a learning opportunity.

When it comes to an argument, however, your difference of opinion has disintegrated into seeing the other person as "wrong" and yourself as "right." When defensiveness takes over and you seek only to validate your opinion, the argument is already lost—by you.

Mindfulness offers a pause to ask the questions:

"Am I listening fully, without defensiveness, or am I only hearing what validates my position?"

"Am I reacting with assumptions or am I responding with clarity?"

"Can I hear the other person's point of view, or am I constantly interrupting with my own?"

"Is connection more important than victory?"

Presence allows both people to feel respected and safe—conditions that make arguments unnecessary.

Mindfulness in Action

The next time tension rises and you find yourself getting hot under the collar with a colleague, friend, or loved one, try incorporating some of these techniques to help diffuse disagreements:

Pause when you feel your voice tightening and the heat rising. In that instant urge to argue, pause, inhale deeply, and exhale slowly. This single act shifts your physiology. The nervous system calms. The brain clears. Your options expand.

Step back, not away. If you need space, say so. This is not withdrawal. It is wisdom. It signals respect for the relationship.

Turn the conversation into **collaboration**, helping to achieve a common goal. Ask curious and grounding questions that include rather than exclude. Consider questions like:

"Help me understand what you're feeling."

"What do you need right now?"

"What matters most here?"

These types of questions disarm conflict because they show willingness—not defensiveness.

Speak in terms of **"I" versus "You"** in conversations. Phrases like "You always ... ," "You never ...," or "You make me ..." incites blame and inflames the nervous system like adding gasoline to a fire.

Mindfulness helps to reframe these statements, replacing accusation with compassion. Instead, try using "I feel ...," "I need ...," or "I'm trying to understand ..."

Mindful Presence

Presence gives you a front-row seat to your own inner patterns—your tone, your triggers, your preferences, and the blind spots you usually overlook. The more intimately you understand yourself, the less driven you are to control others or prove your worth through force. When you learn to notice the earliest signals of tension rising in your body, you can interrupt the spiral before it gains momentum.

This self-awareness—paired with the ability to sense what others are feeling—is the foundation of emotional intelligence. With mindful attention, you begin to recognize the fear hiding beneath someone else's anger. You notice when an old wound is shaping your current reaction. You can discern the difference between what is true in this moment and what is simply emotional distortion from the past.

When conflict stops feeling like a threat and starts looking like an opening for understanding, everything changes. This shift in perception is the quiet power of mindfulness—it's how arguments soften, de-escalate, and often dissolve entirely.

The best way to approach calmer communication is to establish a daily mindfulness practice that strengthens your emotional resilience. You don't have to meditate for hours. Even five minutes of breath awareness, gentle yoga, journaling, or smiling will help regulate the nervous system.

When your inner world is steady, the outer world feels less threatening. When your mind is not racing ahead or falling backward, the present moment becomes easier to navigate. When you are centered, conflicts lose their power over you.

We don't stop arguing because life becomes easier. We stop arguing because we become more balanced.

Conflict will never disappear from the world, but the tension we add to it can. We cannot control how others behave, but mindfulness gives us the profound ability to control how we show up—with clarity instead of chaos, compassion instead of defensiveness, and curiosity instead of fear.

Arguments don't end because one person wins. They end because one person chooses awareness. Often, that is enough to transform the entire conversation. Mindfulness makes the discussion more conscious and helps you choose the path that brings peace.

In the wise words of Dr. Wayne Dyer, "Would you rather be right, or would you rather be kind?"

Heal Trauma

When we hear the word trauma, many of us picture large-scale catastrophes such as war, natural disasters, violent attacks, or abuse. But trauma isn't reserved for dramatic or headline-worthy events. It also hides in unsuspecting everyday moments like breaking your ankle while on vacation, a car accident on the way to work, a painful breakup, a medical diagnosis, or the loss of a beloved pet. Even the shock of losing something you deeply value can be destabilizing.

Trauma is never just the event itself. It is the *aftershock*—the physical and emotional imprint left in the body, mind, and heart when life shifts suddenly and without warning. It's the long stretch of uncertainty that follows as you try to understand what has happened and regain your sense of balance. At its core, trauma is a deeply complex, multi-layered experience that overwhelms your ability to cope, leaving you feeling helpless, ungrounded, and disconnected from yourself. It is not defined by the size of the event, but by how the nervous system experiences it.

Different Forms of Trauma

Trauma shows up in several forms, and recognizing them can help us better understand our own responses.

Acute trauma arises from a sudden, overwhelming event—a tornado warning, an assault, a car crash, a medical emergency. Your sympathetic nervous system fires into action, flooding your body with adrenaline and cortisol to protect you. Once the danger passes, your parasympathetic nervous system guides you back toward calm.

When events like these happen repeatedly, the body doesn't get the same chance to recover. This leads to **chronic trauma**—ongoing exposure to stress that exhausts both body and mind. Think of someone who lives through repeated domestic abuse or cares for an unpredictable family member. This continued stress can settle into the body as anxiety, tension, emotional instability, and physical pain if not addressed and treated.

There is also **secondary trauma**, which affects caregivers, first responders, medical professionals, therapists, and anyone who regularly supports those in distress. You don't have to be the one living the trauma to be shaped by its emotional weight. Secondary trauma involves either hearing about or witnessing someone else's hardship. Family members caring for ill or aging loved ones also experience this deeply. The more emotionally invested you are, the more likely you are to absorb the pain of the person you're caring for.

Trauma: More Common than You Think

It may feel like trauma is something that happens "out there," to other people—but globally, more than 70% of people will experience at least one traumatic event in their lifetime (World Health Organization). In the United States, the CDC estimates that 60–70% of adults have experienced at least one traumatic event, and around 64% have endured at least one form of childhood trauma.

With eight billion people on the planet, there are eight billion different life stories and eight billion ways of experiencing hardship. What overwhelms one person may not overwhelm another. No two nervous systems respond the same way.

One Accident—Two Different Traumas

Consider two friends who crash into a tree during a car accident. One breaks his arm. The other stands beside the wreckage in shock but has no physical injury.

An ambulance arrived on the scene and transported both friends to the hospital where both were treated for their symptoms and released.

Six weeks later, the friend with the broken arm is healed and ready to drive again. The friend who was in shock still can't get into a car without panicking. Which one experienced trauma?

The answer is both, in different ways. The first suffered physical trauma that healed easily. The second suffered emotional trauma that altered his sense of safety.

Trauma is a subjective experience that affects people in varying degrees. It is not weakness. It is biology.

Without awareness and support, emotional trauma can spiral into chronic anxiety, depression, PTSD, or internalized fear. This is why understanding trauma is essential. It helps us meet ourselves and others with compassion and understanding instead of judgment.

Mindfulness Supports Trauma Healing

Mindfulness is not a magic wand, but it is a powerful ally—one that helps you reconnect with your body, calm your nervous system, and meet your inner world with honesty and compassion. When you approach trauma through a mindful lens, you begin to notice your internal landscape more clearly. You learn how to regulate your emotions before they swell beyond your capacity, and you give yourself the space to respond consciously rather than react out of fear or habit. You become more attuned to your physical, emotional, and mental signals, recognizing the cues your body has been trying to share with you all along. Instead of being swept back into the past, you develop the ability to stay rooted in the present moment, where healing can actually occur. In this way, mindfulness gently teaches the body that it is safe again. It becomes a holistic path—one that honors both the emotional depth and physical imprint of trauma, guiding you back to a sense of internal steadiness and wholeness.

Healing Trauma: Mindfulness Practices

Mindfulness techniques that are particularly effective in healing trauma are the body scan, deep breathing, loving-kindness mediation, journaling, grounding in nature, and mindful movement such as qigong, tai chi, or yoga. All of these practices develop more integration between body, mind, and spirit, thus reducing stress and creating overall well-being.

A **body scan** helps reconnect you with sensations you may have learned to fear, ignore, or numb. Trauma often causes disconnection from the body. The body scan slowly repairs this by building safety and awareness.

As you move your attention through the body, you learn to notice tension, discomfort, and emotional holding. With awareness, softening those areas becomes possible. Over time, this activates the parasympathetic nervous system, calming the stress response and easing both physical and emotional pain.

Deep breathing anchors you to the present moment. Large, mindful breaths increase oxygen, improve clarity, strengthen respiratory muscles, and calm the nervous system.

In his teachings, Thich Nhat Hanh sums up perfectly, the power of breath: *"Peace is every breath."* When you breathe consciously, your body remembers that it is not in danger.

Loving-kindness meditation may be one of the most transformative techniques for trauma. It nurtures self-compassion, dissolves self-blame, and softens the emotional armor trauma often creates. It reconnects you to the truth that you—and all beings—are worthy of love and safety.

"May all beings be happy. May all beings be whole. May all beings be at peace."

Mindful journaling helps you process emotions without drowning in them. It allows you to witness your thoughts with curiosity rather than judgment. This kind of writing reveals patterns, stories, and beliefs that may have been shaping your behavior long after the trauma ended.

Awareness is the first step toward release.

Nature offers instant grounding. Bare feet on the earth, your arms around a tree, the aroma of flowers (unless you have allergies) pull you back into your body and the present moment. These sensory experiences trigger present-moment awareness. Grounding counters dissociation and restores a sense of safety.

Mindful movement can take many forms. Yoga, tai chi, and qigong weave breath, movement, and awareness together. These practices regulate emotions, build resilience, release trauma stored in the body, and create a sense of wholeness. Many people describe feeling clearer, calmer, and more connected after even one short session.

Trauma Happens—Mindfulness Heals

The truth is, trauma touches all of us in one way or another. Whether it arrives through a major life event, a series of smaller emotional blows, or a sudden physical shock, each person relates to trauma differently. Not every mindfulness technique in this book will resonate with you, and that's perfectly okay. What matters is finding the practices that feel supportive and sustainable for your life. As you explore and experiment, you'll discover that mindfulness—through awareness, acceptance, and gentle presence—can become a powerful companion on your healing journey, helping you navigate trauma with greater clarity, compassion, and resilience.

If you feel drawn to exploring yoga as part of your healing journey, you may enjoy my book *Empowering Your Life with Yoga*. In it, I show you how to take yogic philosophy off the mat and into your daily life so you can begin living with more purpose, ease, and alignment. If you prefer a guided experience, my audio class Yoga for Deep Relaxation blends mindful movement, deep breathing, and gentle meditation to help you unwind and reconnect with yourself. You can find both of these resources listed in the Reference section of this book.

Trauma is a part of life, but it doesn't have to overwhelm you.

Mindfulness doesn't erase trauma. It helps you *heal* it—gently, patiently, and with compassion.

***Please note:** While contents of this book may be helpful to wellness and recovery, they do not take the place of medical advice. If you are struggling with any form of trauma, seek professional, medical care.

Improve the Taste of Food

If there's one universal truth about modern life, it's this: we are always in a hurry. Meals become pit stops, interruptions, or vague afterthoughts wedged into the blur of a 24/7 schedule. Many people eat standing over a sink, scrolling through their phones, sitting in traffic, or worse—forget to eat at all. In the rush of it all, we often settle for convenience foods made with low-quality ingredients and wrapped in toxic packaging. The body eats these meals, but the mind is somewhere else entirely.

And yet, something remarkable happens when you bring mindfulness to your plate. Simply by paying attention—by eating with your senses awake and your nervous system settled—you can transform not just the *experience* of eating, but the *taste* of the food itself.

Mindfulness slows you down just enough to truly notice what's happening in your mouth, your body, and your mind. It invites you to savor rather than simply swallow, to appreciate rather than rush, and to nourish rather than numb out. With mindful eating, the same strawberry tastes sweeter, the same soup feels richer, and even the simplest meal becomes a quiet conversation with the present moment.

This heightened awareness lets you catch subtleties in flavor and texture that would otherwise slip by unnoticed. Eating slowly gives your brain time to register those distinct tastes and to recognize when you've had enough. When you bring mindfulness to the table, an everyday meal becomes a sensory experience—one that deepens your appreciation for the nourishment, effort, and care that went into each bite.

Conscious Tasting

One of the most surprising benefits of mindful eating is that it literally enhances flavor. Taste isn't just about taste buds; it's about presence. When you're distracted, stressed, or multitasking, your brain cannot fully register the nuances of what you're eating. The mind is too busy managing unfinished business to enjoy the pleasure of a good meal.

But when you slow down and engage your senses—sight, smell, taste, touch, even sound—you awaken your innate ability to savor. Your awareness sharpens. Your perception widens. You begin to taste subtleties you never noticed before: a hint of maple, a trace of nutmeg, a whisper of lemon. Something that once seemed ordinary becomes unexpectedly delightful.

Part of this miracle can be traced back to the relationship between taste and smell. The majority of what we experience as "flavor" actually comes from the olfactory system—your sense of smell. The olfactory system compliments the work of your taste buds (gustatory system) and plays a major role in detecting the flavor of food. When you chew, aromatic molecules travel up into the nasal cavity and communicate with receptors that help decode the full flavor profile of your food.

Think back to a time when you had a cold or allergies. Remember how the world lost its flavor? Even your favorite meal might have felt flat. That's because swollen nasal tissue blocks these scent receptors, diminishing your ability to taste. When your senses are open and fully engaged—when you *smell* as well as *taste*—your food becomes more vibrant.

Mindfulness helps bring your senses online. It invites you to savor texture, aroma, temperature, and sound. Whether your sinuses are clear or not, mindful awareness reconnects you to the sensory richness of eating.

A Blessing for the Meal and the Moment

As you may remember from Part One, one of the simplest mindful eating practices is to pause before your first bite. You don't need a formal blessing—just a moment of acknowledgment. A breath. A quick whisper of gratitude. A prayer.

This tiny pause reconnects you with the reality that your food came from somewhere: from soil, sunlight, rain, seed, harvesters, animals, farmers, truck drivers, grocery store clerks, cooks, and ultimately, your own choice to nourish yourself.

This awareness softens the nervous system and opens the senses. It prepares your mind to taste what your body is about to receive.

Savoring and Body Wisdom

Breathing deeply between bites may seem simple, but it supports your digestive system in profound ways. Slowing your breath activates the parasympathetic nervous system—the branch responsible for rest, repair, and digestion. When your body feels safe, it's able to absorb nutrients more effectively. Your stomach produces the right enzymes. Your intestines move food efficiently. Your brain receives clear signals of fullness.

The result? You eat less, enjoy more, and feel nourished rather than stuffed or sluggish.

When you breathe slowly and chew with intention, you give your brain something essential: time. Time to register flavor. Time to notice texture. Time to appreciate aroma. Time to recognize fullness. With this gentle pause woven into the act of eating, a meal shifts from something you rush through to something you fully experience. Eating becomes a moment of presence, not just another task to check off the list.

Mindfulness, Weight Loss, and Compassionate Awareness

Besides improving the taste of food, mindfulness offers another benefit at the table. It helps clarify your relationship with hunger, fullness, and emotional eating.

According to the CDC, over 40% of US adults experienced obesity as of 2023. Many factors contribute to this epidemic, but one of the most overlooked reasons is disconnection. We have become disconnected from our bodies, from hunger cues, and from the emotional patterns driving our food choices.

Placing more emphasis on mindful eating can help counter the unhealthy patterns so many of us fall into. When you know what you're putting into your body, why you're eating it, and how it affects you in the moment, you begin to break free from automatic, unconscious habits. This simple awareness helps you reconnect with yourself and appreciate the body you inhabit.

Mindfulness doesn't scold you into eating differently. It gently helps you notice. Asking yourself a few mindful questions can bring you back into the present:

Why am I reaching for food right now?
What does my body actually need?
How does this food feel as I eat it?
How does my body feel afterward?

With mindful awareness, you start eating from a place of genuine connection rather than impulse or routine. You become more attuned to the moments when food is being used for comfort instead of nourishment. And because mindfulness cultivates compassion—not judgment—you naturally begin making choices that support your well-being. When you treat yourself with more kindness, you see your body as the home you live in, not a project to correct or control.

Sensory Mealtime Meditation

The next time you sit down to eat, I invite you to turn your meal into a meditation.

Notice what happens before your first bite. Does your stomach tighten or growl? Does your mouth water? Do you feel anticipation? Relief? Gratitude?

As you pick up your fork, pause. Smell the food. Observe the colors and shapes on your plate. Take in the whole sensory environment.

Then, with your first bite, slow down. Notice which sense speaks first—taste, smell, texture? Does each bite feel grounding or uplifting?

Comforting or energizing? Does it evoke a memory? A feeling?

Chew slowly. Breathe between bites. Let your senses have their say. This is mindful eating—a relationship with your body, your senses, your food, and the present moment itself.

One of the sweetest gifts of mindful eating is discernment. When you truly taste your food, you discover what you genuinely enjoy and what you don't. You learn what energizes you and what drains you. You learn which foods soothe your body and which irritate it. You become a kinder companion to yourself simply by paying attention.

Eating mindfully doesn't require special tools or ingredients. It requires presence, and presence transforms even the simplest meal into a feast.

The next time you sit down to eat, let yourself taste—really taste—your food. Let your senses awaken. Let the simple act of eating become a pathway to nourishment, gratitude, and inner peace. Because when you eat mindfully, food doesn't just taste better. Life does, too.

Create Mastery

"To practice a thing diligently is to know it deeply."
— PHILIP TOSHIO SUDO (ZEN GUITAR)

There is an innate desire in each of us to become the best version of ourselves. Abraham Maslow, one of the great voices in human psychology, called this longing self-actualization—the continual process of growing into everything we are capable of becoming. It involves the pursuit of personal growth, self-improvement, and the realization of one's abilities and talents. It isn't a finish line we cross or a certificate we earn. It's more like an unfolding—an ongoing movement toward our potential through curiosity, self-honesty, and conscious participation in our own evolution.

Mastery lives inside this larger journey. Where self-actualization is the whole landscape, mastery is the path we carve through it. It involves cultivating a particular skill or ability with intention, devotion, and a willingness to stretch beyond what we already know. Mastery isn't simply knowing *about* something, it is knowing it in your bones. Mastery is the difference between memorizing a recipe and cooking by intuition, or between sounding out a note and hearing music in your imagination before you ever touch the instrument.

A person on the path to mastery displays a rare blend of passion, discipline, and humility. They set clear goals, practice with purpose, and accept setbacks as part of the learning curve rather than as a verdict of their worth. They understand that failure isn't the opposite of mastery—it's one of its most valuable teachers. Mindfulness deepens this understanding by helping us stay present with both progress and disappointment, allowing each experience to shape us rather than stop us.

Mastery is not a straight line from inspiration to excellence. Life is full of noise, distraction, and emotional detours that pull our attention away from what matters. Without mindful awareness, it's easy to slip into autopilot and lose contact with our deeper desires and the slow, steady work required to cultivate them. Mindfulness becomes the anchor—returning us to the moment where real learning happens.

When you're mindful, you see your progress more clearly. You can receive feedback without shrinking or bristling, and you learn to work with your limitations rather than treating them like enemies. Mindfulness also keeps discouragement at bay because it shifts your focus from perfection to presence. You begin to understand that mastery isn't built in grand leaps but in small, intentional repetitions that accumulate over time.

The masterful individual knows this truth: the journey *is* the practice.

Consider an opera singer training for a debut at the Metropolitan Opera House. She spends years studying breath work, refining vocal technique, drilling scales, and stretching the limits of her range. She also spends just as much time listening—to her coaches, to her body, and to the subtle shifts in tone that only a quiet, attentive mind can perceive. Rest, reflection, and mindfulness become as essential to her progress as the hours spent warming up her voice. It is this union of discipline and presence that shapes her into an artist rather than a performer.

Or think of a professional baseball player pursuing a place in the World Series. He throws thousands of fastballs, trains his body, and sharpens his reflexes. He also visualizes plays, regulates his emotions, and stays mentally agile when the pressure rises. When his team loses, he doesn't unravel—he recalibrates. This mindful approach helps him slip into that elusive state athletes call "the zone," where skill meets awareness in a fluid, almost effortless harmony.

Even the iconic Thomas Edison understood this. "I have not failed," he said. "I've just found 10,000 ways that won't work." His confidence wasn't arrogance—it was the wisdom of someone who understood the power of deliberate, mindful experimentation. Decades later, Malcolm Gladwell's "10,000-Hour Rule" offers a modern echo of that same truth: it takes intentional action and regular practice to achieve mastery.

And here's the encouraging part: you don't have to be an opera singer, a baseball star, or an inventor to create mastery in your own life. Whether you're learning a language, improving your communication skills, deepening your relationships, or developing emotional resilience, mindfulness strengthens your ability to stay focused, receptive, and engaged. It keeps you anchored in the present moment—where skill is shaped, choices are made, and growth actually happens.

When you integrate mindfulness into your daily routine, your life becomes your training ground. Your thoughts, actions, and habits come into clearer view. You begin to practice with intention rather than out of habit. Over time, clarity sharpens, patience expands, and excellence becomes a natural outcome because you *show up for it* with awareness.

While "practice makes perfect," mindfulness creates mastery.

PART THREE

Developing a Mindfulness Practice

"See each day as a gift when you wake up."
— TANVI GANDHI

Life in the modern world rarely moves at a gentle pace. It pulls us in a dozen directions at once, filling our days with noise, pressure, and responsibilities that can easily knock us off balance. In that whirlwind, the idea of starting a mindfulness practice can feel unrealistic—like something you'll get to "someday," when things finally calm down. The truth is, however, incorporating mindfulness into your daily life is not another task to manage; it's the steadiness that helps you manage everything else. When woven into ordinary moments, mindfulness brings clarity, calm, and a renewed sense of alignment with what matters most.

A regular mindfulness practice supports emotional regulation, improves mental clarity, and strengthens overall well-being. Beyond its mental benefits, mindfulness also contributes to physical health—research shows it can help lower blood pressure, improve sleep quality, and even strengthen your immune system. In many ways, mindfulness is the foundation of a life well-lived. It trains your awareness so that you actually experience the moments that make up your life, instead of rushing past them.

There are countless ways to cultivate mindfulness, from simple breathing techniques to meditation, yoga, journaling, and mindful time in nature. The methods in this book offer a small but effective collection of tools designed to help anchor you in the present moment. Practiced regularly, any one of them can help you reconnect with your true self and meet life as it unfolds—one breath, one moment at a time.

You don't need to have everything figured out before you begin. In fact, perfection isn't the goal at all. Start gently. Start small. Choose shorter sessions that naturally fit into your day. Even five minutes of intentional practice can shift your energy and improve your focus.

As you build your practice, remember that consistency matters far more than duration. A few mindful minutes each day offer far more benefit than one long session squeezed in once a week. Over time, as the habit takes root, you may find yourself naturally extending your practice without effort or strain.

Be patient with yourself. New habits take time to form, and mindfulness itself will help you cultivate the very patience that supports the journey. As your life changes, your practice will likely need to change with it. Being flexible ensures that your mindfulness routine remains both meaningful and sustainable. When you weave mindfulness into the fabric of daily living—your commute, your meals, your conversations, your morning routine—you create a supportive rhythm that helps you meet the day with greater ease and clarity.

In the pages ahead, you'll find guided meditations, breathing practices, yoga postures, journaling prompts, and mindful nature exercises. These practices are some of my personal favorites, but they represent only a small fraction of what is available to you. Feel free to adapt them based on your needs, your schedule, and your curiosities. As you explore, I encourage you to continue learning, experimenting, and discovering what truly supports the life you want to create.

Mindfulness is not just something you do—it's a way of being. Your practice, in whatever shape it takes, can become one of the most loving gifts you offer yourself.

Meditation Practice

Meditation has a primordial, richly layered history that began long before its techniques were ever written down. Rooted in numerous spiritual and philosophical traditions, early meditation practices were passed from generation to generation through oral teachings, and evolved across cultures. Some of the earliest depictions of meditation appear in Indian wall art dating back roughly 5,000 years, with written references emerging in the Hindu Vedas around 1500 BCE. Similar contemplative practices also appear in the Jewish Torah, the Chinese Tao tradition, and in Buddhist communities of India and Japan from 1500 BCE onward.

In the Western world, meditation gained influence in Europe between the 14th and 18th centuries with the rise of Catholic Christian teachings. By the 19th century, Buddhist and Vedic philosophies had traveled to Europe and the United Kingdom, eventually reaching the United States through Hindu holy teachers and Western scholars. By the mid-1950s, meditation had become firmly woven into modern Western culture, and its influence continues to grow. Today, meditation is recognized worldwide as a powerful doorway to mindful awareness and inner peace.

The landscape of meditation is vast—far too expansive to capture in a single book. Still, the practices included here offer a meaningful place to begin. Think of them as invitations rather than prescriptions. Explore each technique gently, choosing one or two that resonate with you and practice them for a week or two. Notice how they affect your physical body, your emotional state, and the quality of your thoughts.

Beyond personal changes, you may also notice positive differences in your environment. Are your relationships shifting? Do conversations feel softer or more honest? Are you more tolerant of those around you? Can you see beauty in places where you once rushed by?

Use the samples in the pages ahead as stepping stones. Try the ones that call to you, return to them as often as you need, and feel free to discover new approaches that suit your life and personality. Meditation is an ancient practice, but its greatest gifts arrive in the present moment—one breath, one experience, one insight at a time.

Guided Meditation

Guided meditation is a practice where an instructor or recording leads you through steps of relaxing your body, focusing your mind, and settling into present-moment awareness. It's especially helpful for beginners or for anyone who feels intimidated by meditating in silence. Instead of trying to figure out what to do, you simply follow the guidance and allow yourself to be led.

Today, guided meditations are widely accessible. You can find practices for relaxation, stress reduction, emotional healing, spiritual growth, creativity, business success, and more. Platforms like *Insight Timer* and *Calm* offer thousands of options, and many gyms and yoga studios provide live guided sessions.

One of the biggest benefits of guided practice is structure. When your mind has a tendency to wander—or bolt entirely—the step-by-step instructions help you stay engaged. The guidance creates a sense of safety and support, which allows your body to soften and your attention to deepen.

To make the most of your guided meditation, choose a quiet, comfortable space where you won't be disturbed. Begin your session with an open mind and a willingness to follow the experience where it leads. Breathe intentionally as you're guided through visualizations, body scans, or relaxation cues.

When the meditation ends, take a moment before jumping back into your day. Notice any shifts—are you calmer, clearer, more grounded? Even a subtle softening is a sign that your practice is working.

The guided meditation included below is taken from my recording *"Yoga for Deep Relaxation."* It is the final track, titled **"Heart**

Meditation," and is available on all major streaming platforms and in CD format through CDBaby.com.

Let's begin:

Find a quiet and comfortable space where you won't be disturbed. Sit or lie down to your preference.

Bring your awareness to your chest and notice your beating heart.

Without judging yourself, allow your awareness to rest in your chest and breathe into your heart center, a beautiful emerald green color.

Visualize your heart center filling with this beautiful color as you feel love filling your heart. Let this Emerald green expand outward to surround your whole body.

Your heart center is the area of your body where you hold feelings of compassion, acceptance and unconditional love.

Become aware of these feelings that are filling your heart.

Feel the compassion, acceptance, and unconditional love that you have for yourself. Allow yourself to rest in complete acceptance.

Now, visualize the expanding emerald green outward, encompassing your family, friends, acquaintances ... even people you don't know.

Expand your compassion to them.

Send unconditional love outward and be open to receiving these feelings returned to you.

Feel the connection you have to all beings. Notice the expansion you feel in your heart through the connection of unconditional love.

Breathe

Now, bring your awareness back into your own body, to your own heart center, still feeling the connection with all beings.

Allow yourself to rest in the awareness of your own body.

Rest in the awareness of compassion, connection, and unconditional love.

Breathe in and out, resting in the loving energy of emerald green light.

Begin to wiggle your toes and fingers. Stretch your body in ways that it is asking you to move.

Bring your hands to your heart in the prayer position and bow your head to the Divine within yourself.

NAMASTE *(I honor the place in you, which is the same in me. We are one.)*

Guided meditation offers supportive structure that makes meditation easier to explore and deepens mindful awareness.

Visual Meditation

Visual meditations are open-eye practices that involve maintaining a soft focus and relaxed gaze while still being aware of your surroundings. Less commonly known than closed-eye meditation, they offer unique benefits. Especially good for beginning meditators who have difficulty keeping their eyes closed, visual meditations make it easier to focus. They can sharpen concentration, soothe the nervous system, and even ease eye strain by encouraging a softer, more intentional gaze. Because your eyes remain open, the mind has a simple point of reference—making it easier to stay present.

In this chapter, I offer three forms of visual meditation: open-eye meditation, tratak, and yantra meditation. While each method shares the same foundation of soft focus and steady attention, they offer distinct ways to quiet the mind, release tension, and cultivate clarity. Together they provide accessible options for deepening mindfulness through the power of sight.

Open-eye meditation

As the name suggests, open-eye meditation involves meditating with your eyes open while maintaining a soft, relaxed gaze. Rather than turning inward and shutting out the world, this practice invites you to stay present with your surroundings. It's especially helpful for people who struggle with closed-eye meditation or who want to weave mindfulness more naturally into daily life.

Because it keeps you visually connected to the world around you, open-eye meditation makes mindfulness feel less like a separate "practice" and more like a way of being. You can do it almost anywhere—at your desk, in a park, at home, or while waiting in line—making it one of the most flexible forms of meditation.

To begin, find a comfortable position where you can settle—standing, sitting, or lying down. There's no required posture; ease is what matters most. Once you're comfortable, let your eyes soften. Rather than focusing on a single point, allow your gaze to widen so that you're taking in your entire field of vision. Slightly lowering your eyelids can help quiet the mind and soften any tendency to stare or judge.

Nature is one of my favorite places to practice this meditation. Earlier in this book, I mentioned how much I love watching clouds. On a warm summer day, nothing grounds me more quickly than lying on the grass, looking up at a sky full of shifting clouds, and letting my breath and gaze settle me into the present moment. Open-eye meditation turns those simple moments into rich opportunities for peace.

As you rest your gaze, become aware of your breathing. Let it be natural. Notice the colors, shapes, sounds, and movements around you—without clinging to them or pushing them away. Your only job is to witness. If your mind wanders, gently return to your breath and your softened gaze.

If you're new to meditation, start with just five to ten minutes. Over time, you may find that this practice helps you stay more grounded and attentive throughout your day—not only during designated meditation sessions. Open-eye meditation is a simple yet powerful way to carry mindfulness with you, creating pockets of calm even in the midst of your busiest moments.

Tratak

Tratak, a Sanskrit word meaning "to gaze," is a focused visual meditation in which you rest your eyes on a single point without blinking. This simple practice strengthens concentration, steadies the mind, and heightens inner awareness. Over time, tratak can ease anxiety, clarify thinking, deepen spiritual focus, and even strengthen the eye muscles. Some traditions also suggest that a dedicated practice enhances intuition.

A candle flame is the most common focal point, though other objects—such as a flower, an object of worship, the moon, and even the sun—may be used. **If you choose to practice with the sun, do so ONLY at sunrise or sunset, when the atmosphere naturally filters out the harsher blue light and makes gazing safer.** Still, be mindful when gazing toward the sun at any time. During sunrise and sunset, the sun's angle is lower in the sky, which means its rays must cross through a longer distance of the atmosphere to reach your eyes.

I've practiced tratak for more than twenty years, and I still find it to be one of the most peaceful forms of meditation I know. I've gazed at sunsets across the world, but nothing compares to the quiet clarity of watching a single candle flame flicker in a darkened room. Some of my deepest moments of insight have emerged from that simple glow.

How to Practice Tratak:

Find a quiet, dimly lit room where you won't be interrupted. Sit comfortably—either cross-legged on the floor or upright in a chair, feet grounded and arms relaxed. Place a candle two to three feet in front of you at eye level. Try not to strain your body toward the flame, but completely relax in your seated position.

Light the candle. Settle your breath. Then gently fix your gaze on the flame, keeping your eyes soft but steady. Try not to blink. It's perfectly normal—even beneficial—if your eyes water; that's part of the cleansing effect.

If you are new to tratak, your eyes may blink sooner than you'd like. Don't force anything. With practice, your ability to hold a steady gaze will naturally increase.

As you continue to watch the flame, allow thoughts to drift through without following them. Each time you notice your mind wander, return your attention to the candle flame and the rhythm of your breath.

When your eyes begin to tear, blow out the candle and close your eyes. Notice the after-image that appears in your mind's eye—this subtle inner glow is often the most profound part of the practice. Keep your eyes closed, focusing on the image until it fades.

Gently open your eyes, and take a few slow breaths, letting yourself reorient. Notice how you feel. More grounded? More spacious? More at ease? Give yourself a moment to integrate whatever has shifted.

Tratak is a simple practice, yet its effects ripple through the mind, body, and spirit with surprising depth. Whenever you need clarity or calm, return to the flame. Sometimes the smallest light reveals the most profound insight.

Yantra

The word *yantra* comes from the Sanskrit root *yam*, (to sustain) and the suffix tra (instrument or tool), together meaning "a tool that sustains conscious awareness." Yantras are geometric designs used for thousands of years in Hindu, Buddhist, and Tantric traditions to support meditation, concentration, and spiritual growth. Each pattern symbolizes universal principles, while the central point—the *bindu*—represents the meeting place between the physical and spiritual realms and is typically the focus of meditation.

Yantra meditation is the open-eye practice in which you gently gaze at the geometric design, allowing its symmetry and patterns to draw the mind inward. This steady visual focus helps quiet mental chatter, deepen concentration, and cultivate present-moment awareness.

The philosophy behind yantras rests on the idea that symbols carry energetic and psychological influence. Their shapes are said to reflect the structures of the cosmos and the deeper aspects of consciousness. Whether or not you subscribe to these spiritual teachings, yantra meditation provides practical benefits: it reduces stress, sharpens focus, and promotes a grounded sense of calm as attention settles on a single image.

Physiologically, the practice engages the parasympathetic nervous system, lowering stress hormones and supporting healthy autonomic function. This can lead to lowered blood pressure, improved immunity, and enhanced emotional regulation. Over time, yantra meditation becomes a steadying tool for mental clarity and overall well-being.

There are many yantras to choose from, each associated with traditional qualities. The Sri Yantra symbolizes abundance and spiritual expansion; the Ganesha Yantra represents the removal of obstacles; the Durga Yantra is linked with protection and inner strength; and the Hanuman Yantra supports courage and determination. If you prefer a personal touch, you can even create your own geometric design to serve as a focal point.

Below is an example of a yantra. You are welcome to use this image for your meditation practice, or find one that resonates more closely with you. Once you settle on a design, take a moment to look at the image and notice where you rest your gaze.

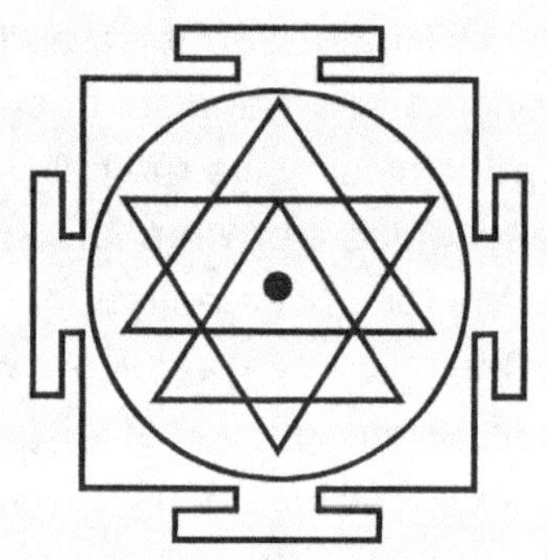

Fig. 1 yantra

How to Practice Yantra Meditation:

1. **Set your intention** or select a yantra that resonates with your purpose.

2. **Sit comfortably** in a quiet space and place the image at eye level.

3. **Rest your gaze softly** on the bindu or central point. Let the entire pattern come into awareness without strain.

4. **Allow your breath to settle** into a slow, steady rhythm as you continue to gaze.

5. **Notice any sensations**, emotions, or insights that arise as the mind grows quiet.

6. **Begin with a few minutes** and extend the duration as the practice becomes more natural.

7. When you finish, **close your eyes and observe the after-image** in your mind's eye. Let it fade naturally before returning attention to the room and moving on with your day.

Some practitioners pair yantras with mantra chanting to deepen concentration, a topic addressed in the following section.

Yantra meditation blends art, symbolism, and mindfulness into a single practice that nurtures clarity, creativity, and self-discovery. Compared with other open-eye practices—such as general open-eye meditation or tratak—yantra meditation has the strongest spiritual roots. Open-eye meditation takes in the full visual field, tratak narrows attention to a single point (often a flame), and yantra meditation focuses on a symbolic image. Despite these differences, all three can reduce stress, support nervous-system balance, and strengthen mindful awareness.

What matters most is choosing the practice that resonates with you. Begin where you are, explore with curiosity, and let the benefits unfold.

Mantra Meditation

A mantra is a word, sound, or phrase repeated to steady the mind and deepen meditation. Its Sanskrit roots—*manas* (mind) and *tra* (tool)—reflect its purpose: a mantra is simply a tool that anchors your awareness in the present moment.

Originating in ancient Hindu and Buddhist traditions as early as 1500 BCE, mantras have since crossed cultures and spiritual paths. While Christianity does not use mantras in the traditional sense, repetitive prayer and sacred phrasing echo the same intention of devotion, presence, and inner stillness. Whether one recites the Gayatri Mantra, the Nembutsu, or a biblical verse such as "Give thanks to the Lord, for He is good" (Psalms 107:1), the principle is the same: Repetition quiets the mind and focuses awareness.

Mantras offer both spiritual and psychological benefits. Their steady rhythm helps calm the nervous system, interrupt negative thought patterns, and create new neural pathways associated with peace and clarity. Many people also use mantras as affirmations to cultivate positive habits or attitudes. Through vocal vibration, breath, and repetition, mantra practice can shift mental states, regulate emotions, and support spiritual growth. Some believe that the sound waves generated by chanting contribute healing energy to all beings.

Research supports these effects. Studies conducted between 1979 to 2020 reveal that repetitive chanting can reduce stress, anxiety, and hypertension while improving immune function. Honoring its ancient roots, mantra practice remains a powerful tool for well-being across traditions.

Below are several mantras you may wish to explore. While some are tied to specific spiritual lineages, all can be practiced by anyone seeking mindfulness, emotional balance, and inner peace. Many sacred sounds—known as *bija* (seed) mantras—carry no literal meaning but are valued for their vibrational impact on the body and mind.

I have practiced Primordial Sound™ meditation for more than thirty years, and mantra has continually deepened my understanding of equanimity and compassion. It is one of the practices that has most profoundly shaped my life. I offer the following mantras in that spirit.

Buddhism

Nam Myoho Renge Kyo *(Nam-Myo-Ho-Ren-Ge-Kyo):* This mantra expresses devotion to the interconnectedness of all beings and the universal potential for enlightenment.

- **Nam**– devotion or dedication; committing oneself to spiritual awakening.

- **Myoho**– "Mystic Law," the principle that all beings can transform suffering to attain enlightenment.

- **Renge** – "to blossom like a lotus flower," symbolizes our potential for enlightenment and purity amidst the challenges of life. Like the lotus flower, each of us pushes through the "mud" of our challenges, to create a mindful life of compassion and awareness.

- **Kyo** – sutra or teaching; the expression of awakened truth as taught by the Enlightened Being.

Chanting this mantra is said to awaken one's innate Buddha nature and transform challenges—including illness or emotional difficulty—into opportunities for growth. Practitioners often report increased clarity, focus, courage, and compassion.

Nam Myoho Renge Kyo is thought to attract positive energy into one's life by burning away ignorance and developing a compassionate nature, thus ensuring happiness and success. This is a good mantra to practice when you are feeling anxious or worried as it can help to refocus your awareness to the present moment, finding a sense of inner peace and calm.

To practice, sit comfortably with hands at your heart. Keep a soft gaze or close your eyes. Hold an intention—for yourself or for someone else—and repeat the mantra slowly: *Nam-Myo-Ho-Ren-Ge-Kyo.* Traditionally, 108 repetitions are used, though you may begin with whatever feels comfortable. After you have completed the mantra, rest in silence for a few moments.

Om Mani Padme Hum *(Om-Ma-Ni-Pad-Me-Hum)*: Known as the mantra of compassion, it is often known as the Avalokitesvara mantra, or Compassionate Buddha mantra, Om Mani Padme Hum literally translates as "Hail to the Jewel in the Lotus." It symbolizes the wish to transform suffering through wisdom and compassionate action. This mantra is known as the "destroyer of all evil," providing liberation and relief from suffering for those who recite it.

Each syllable carries a specific purification vibration:

- **Om** – the primordial sound of the Universe that encompasses all of existence. It purifies pride and ego.
- **Ma** – ethics; establishes patience and reduces jealousy.
- **Ni** – patience; purifies one from excess passion and desire, balancing emotions.
- **Pad** – diligence; overcomes ignorance and prejudice, cultivating wisdom.
- **Me** – concentration and renunciation; overcomes possessiveness and greed, develops compassion and generosity.
- **Hum** – wisdom and integration; dissolves anger and aggression.

Although Buddhist in origin, this mantra is widely embraced as a healing chant that opens the heart and fosters empathy. Many recite it for the well-being of others.

Whenever I come across someone who is suffering, whether I meet them in person, see them from a distance, or watch them on television, I extend the mantra toward the distressed individual (or group), intending their relief from suffering. I quietly recite *"Om Mani Padme Hum,"* focusing my attention toward them and intending their highest good.

To practice, sit comfortably and establish a steady breath. Chant aloud, softly, or silently. I would suggest trying each level of sound, as they all offer different vibrations and feelings in your body. Use a mala (prayer beads) if you wish to track repetitions. One hundred eight repetitions is traditional; however, repeat the mantra for as many times as you are comfortable.

Visualizing a lotus blooming at the heart can deepen the experience. Remain in silence afterward, noticing any shifts in awareness.

For best results, recite the mantra daily. Regular practice can deepen your connection with the mantra and enhance its benefits.

Hinduism

Om: In the Vedic tradition, *Om* is considered the primordial sound from which all creation was born. It is the constant vibration of the Universe, which is the essence of all things. Invoked before any chant or auspicious beginning, Om is considered the vibration of ultimate truth. Considered the most sacred sound of the cosmos, it can help calm the mind and connect you with a higher state of consciousness.

If you are new to the practice of mantra, *Om* is the perfect place to begin. The simple, one-syllable sound offers a positive and powerful vibration that resonates a feeling of deep peace throughout the mind and body.

To practice, sit quietly and set a timer for three to five minutes. Chant "Om," allowing the sound to lengthen naturally and feeling the vibration resonate through your body. Repeat until your timer rings. Afterward, sit quietly for a moment, feeling the resonance throughout your body.

Shanti Mantra *(Om Shanti, Shanti, Shanti, Om):* The Sanskrit word for "peace," Shanti is a simple and widely used prayer for peace. Widely used in meditation, yoga, and spiritual practices, the Shanti Mantra consists of a beginning and ending *Om* with *Shanti* spoken three times in between.

> *The first **Shanti** is spoken to purify the body.*
> *The second calms and cleanses the mind.*
> *The third brings peace to one's soul.*

Chanting *Shanti* three times also affects the past, present, and future, thus healing all directions of the Universe. Chanting this mantra can dissolve emotional tension, harmonize environments, and restore balance after conflict. It is believed to create a positive and peaceful atmosphere wherever it is chanted.

When practicing, sit comfortably and breathe deeply. Chant Om, Shanti, Shanti, Shanti, Om aloud or silently as many times as you wish. When your practice comes to a close, sit in silence for a few moments, reflecting on the peace and harmony that you feel in your body, mind, and spirit.

Bija (Seed) Mantras: The term *bija* is a Sanskrit word that means "seed" and symbolizes the potential or original essence within something. Bija mantras are single-syllable sounds representing elemental forces and energetic qualities within the body. Their vibrations support emotional balance, physical well-being, and spiritual awakening.

Typically associated with the core energy centers of the body (chakras), the most notable bija mantras are:

- **Lam** (earth) – spine and coccyx; grounding, stability; supports the bones, legs, feet, and immune system. Use this mantra when you are feeling anxious and off-balance, or when you have issues with your lower extremities.

- **Vam** (water) – lower abdomen; fluidity and emotional ease, pleasure and joy; encourages adaptability and healthy relationships. Use this mantra to ease trauma.

- **Ram** (fire) – solar plexus; confidence and determination; improves digestion and metabolism. Use this mantra to increase self-confidence and willpower.

- **Yam** (air) – chest and heart; love, compassion, forgiveness; supports the heart and emotional equanimity. Pronounced "yum," use this mantra to dissipate resentment and anger.

- **Ham** (ether) – throat and mouth; expression, clarity, integrity, and authenticity; supports communication and the throat. This is a great mantra for singers and speakers. Use this mantra to help speak your truth.

These primordial vibrations harness and activate specific energies that enable wellness, personal growth, and spiritual enlightenment.

For example, if you're facing instability—such as a job loss or a major life transition—the combination of grounding (Lam), emotional flexibility (Vam), and confidence (Ram) can be especially supportive.

To practice bijas, sit comfortably, take a few full breaths, and chant each sound three times, observing the sensations they generate. You may repeat them individually or as one continuous sequence.

These mantras are simple yet powerful tools for cultivating presence, clarity, and inner peace. Whether spoken aloud, whispered, or repeated silently throughout the day, they steady the mind and open the heart. With regular practice, these sounds become companions—gentle reminders of resilience, compassion, and the deeper wisdom that lives within us all.

Christianity

While the word *mantra* isn't part of Christian tradition, Christians have long used repetitive prayer to quiet the mind and deepen spiritual connection. These practices function much like mantra meditation—steadying attention, opening the heart, and creating space for contemplative awareness. **Centering Prayer** is a silent prayer practice that uses a chosen sacred word to return the mind to God's presence. What word makes you feel closer to God?

The Rosary (Catholic)

Catholics use the Rosary, a sequence of repeated prayers including the *Hail Mary, Our Father,* and *Glory Be,* to enter a meditative state while reflecting on the life of Christ and the intercession of the Virgin Mother (Mary). Prayer beads—similar to a *mala*—guide the rhythm of repetition, inviting the practitioner to settle into focused devotion.

The Jesus Prayer (Eastern Orthodox)

Eastern Orthodox use of repetitive prayer, most notably the *Jesus Prayer,* is used as a way to focus one's mind and heart on the presence of God. **"Lord Jesus Christ, Son of God, have mercy on me, a sinner"** is recited continuously to align the mind and heart with God, seeking mercy for one's sinful ways. Its steady repetition softens distraction, cultivates humility, and strengthens the inner awareness of divine presence.

Taizé Prayer

A relatively new meditative practice, originating from the ecumenical monastic Taizé Community in France, Taizé Prayer was founded in the 1950s by a Swiss-born Protestant pastor Brother Roger of Taizé.

Taizé Prayer blends simple, repetitive chants with silence. These short biblical phrases, sung in a meditative rhythm, create a spacious inner stillness that encourages reflection and connection with God.

Taizé has become a global expression of contemplative worship, especially among young people, drawing thousands to its monastic home in France each year. Many churches incorporate Taizé services for those seeking a more reflective spiritual experience.

Parishes worldwide are increasingly incorporating this form of meditative prayer in order to provide a deeper connection with God for their parishioners. Often accompanied by music, the simple, repetitive chants are either sung a cappella or accompanied by soundtracks or musical instruments.

One example comes from Reverend Donna Michael, whose chants offer peaceful, mantra-like repetition:

I am a light, I am a light, I am a light in this world …
… and I shine, and I shine, and I shine so bright.

Besides being a devoted peacemaker, she writes and produces her own beautiful chants and even hosts live Taizé ceremonies. Look for her chants on YouTube or through her website in the Foreword section of this book.

Christian Chanting

Gregorian chant and other forms of liturgical music also mirror the meditative effect of mantra through repetitive singing of scripture and sacred text. Composers such as **Dame Hildegard von Bingen** created soaring chants in the 12th century that still draw listeners into deep stillness today, inviting a mindful awareness of the sacred.

Even though these Christian practices may not be labeled as "mantra" their purpose is similar. They use repetition as a spiritual anchor, quiet the mind, and focus on the Divine to enter into present-moment awareness.

No matter the tradition, both mantras and Christian contemplative practices guide practitioners toward inner stillness, mindful presence, and a deeper experience of the sacred.

Walking Meditation

Walking meditation is mindfulness in motion. Unlike sitting meditation, it blends gentle movement with present-moment awareness, making it especially accessible for people who struggle to sit still or prefer a more active practice.

Rooted in Buddhist tradition, walking meditation was originally paired with sitting meditation to help practitioners carry their mindfulness into everyday activity. The simple intention is to stay aware of each step, each breath, and each moment as the body moves through space.

My first experience with walking meditation was with Thich Nhat Hanh in Memphis, Tennessee, in the early 2000s. Before giving a talk, he invited us to walk with him, contemplating our breath and stepping mindfully in what he called, the "present moment-wonderful moment." There we were, hundreds of us, silently walking across Overton Park, following our beloved teacher—one mindful step at a time. Even among a large crowd, the practice felt intimate and deeply grounding.

Thich Nhat Hanh emphasized walking with full awareness—feeling the lifting and placing of each foot, noticing the movement of the legs, and staying connected to the environment with gratitude. He often described walking meditation as "walking as if you are kissing the earth with your feet," a poetic encouragement to move with tenderness, reverence, and presence.

Like other forms of meditation, walking meditation calms the mind and reduces stress. It also strengthens the body, supports emotional regulation, and can be practiced almost anywhere. Its simplicity makes it a versatile tool for cultivating peace and clarity throughout the day.

Practicing Walking Meditation

Choose a location: Find a quiet, safe place where you can walk without interruption. This could be in a garden, a park, your own backyard, or even a long hallway.

Stand still: Begin standing with your feet hip-width apart. Ground yourself by noticing the contact between your feet and the earth. Shoes or bare feet are both fine; just be mindful of the surface.

Set your intention: Take a few deep breaths. Choose a simple intention: to calm your mind, release tension, or practice gratitude. Ultimately, your aim is to remain mindful.

Begin walking slowly: Walk at a slow and deliberate pace. Pay attention to each step: lifting, moving, and placing your foot. Notice the shifting of your weight and the sensations in your legs and feet.

Optional: Place your hands together in the prayer position as you walk.

Coordinate breaths and steps: If it feels comfortable, match your steps with your breath—perhaps two steps per inhale and two per exhale. Adjust according to your natural gait.

Maintain awareness: Keep your awareness on the act of walking. If your mind wanders, gently return your focus to the sensations of walking.

Observe your surroundings: Stay aware of your surroundings without getting pulled into stories. While walking, notice the sights, sounds, and smells around you. If you hear laughter or smell food at a nearby picnic, notice it ... and let it move to the background as you return to your steps.

Practice Gratitude: Let each step be an opportunity to appreciate your ability to move, breathe, sense, and experience the world around you. Walking meditation naturally reveals countless moments of gratitude.

Conclude the practice: After five to ten minutes (or longer, if you wish), come to a stop. Stand quietly. Take a few deep breaths and observe how your body and mind feel.

Carry peace into your day: See how long you can maintain the calm presence you cultivated. Even a few mindful steps later in the day can reconnect you to this peaceful state ... and to yourself.

Body Scan / Yoga Nidra

As I discussed in Part One, the body scan is a foundational mindfulness practice that guides your attention systematically through the body. Yoga Nidra deepens the practice and benefits of the body scan.

Noticing sensations with curiosity and without judgment, the mind and body naturally shift into deeper relaxation. You can guide yourself through the practice, work with a teacher, or follow any number of quality recordings. Below is a simplified script you can use or record in your own voice.

Body Scan

Begin by sitting or lying down in a quiet, comfortable place. Close your eyes and take a few slow breaths to anchor your awareness in your body.

Bring your awareness to all ten toes. Notice their sensations—warmth, coolness, tingling, or stillness. Gently wiggle them and sense the space between each toe.

Shift your awareness to your feet. Feel the tops, the soles, and the heels resting on the surface beneath you. Breathe slowly and soften your feet.

Move your awareness to your ankles. Notice the inner and outer ankle bones. Rotate them gently and feel any subtle movement or sensation. Let them relax.

Guide your attention up your shins and calves. Feel the shin bones settle toward the calves and the calves soften toward the earth. Allow your whole lower leg to release.

Bring awareness to your thighs and hamstrings. Sense where your legs touch the ground and where they float. Soften the muscles and let the weight of your legs soften even more.

Move awareness into your hips and abdomen. Feel the strength of your hips and the softness of your belly. Let the abdomen relax toward your spine and allow your whole midsection to relax, feeling supported. Breathe.

Shift awareness to your chest, upper back, and shoulders. Inhale into your chest and ribcage; exhale and feel the torso soften. Allow your shoulders to drop and the upper back to settle into the earth.

Move your attention down your arms—from shoulders to elbows, and elbows to wrists. Let the arms grow heavy.

Bring awareness to your wrists, hands, fingers, and thumbs. With each breath, feel them soften and let go.

Move your awareness to your neck, face, and head. Feeling your breath move through your throat, into your face, and head.

Feel your head supported by the surface beneath you.

Inhale ease throughout your face and brain; exhale and allow the back of your head to rest more fully.

Breathe naturally and sense your entire body at once. Notice heaviness or lightness, warmth or coolness, and the overall texture of your experience. Let yourself surrender completely.

Let go. Let go. Let go.

Pause. Rest in silence.

When you're ready, deepen your breath. Gently wiggle your finger and toes, allow movement to spread through your body, and slowly stretch.

Take your time returning to full awareness.

Notice how your breathing feels now. Has physical tension loosened? Is your mind quieter? Did any insights surface?

The body scan not only relaxes the body but also slows mental activity, returning you to the present moment. Avoid rushing back into activity—give your body time to transition.

You can make the body scan brief or detailed depending on your time. If you want to go further into mind-body awareness, the next step is *Yoga Nidra.*

Yoga Nidra

Yoga Nidra, or *"yogic sleep,"* is a guided practice designed to induce deep physical relaxation while keeping the mind awake. Ideally, you practice it after yoga or physical movement so the body is primed to relax. Although similar to the body scan, Yoga Nidra must be guided by a teacher or recording. The body scan is only one part of the larger experience of Yoga Nidra.

Yoga Nidra typically includes several stages that guide the practitioner toward a state between wakefulness and sleep. In this state, brain waves shift into alpha, theta, and even delta patterns—deeply restorative frequencies associated with healing, emotional balance, and intuitive insight.

Preparation is essential. Practice lying down with support under your knees, head, and lower back. A soft, supportive surface and a warm blanket help the body relax fully. Comfort is not optional in Yoga Nidra—it is foundational.

Once you have settled into your "Nidra nest," the practice begins with a personal intention or affirmation. This is known as a **sankalpa**, a heartfelt intention or affirmation. This intention serves as your goal or guiding principle for your practice. Choose a brief sentence or phrase that is meaningful for you.

Your guide will then move into the **rotation of consciousness**—a systematic body scan from feet to crown. Next, the practice typically progresses into breath awareness, counting or observing the breath's natural rhythm to deepen relaxation, followed by a short period of silence.

The next stage involves accessing sensation awareness, exploring opposites such as heavy and light, warm and cool, or tense and relaxed.

As relaxation deepens, another short period of silence is then followed with the **visualization**. This may include imagery, symbols, or scenes designed to access the subconscious mind and encourage emotional clarity. With the mind relaxed and open, long-held patterns may surface for healing.

Before concluding, your guide will ask you to reaffirm your **sankalpa** three times, allowing it to imprint more deeply on your subconscious.

The session concludes with a slow return to wakefulness, giving you time to reorient gently.

Yoga Nidra can produce profound insights and a sense of rejuvenation similar to waking from an exceptionally restful sleep. Many practitioners experience emotional release or clarity about issues they've been struggling with. Others may feel restless or experience physical discomfort during early sessions—this is normal and often related to unfamiliar stillness or insufficient physical support.

Each stage of Yoga Nidra is designed to guide you into progressively deeper states of relaxation, ultimately reaching a state of conscious awareness that is both restful and rejuvenating, what some call superconsciousness. Superconsciousness is a heightened state of awareness that transcends ordinary consciousness, often likened to intuition or universal wisdom.

If Yoga Nidra interests you, many excellent books and recordings are available to deepen your practice. It is a powerful technique that can truly transform your understanding of rest and mindful awareness.

Both the body scan and Yoga Nidra support stress relief, improved sleep, emotional balance, and greater self-awareness. However, Yoga Nidra guides the mind into deeper healing states of theta and delta brain waves, which support memory consolidation, immune function, and overall rejuvenation.

Gentle and accessible for all age groups and fitness levels, both practices help you anchor into the present moment and cultivate a nourishing sense of inner peace.

Breathing Meditation

Breathing meditation is one of the simplest and most accessible mindfulness practices. Known in Buddhism as *Anapanasati,* or "mindfulness of breathing," it has been used for more than 2,500 years to steady the mind, clarify emotions, and support overall well-being. Rooted in the Buddha's original teachings, it remains a central practice for cultivating presence and calm.

At its core, breathing meditation asks you to rest your awareness on the natural flow of your breath. Observe each inhale and exhale without trying to change anything. This gentle focus anchors the mind in the present moment, quiets distraction, and nurtures a sense of ease and clarity.

While originally developed for spiritual insight and liberation from suffering, breathing meditation is now widely practiced for stress reduction, anxiety relief, and emotional balance. It can be done anywhere—while working, commuting, waiting in line, or moving through daily routines—which makes it both practical and deeply healing.

Thich Nhat Hanh played a major role in sharing this practice with the modern world. Through simple, compassionate guidance, he emphasized using the breath to stay grounded, present, and connected to everyday life. His teachings helped people everywhere integrate mindful breathing into moments big and small.

Because it is so adaptable, breathing meditation can support students, professionals, and anyone navigating stress. Focusing on the breath steadies the mind, softens emotional reactivity, and fosters clearer communication—helping to diffuse tension before it escalates.

To practice, keep your eyes open or closed and place gentle attention on your breath. Notice its temperature as it enters your nose, the rise of your chest, and the softening that occurs with each exhale. Let the sensations speak for themselves. Simply witness what the breath is doing in your mind and body.

If you prefer a traditional seated practice, find a quiet place where you can sit comfortably with a relaxed, upright spine. Settle in, close your eyes, and rest your awareness on the rhythm of your breathing. Silently acknowledge each inhalation and exhalation. Below is a simple script you may use during practice:

"Breathing in, I am breathing in."

"Breathing out, I am breathing out."

As the rhythm becomes familiar, you can shorten the phrases:

"Breathing in."

"Breathing out."

Or even:

"In."

"Out."

You may also choose words that support your intention—such as calm, ease, peace, or release. Find the words that are most helpful for you.

For example:

Breathing in, I am calm.

Breathing out, I am at ease.

Breathing in, calm.

Breathing out, ease.

Calm.

Ease.

As thoughts arise, let them pass without judgment. Gently guide your attention back to the breath. Thich Nhat Hanh often encouraged smiling during practice—a small gesture that releases tension and opens the heart. Try it, and notice the quiet joy it brings.

Consistency matters more than duration. Even a few minutes each day can shift your baseline toward peace and mindfulness. Morning practice is especially supportive, as your brain is still in receptive, slower-wave states. Starting the day with conscious breathing sets the tone for clarity and calm.

Thich Nhat Hanh described mindful breathing as a pathway to compassion, inner freedom, and a deep appreciation for the present moment:

Breathing in, I calm my body.
Breathing out, I smile.
Dwelling in the present moment,
I know this is a wonderful moment.
—Thich Nhat Hanh

Pranayama

Pranayama is the yogic practice of consciously regulating the breath. The word comes from the Sanskrit word prana, meaning "life force," and *ayama*, meaning "to extend or direct." Together, they describe breath work as the art of expanding and guiding your vital energy through intentional breathing.

Rooted in the Vedic traditions of India and outlined in Patanjali's *Yoga Sutras*, pranayama is one of yoga's eight limbs—a key step on the path toward inner clarity and spiritual freedom. Traditionally, these breathing techniques prepare the body and mind for meditation by steadying the nervous system, sharpening focus, and creating a sense of internal spaciousness. When paired with yoga postures, pranayama deepens awareness and supports a more meditative state.

Pranayama includes a variety of powerful breathing techniques, each with its own rhythm, purpose, and effect. Because breath has a direct influence on the brain and nervous system, it's important to practice with intention. Choosing a technique starts with understanding what you want to shift—your energy, your mood, or the physical state of your body.

For example, an energizing practice such as **Kapalabhati** generates heat, stimulates circulation, increases oxygen intake, and improves blood flow to the brain. It is helpful when you need a boost, but not ideal if you're already overheated, stressed, or agitated. In those cases, cooling breaths like **Sitali** or **Sitkari** are better suited. They soothe the body and calm emotional reactivity by drawing air across the tongue or teeth, cooling as you inhale.

Beyond regulating temperature and mood, pranayama supports overall physical and emotional well-being. Slow, steady methods such as **Ujjayi** and **Dirga** pranayamas expand lung capacity, quiet the mind, and help stabilize the breath. More vigorous practices, like **Bhastrika**, strengthen the diaphragm, tone the intercostal muscles, stimulate digestion, and support healthier metabolic function. Together, these effects can elevate energy, improve resilience, and enhance emotional balance.

Yogic philosophy teaches that the breath is the bridge between the mind and body. When breath is calm, the mind follows. When breath is scattered, the mind becomes unsettled. Pranayama helps harmonize the two, creating the internal coherence necessary for mindfulness to flourish.

At its core, pranayama is about balance—balancing energy, emotions, and the subtle patterns that shape daily experience. Its techniques offer a practical way to feel more grounded, present, and internally attuned. Used regularly, pranayama can enrich your daily life with clarity, steadiness, and renewed vitality.

In the upcoming sections, you'll find simple explanations and step-by-step instructions for six accessible pranayama techniques. Whether you're preparing for meditation, easing stress in traffic, or needing midday focus, these practices can help you recenter and reconnect with the present moment.

Three-Part Breath *(Dirga Pranayama)*

Dirga Pranayama—often called *Three-Part Breath*—is a calming technique that deeply engages all lobes of the lungs, promoting relaxation and focus. The right lung has three lobes, while the left has two, making room for the heart. This practice involves deep inhalations and exhalations that expand the abdomen, ribcage, and chest. This deep, layered breath creates an immediate sense of calm by reconnecting the mind and body through slow, intentional breathing.

The name *dirga* comes from Sanskrit, meaning "long" or "extended," describing both the length of the breath and the spacious quality it brings to the body. As you inhale, the breath gently expands the abdomen, then the ribcage, and finally the upper chest. Exhaling reverses this order, relaxing the abdomen, ribcage, and chest. This rhythmic sequence is soothing and fosters mind–body coherence as it regulates the nervous system.

Three-Part Breath is often the first technique I teach to yoga and meditation students because it's simple, effective, and immediately brings the mind into the present moment. It can be practiced any-where, anytime, and is an excellent tool for easing stress, increasing focus, and supporting emotional clarity.

Physically, Dirga Pranayama strengthens respiratory muscles, increases oxygenation, and improves digestive function by gently massaging the abdominal organs with each full breath. The rhythmic expansion and release also stimulates the lymphatic system, helping the body clear metabolic waste and reduce muscular tension. As the body relaxes, the mind naturally follows, allowing space for clarity, balance, and emotional steadiness.

Mentally and emotionally, the slow, deep rhythm of Three-Part Breath triggers the release of calming endorphins, promoting ease, stability, and a sense of inner safety. When practiced regularly, it becomes a powerful doorway to mindfulness—the foundation of self-awareness and presence.

How to Practice Dirga Pranayama (Three-Part Breath)

1. **Find a comfortable position:** Sit or lie down somewhere quiet where your spine is straight and feels supported. If lying down, place a bolster under your knees.

2. **Begin with awareness:** Gently close your eyes and observe the natural rhythm of your breath. Notice the rise and fall of your chest and abdomen without altering your breath.

3. **Abdominal breathing:** Place a hand on your belly. Inhale through your nose and let the belly rise softly. Exhale and feel it fall. Repeat until you can feel the breath filling your lower lungs with ease.

4. **Thoracic breathing:** Keep one hand on your belly and place the other on your ribcage. Inhale: belly first, then ribs expanding outward. Exhale slowly, contracting the

ribcage first, then relaxing the abdomen. Repeat for a few cycles.

5. **Clavicular breathing:** Place a hand on your chest. Inhale deeply, filling the abdomen, ribcage, and finally the chest, allowing your collarbones to rise. Exhale from your chest, then the ribcage, and finally the abdomen.

6. **Full Cycle:** Continue this three-part breathing cycle, maintaining a smooth, continuous wave-like breath. Focus on the rhythmic flow: inhale (abdomen-ribcage-chest), exhale (chest-ribcage-abdomen).

If you lose the rhythm, simply begin again. With practice, Dirga Pranayama will become a natural, calming rhythm that anchors you in the present moment.

Victorious/Ocean Breath (Ujjayi Pranayama)

Ujjayi Pranayama, or *Victorious Breath,* is a powerful breathing technique that fosters mental and physical harmony. Its name, meaning "victorious" in Sanskrit, reflects the mastery of connecting mind and body through conscious breathing. The practice's rhythmic sound resembles ocean waves, earning it the nickname *Ocean Breath.*

This pranayama enhances the mind–body connection, balancing energy flow, boosting concentration, and promoting inner peace. Think of it as a trinity: the mind creates ideas, the body manifests them, and the breath acts as the spirit connecting both, turning ideas into reality. Breath becomes the bridge that transforms intention into action.

The acronym **"I AM"** symbolizes this mind–body–spirit connection:

I — idea (mind)

A — action (breath)

M — manifestation (body)

Ujjayi Breath embodies this principle, reminding us of the creative power that arises when mind, breath, and body work together.

Rooted in ancient yogic tradition, Ujjayi was originally used to sharpen focus and guide prana during meditation and yoga practice. Today, it's embraced far beyond the yoga mat, benefitting everyone, calming stress, improving concentration and easing discomfort.

Use Ujjayi whenever your mind feels scattered, your temper flares, or you need to reconnect with the present moment. It softens anxiety, steadies the nervous system, and prepares the mind for rest, making it an excellent bedtime practice as well. The more consistently you use it, the more naturally mindfulness begins weaving into everyday life.

Like Dirga Pranayama, Ujjayi is simple to learn and deeply rewarding once it becomes familiar. Its signature whisper-like sound encourages concentration and helps cultivate a meditative state through slow, steady breathing.

How to Practice Ujjayi Pranayama

1. **Preparation:** Find a comfortable position—lying down, seated, or standing with your feet firmly grounded. Keep your spine long, your chest open, and your shoulders relaxed for optimal lung expansion.

2. **Focus:** If you're new to this breath, closing your eyes may help sharpen your focus. Breathe normally through your nose and notice the sensations: the movement in your throat, the air flowing through your nostrils, and the expansion of your lungs.

3. **Technique:** Inhale deeply through your nose, fully filling your lungs. Exhale through your nostrils. On the following breath, gently narrow the back of your throat as if whispering or fogging a mirror—without opening your mouth. This slight constriction creates the signature oceanic sound. Maintain that throat texture as you inhale and exhale, keeping your breath long, smooth, and even.

4. **Practice:** Focus on the ocean sound and the breath's rhythm. Continue for three to five minutes or eight slow rounds of breath. When finished, let your breathing return to normal and notice any shifts in your body, mood, or mind. You may feel more spacious, calmer, or simply more aware.

If you feel lightheaded at any point, release the technique and breathe normally. Deep breathing increases oxygen intake, which can momentarily disrupt the balance of oxygen and carbon dioxide—especially if you're not used to breathing deeply. With practice, your system will adapt. If dizziness persists, consider practicing with a teacher or consulting a healthcare professional.

The practice of Ujjayi Pranayama offers conscious control over your breath and greater mastery of your mind and emotions. Whether paired with yoga or other forms of exercise, used as a midday reset, as an aid for falling asleep, or practiced quietly your during daily life, it strengthens respiratory and cardiovascular health, sharpens awareness, and reduces stress. With steady practice, this "victorious breath" helps cultivate the clarity and centeredness that define a mindful life.

Equal Breath (Sama Vritti Pranayama) / *Box Breath* (Chatur Vritti Pranayama)

Equal Breath (Sama Vritti) and Box Breath (Chatur Vritti) are two of the simplest—and most effective—breathing practices for calming the mind, easing stress, and restoring emotional balance. While they share the same foundation, the key difference lies in breath retention: Sama Vritti keeps the breath moving, while Chatur Vritti adds pauses after each inhalation and exhalation.

Sama Vritti (Equal Breath) comes from the Sanskrit words *sama* (equal) and *vritti* (movement). True to its name, this practice balances the breath by matching the length of the inhalation to the exhalation. A basic version might look like inhaling for a count of four and exhaling for the same four-count rhythm.

Chatur Vritti (Box Breath) builds on this pattern by adding four equal movements—inhale, hold, exhale, hold—each for the same count. For example, inhale for four, hold for four, exhale for four, hold for four.

Although four counts are commonly used, your breath should always match your comfort level. Over time, as your lung capacity expands, you may naturally increase the length of each phase. The real aim is equality—not perfection—allowing the breath to steady the mind and regulate the nervous system.

Both practices promote clarity and calm, yet they offer slightly different benefits. **Equal Breath** is ideal for soothing the nervous system, quieting mental chatter, and resetting emotional equilibrium. **Box Breath**, with its gentle breath retention, helps strengthen the lungs, builds stress resilience, and sharpens focus. This is why it's often used by athletes, first responders, and military personnel during high-pressure situations.

These practices shine during a morning mindfulness routine, preparing the mind and body for the day ahead. Because they oxygenate the bloodstream and quiet scattered thoughts, they create a more serene mind from the moment you wake. They are equally supportive during stressful moments or as a way to unwind before sleep.

Let's explore each technique more closely, beginning with Equal Breath.

EXERCISE — *Equal Breath* (Sama Vritti Pranayama)

Equal Breath has two simple parts—inhale and exhale—kept at equal length.

1. **Inhale** slowly through the nose for a comfortable count (for example, four).
2. **Exhale** through the nose for the same count.

Continue for about five minutes or as long as you remain comfortable. Notice how the breath begins to smooth out your energy. Does your body feel more relaxed? Does your mind feel clearer? Because Equal Breath is both simple and adaptable, it becomes a reliable tool whenever you crave emotional steadiness or a mental reset.

Benefits — *Equal Breath*

- Balances the body and mind by equalizing the breath
- Activates the parasympathetic nervous system, easing stress and anxiety
- Supports respiratory health and improves lung efficiency
- Encourages emotional stability and mindful awareness
- It is gentle, grounding, and easy to integrate into everyday life.

EXERCISE — *Box Breath (Chatur Vritti)*

Box Breath expands upon Equal Breath by adding two pauses. These four equal parts create the "box."

Before beginning, settle into a comfortable position where you can focus.

1. **Sit upright** with your spine supported and feet grounded, or lie comfortably with support under your knees.

2. **Inhale** through your nose for a count of four.

3. **Hold** your breath for a count of four, keeping your face, neck, and shoulders relaxed.

4. **Exhale** through your nose (or mouth, if preferred) for a count of four.

5. **Hold** again for four counts before beginning the next round.

Repeat several cycles, maintaining a steady, easeful pace. Practice for at least five minutes to experience its full benefits. You may adjust the count as needed—just keep all four parts equal.

Benefits — Box Breath

- Includes all the benefits of Sama Vritti
- Strengthens the lungs through gentle retention
- Builds stress resilience by training the nervous system to stay calm under pressure
- Lowers heart rate and quiets the body's stress response
- Enhances mental focus and emotional regulation

It's especially handy for those nerve-wracking moments, whether you're gearing up for a big event, on the move, or when anxiety decides to pay an unexpected visit. It's also a wonderful midday refresher, improving alertness and productivity without the need for caffeine. Practiced at night, Box Breath helps release the day's tension and prepare you for deep, restorative sleep.

Because it anchors the mind to counting and smooth breathing, Box Breath can even serve as a meditation on its own.

Sama Vritti and Chatur Vritti are simple yet powerful pranayamas for cultivating mindfulness. Whether you're new to breath-work or a seasoned practitioner, these techniques help regulate emotions, improve concentration, and enhance your overall quality of life.

Alternate Nostril Breathing (Nadi Shodhana/Anulom Vilom)

Alternate Nostril Breath is one of the most balancing practices in the yogic tradition. Known in Sanskrit as *Nadi Shodhana* and *Anulom Vilom*, these two variations help harmonize the mind and body by regulating the flow of prana (life force) through subtle energy channels called *nadis.*

To appreciate this breath, it helps to understand the nadis. The Sanskrit root *nad* means "flow" or "channel." Nadis are not physical structures but part of the subtle energetic body that includes chakras, auras, and consciousness. They guide the movement of life force throughout the body, influencing physical vitality, emotional stability, and spiritual awareness. Yogic texts describe as many as 72,000 of these channels throughout the human body. The *Ida, Pingala*, and *Shushumna* nadis are considered primary, and extend from the base of the spine to the head.

Ida nadi, meaning "comfort," originates on the left side of the body and carries cooling, restorative, parasympathetic energy. Considered "feminine" in nature, it is linked with intuition and receptivity. It crisscrosses the spine at the junctions of the chakras.

Pingala nadi originates on the right side of the body, carrying warming, active, sympathetic energy. Translated as "tawny," it is considered "masculine" in nature and is linked with vitality, focus, and logic. It, too, crisscrosses the spine at the junctions of the chakras.

Sushumna channel runs through the center of the spine and is considered the most important nadi, integrating the opposite forces of Ida (feminine) and Pingla (masculine) and connecting the base chakra to the crown chakra. Associated with harmony, neutrality, and balance, Sushumna is translated to mean "joyful mind."

Because Nadi Shodhana and Anulom Vilom alternate the breath between nostrils, they directly influence these channels, gently balancing both hemispheres of the brain and both branches of the nervous system. This is why Alternate Nostril Breath reliably brings calm, clarity, and emotional stability.

While the practices look similar, there is one important distinction: **Anulom Vilom** does not include breath retention, making it accessible for beginners. **Nadi Shodhana** incorporates gentle holds to deepen purification and energetic balance.

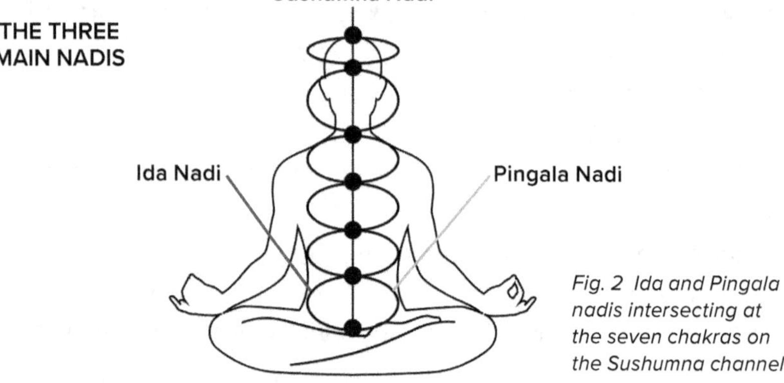

Fig. 2 Ida and Pingala nadis intersecting at the seven chakras on the Sushumna channel.

EXERCISE — Anulom Vilom
(Alternate Nostril Breath — without retention)

Anulom Vilom translates to "with the grain, against the grain," reflecting the alternating nature of the breath. Straightforward and soothing, it balances Ida and Pingala, steadies emotions, and supports focus. Many practitioners describe feeling more spacious, centered, and mentally clear after only a few rounds.

Follow these directions to practice **Anulom Vilom**:

1. **Sit comfortably** with your spine erect and shoulders relaxed.

2. **Curl your index and middle fingers** into your palm, keeping your thumb, ring, and little fingers extended.

3. **Close your right nostril** with your thumb and inhale through your left nostril.

4. **Close the left nostril** with your ring finger and release your thumb.

5. **Exhale slowly** through your right nostril.

6. **Inhale slowly and deeply** through your right nostril.

7. **Close your right nostril** and exhale through **the left** nostril. This completes one round.

8. **Continue** for five to ten minutes or as long as it is comfortable.

When you have completed your practice, sit quietly and notice the effects. Are you feeling calmer and more relaxed? Allow yourself a moment to integrate before moving on with your day.

EXERCISE — Nadi Shodhana
(Alternate Nostril Breath — with retention)

Nadi Shodhana means "purification of energy channels." With the addition of gentle breath retention, the practice becomes more focused and cleansing. Many people report heightened clarity, a sense of inner spaciousness, and deeper emotional balance. Beginners may feel slightly lightheaded at first. If so, simply release the holds and breathe normally.

Follow these directions to practice Nadi Shodhana:

1. **Sit comfortably with a long spine and relaxed shoulders.**

2. **Form the same hand position** as for Anulom Vilom. Exhale.

3. **Close your right nostril and inhale** through your left nostril. Hold for two to three counts.

4. **Close your left nostril and exhale** through your right nostril. Hold for two to three counts.

5. **Inhale slowly through your right nostril.** Hold for two to three counts.

6. **Close the right nostril and exhale through the left**. Hold for two to three counts.

7. **Continue for five to ten minutes**, adjusting the time for your comfort.

After your practice, sit quietly and observe your breath. Notice any shifts in your emotional or mental state. Can you feel a sense of ease moving through your body?

If this is your first introduction to alternate nostril breathing, you may wish to practicing for a shorter amount of time until you can acclimate to the breath.

Both forms of Alternate Nostril Breath offer readily available and profound benefits:

Anulom Vilom

- Calms the mind and steadies emotions
- Enhances concentration
- Improves lung function and oxygenation
- Reduces stress and supports better sleep
- Ideal for beginners and daily use

Nadi Shodhana

- Includes all benefits of Anulom Vilom
- Creates better respiratory function
- Enhances mental clarity and inner stillness
- Supports spiritual growth and expands awareness
- Best for practitioners with some pranayama experience

Alternate nostril breathing is a powerful tool for cultivating mindfulness and restoring balance to the entire system. Whether you choose the simplicity of Anulom Vilom or the deeper purification of Nadi Shodhana, this practice can become a steady anchor in your daily life—bringing calm, presence, and harmony to every moment.

Humming Bee Breath (*Bhramari Pranayama*)

Bhramari Pranayama, also known as Humming Bee Breath, is one of the most soothing practices in yoga. Derived from the Sanskrit word *bhramara*, which means "bee," ancient yogic practitioners primarily used this technique to promote mental relaxation and clarity. As it turns out, this aptly named practice offers more than mental clarity. In addition to quieting the mind, it is particularly effective for reducing stress and anxiety, lowering blood pressure, and improving sleep quality. The soft humming sound mimics the steady resonance of a bee and naturally draws awareness inward, creating a sense of calm that feels both grounding and comforting.

The practice works by extending the exhalation and adding vibration, moving oxygen through your body, which stimulates the parasympathetic nervous system and encourages the mind to settle. Even a few rounds provide noticeable relief from anxiety, restlessness, and mental overload.

Because this breath gently massages the brain and facial muscles, it is especially helpful to practice when you feel overwhelmed or overstimulated. The sound also drowns out external noise so you are better able to connect with your own inner stillness.

EXERCISE — Humming Bee Breath (Bhramari Pranayama)

Practice Bhramari Pranayama in a quiet and comfortable environment. A dedicated space for meditation, under a tree in the backyard, or sitting on the front porch at sunrise are good options to consider. Consistency is important. Try to incorporate this powerful breath into a daily routine. If you do, the benefits you can reap will be life-changing.

1. **Sit comfortably with your spine straight,** shoulders relaxed, and eyes closed. Bhramari should not be practiced lying down.

2. **Rest the tip of your tongue behind your upper front teeth.** Gently close your lips, keeping your teeth slightly separated. This position helps the humming vibration resonate more fully in your head and brain.

3. **Gently press the tragus**—the small flap of cartilage just in front of your ear canal—over your ears with your index fingers to muffle outward sound. Keep your hands and fingers as relaxed as possible.

4. **For a deeper experience, use Shanmukhi Mudra** (hand position) to produce a more meditative state. Place your thumbs over both ear canals so that outside sounds become muffled. Rest your index fingers at the middle of your forehead. Reaching your middle, ring, and pinky fingers over the eyes, place the tips of each finger gently on the bridge of your nose.

5. **Inhale slowly** through your nose.

6. **Exhale slowly as you lower your chin** toward your chest, making a low humming sound like a bee. Keep the sound steady and smooth, focusing at the center of your head.

7. **Inhale** as you lift your chin.

8. **Continue for five to ten rounds** or as long as it feels soothing.

Release your fingers from your ears on the final repetition and breathe normally. Remain still for a moment. Keeping your eyes closed, notice the silence that follows the vibration. What has shifted for you?

Take a few moments to acclimate back into your practice space. Slowly move into your day with calm awareness.

Benefits—Bhramari Pranayama

Bhramari Pranayama naturally slows the breath, reduces anxiety, quiets looping thoughts, and supports emotional regulation.

The resonating vibrations stimulate the vagus nerve, which runs from the brainstem through the neck and into the chest and abdomen. This calming effect counteracts the *"fight/flight/freeze"* response, reducing stress and promoting relaxation.

Prolonged practice of Bhramari can train your nervous system away from "fight/flight/freeze" reactions and into conscious and mindful awareness. It is even used to promote better sleep.

Bhramari Pranayama encourages better throat health and a stronger voice by reducing irritation and discomfort, while creating a natural anti-inflammatory effect. The gentle vibrations in the throat function as a natural massage that soothes and relaxes your larynx, vocal cords, and throat muscles.

Because Bhramari utilizes nostril breathing, it also moisturizes the sinuses and respiratory system, preventing added dryness and irritation in your nose and throat.

During nasal breathing, especially when humming, the paranasal sinuses produce nitric oxide (NO). This naturally occurring gas has antimicrobial properties that can help reduce pathogens in your lungs, thus minimizing the risk of infections that could lead to throat irritation. Nitric oxide enhances oxygen delivery to the tissues in your throat which can help reduce inflammation and soothe irritation, aiding in quicker recovery from discomfort.

Regular Practice

The regular practice of Bhramari (Humming Bee Breath) builds stamina and improves breath control and projection. It conditions the throat muscles, which enhance vocal resonance and tone, thus helping to make the voice clearer and more melodious. This pranayama is particularly beneficial for singers, public speakers, teachers, and anyone who uses their voice often.

Incorporating Humming Bee Breath into your routine can be a simple yet effective way to support throat health, enhance vocal quality, and create a life filled with mindful awareness. Whether you use your voice professionally or are simply looking to improve your mindfulness practice, this technique provides valuable benefits. Humming Bee Breath is a simple and powerful technique that enhances mental clarity, emotional balance, and physical well-being.

Breath of Fire (*Kapalabhati Pranayama*)

Kapalabhati Pranayama—often called *Skull-Shining Breath or Breath of Fire*—is a dynamic yogic technique known for its cleansing, heating, and energizing qualities. The Sanskrit words *kapala* (skull) and *bhati* (shining or illuminating) describe the bright, uplifted feeling this breath inspires. Traditionally referenced in the *Hatha Yoga Pradipika* as a purifying practice for meditation, Kapalabhati is still valued today for its powerful effects on physical vitality, mental clarity.

Modern research supports what ancient yogis understood intuitively. A study published in the *International Journal of Medical and Health Research* found that Kapalabhati strengthens the diaphragm, increases oxygen saturation, and improves overall lung capacity. Because the diaphragm and respiratory muscles work vigorously during this practice, they become stronger and more efficient, improving breathing patterns and core stability.

Another study, from the *Journal of Family Medicine and Primary Care*, revealed Kapalabhati's impact on heart-rate variability (HRV)—a key measure of the body's stress response. Breath of Fire was shown to activate the sympathetic nervous system, increasing alertness, mental sharpness, and internal energy. In other words, this breath wakes up both the body and the mind, placing you in a heightened state of focus and performance.

This makes Kapalabhati a powerful tool on days when you need clarity, stamina, or motivation—before a big presentation, an athletic event, or simply a busy day of tasks that require sharp attention and steady energy. Breath of Fire helps you meet the moment with intention and presence.

CAUTIONS

As dynamic and invigorating as Kapalabhati is, it's also important to approach it with care. Because it creates rapid changes in breathing, heart rate, and internal pressure, certain conditions require caution or medical guidance. The breath's vigorous nature increases blood pressure, which is fine if yours is in a normal range. However, if you already have high blood pressure, it is probably best to consult with your doctor before attempting this technique, as it can put additional strain on the heart.

If you are menstruating, healing from a recent procedure, or feeling dizzy or unwell, wait until you feel stable before attempting this breath.

Consult your healthcare provider before practicing if you are pregnant, have high blood pressure, heart conditions, epilepsy, stomach ulcers, or hernias. The forceful abdominal contractions are not recommended during pregnancy or when recovering from abdominal surgeries.

As with all pranayama, self-awareness is your greatest teacher—if something feels uncomfortable or overwhelming, pause and return to a natural breath.

Benefits — Breath of Fire (*Kapalabhati Pranayama*)

While it is a mindful practice to know your limitations and needs, please don't let these contraindications frighten you, especially if you don't suffer from any of the above conditions. The benefits of this powerful practice can transform your life. They can cleanse and energize your physical body and purify your mind and spirit.

For those who can practice safely, Kapalabhati offers transformative benefits. It clears the nasal passages, increases lung capacity, and removes stale air and impurities from the respiratory system. The sharp exhalations stimulate circulation, awaken mental clarity, and boost energy levels. Many practitioners experience improved digestion as well—the rhythmic abdominal pumping gently massages the internal organs and supports healthy elimination.

Beyond the physical benefits, Kapalabhati can sharpen concentration and uplift your mood. The breath's intensity has a way of burning through mental fog, revealing a state of focus, motivation, and emotional resilience. Practiced consistently, Breath of Fire becomes a powerful ally in cultivating mindful awareness and inner strength.

Let's practice.

EXERCISE — Breath of Fire (Kapalabhati Pranayama)

1. **Sit comfortably**—either on a chair with your feet grounded or cross-legged on a mat. Keep your spine tall and shoulders relaxed. Rest your hands in your lap or at your heart.

2. **Take a few slow breaths** to settle in and center your awareness.

3. **When you're ready, inhale naturally.** Begin sharp, quick exhalations through the nose by snapping the belly inward. Each inhalation happens automatically between the forceful exhalations.

4. **Start at a moderate pace and gradually increase** speed as it feels natural. Aim for 20-30 exhalations per round.

5. **Practice 3-5 rounds**, pausing in between to breathe normally and notice how you feel.

6. **Keep your awareness on your abdomen** moving in and out. It's normal to need a tissue afterward (or during) the practice. Consider clearing your nose before starting.

7. **For comfort and safety**, practice Kapalabhati on an empty stomach.

If you're new to this pranayama, consider learning from a qualified yoga instructor. If you have high blood pressure, heart concerns, or respiratory conditions, consult a medical professional before beginning. Breath of Fire should support your wellness—not strain it.

Kapalabhati is one of many mindfulness tools available to you. Practiced with awareness, it builds strength, sharpens focus, and awakens a sense of purposeful presence—helping you meet your life with clarity and intention.

Yoga

Yoga traces its origins to ancient India more than 5,000 years ago, shaped over centuries by sages, scholars, and devoted practitioners. Among them, Patanjali stands out as one of the most influential. Variously dated between 500 BCE to 450 CE, he compiled the Yoga Sutras—196 concise teachings that form the philosophical heart of yoga and continue to guide practitioners today.

The *Yoga Sutras* are divided into four chapters, each outlining a stage of inner transformation.

Samadhi Pada explores concentration and the discipline of calming the mind's fluctuations, ultimately guiding the practitioner toward *Samadhi*, a state of deep, meditative absorption.

Sadhana Pada describes the importance of consistent practice and introduces the Eight Limbs of Yoga (Ashtanga Yoga)—ethical foundations, postures, breathwork, sensory withdrawal, concentration, meditation, and union.

Vibhuti Pada examines the extraordinary abilities (siddhis) that can arise from advanced practice, reminding us not to confuse special experiences with the true goal.

Finally, **Kaivalya Pada** focuses on liberation—freedom from the cycles of karma and identification with the mind—revealing the enduring state of pure awareness that yoga ultimately seeks.

While yoga offers a vast and profound spiritual path, this chapter emphasizes asana, the third limb of Patanjali's system and the most familiar aspect of yoga in modern practice. Asana involves mindful movement and intentional postures. Though physical in appearance, its purpose extends far beyond exercise—asana strengthens and steadies the body so the mind can settle into meditation with comfort and clarity.

Asana also cultivates discipline, concentration, and a deeper awareness of the breath. It acts as a bridge between the physical and subtle layers of the self, supporting emotional balance, inner steadiness, and the capacity to be present. For thousands of years, yogis have recognized that harmony of body and mind creates the foundation for spiritual and personal growth.

One of the greatest strengths of yoga asana is its adaptability. It can be shaped to meet different bodies, abilities, and intentions, which makes yoga accessible to people of all backgrounds. With regular practice, yoga becomes a journey of self-discovery—one that fosters mindfulness, resilience, and a sense of connection to something deeper than daily routine. Its timeless teachings remain relevant in our fast-paced culture because they offer a path toward clarity and grounded living.

The sequence of postures in this chapter forms a complete, beginner-friendly routine that stretches, strengthens, and balances the entire body. Whether this is your first experience with yoga or you've practiced for years, approaching each posture with a "beginner's mind" invites curiosity and presence. This mindset allows you to discover new layers of awareness and reconnect with yourself in meaningful ways.

Before beginning any yoga practice, especially if you have conditions involving the heart, blood pressure, balance, or recent injuries, consult with your healthcare provider. As with all mindful movement, safety and awareness come first.

In the following pages, you'll find each posture listed with its Sanskrit and English names, along with a brief description. Step-by-step instructions will guide you safely in and out of the pose. Take a moment after each asana to notice how your body feels, how your breath moves, and what has shifted within your mind. Learning to listen to your body is one of the foundations of a mindful and meaningful yoga practice.

Easy Pose (Sukhasana)

Sukhasana, often called "Easy Pose," is a simple cross-legged seated position commonly used in yoga and meditation. It's one of the most basic and accessible seated postures, often used as a starting point for meditation and pranayama practices. Sukhasana symbolizes ease, comfort, and stability, reflecting the yogic principle of finding peace and stillness within the body and mind.

Fig.3 Sukhasana (Easy Pose)

Benefits—Easy Pose (Sukhasana)

Despite its simplicity, Sukhasana offers meaningful physical and mental benefits. It gently opens the hips, knees, and ankles, and encourages a long, aligned spine, which can ease back tension. The steady base created by Easy Pose supports calm breathing and focused attention—an ideal set-up for meditation, pranayama, or simply settling into the present moment. Over time, this posture cultivates groundedness, clarity, and inner ease.

CAUTIONS

Sukhasana may not feel "easy" for everyone. If you have knee, hip, or ankle discomfort, modify the pose by sitting on a cushion, block, or folded blanket to elevate your hips. Cushioning under the ankles can relieve pressure there as well. If keeping your spine upright is difficult, additional height under your seat can make a dramatic difference.

Pregnant practitioners may need extra support and should only sit on the floor if getting up and down feels safe.

Avoid Easy Pose if you have recent injuries or surgeries involving the knees, hips, ankles, or spine. Conditions such as scoliosis, sciatica, arthritis, and lower back pain may require adjustments—or a different posture entirely. As always, listen to your body and honor its limits.

EXERCISE—Easy Pose (Sukhasana)

1. **Sit on the floor** with your legs loosely crossed at the shins. If needed, elevate your hips with a cushion to reduce strain on the knees and lower back. Feel your weight settle evenly across your sit bones.

2. **Gently draw your navel inward** to support a tall but relaxed spine.

3. **Lengthen upward through the crown** of your head, keeping your shoulders soft and your chin parallel to the floor.

4. **Rest your hands on your knees or thighs.** You may take Gyan Mudra (Seal of Knowledge) by touching the index finger to the thumb on each hand.

5. **Keep your gaze soft or close your eyes.** Breathe naturally, or use Ujjayi Pranayama to deepen your inward focus.

6. **Stay for as long as you feel comfortable.** Change the cross of your legs occasionally to promote balanced flexibility.

7. **To exit, extend the top leg forward**, turn slightly toward your bent knee, and press your hand into the floor as you rise to hands and knees.

8. **Step one foot forward** and come to standing, using a chair or wall for support if needed.

9. **Pause for a moment** and notice how your body and mind feel before continuing with your day.

Sukhasana is often the first seated posture a person learns, but its depth grows with practice. Start with short sessions, especially if you're new to meditation or sitting on the floor. With time, ease and comfort naturally increase. As a foundational posture, Easy Pose supports beginners and experienced practitioners alike, offering a simple yet powerful pathway to inner stillness and mindful awareness.

Circle of Joy (Ananda Mandalasana)

Ananda Mandalasana, or *Circle of Joy*, is a simple seated sequence traditionally practiced in Sukhasana. It gently warms the upper body through a flowing series of arm and shoulder movements that open the chest and brighten the heart. This short sequence stretches and strengthens the shoulders, arms, chest, and neck, making it an ideal morning practice to wake up the body, deepen the breath, and lift the spirit.

Fig. 4 Circle of Joy (Ananda Mandalasana)

Benefits—Circle of Joy (Ananda Mandalasana)

Though subtle, *Circle of Joy* offers a surprisingly wide-ranging benefits. The slow, circular movements improve mobility in the shoulders, elbows, wrists, and upper spine while gently strengthening the core and upper back. These mindful motions enhance posture, increase circulation, and support respiratory health by expanding the rib cage and improving lung capacity.

Circle of Joy also stimulates the flow of lymph, synovial fluid, and blood—helping clear toxins, lubricate joints, and oxygenate the body. Equally important are its mental and emotional effects: the rhythm of breath and movement calms the mind, reduces stress, and provides a gentle emotional uplift. This sequence encourages presence, softens tension, and fosters a sense of grounded, heart-centered well-being.

CAUTIONS

Because Circle of Joy is practiced in Sukhasana, avoid it if you've recently experienced hip, knee, or ankle injuries or surgeries. Likewise, shoulder, elbow, wrist, or upper-back injuries need adequate healing time before attempting these movements.

If you have arthritis, rotator cuff limitations, tendonitis, vertigo, or high blood pressure, approach this sequence with care and check with your healthcare provider if needed. Comfort and steadiness should always guide your practice.

EXERCISE—Circle of Joy *(Ananda Mandalasana)*

If you are ready to experience the gentle lift of *Circle of Joy*, settle into a comfortable cross-legged seat and begin.

1. **Sit in Sukhasana** with your spine tall. Bring your hands to your heart in Anjali Mudra and take a deep, steady breath in.

2. **Exhale** as you interlace your fingers, turn your palms outward, and extend your arms straight forward.

3. **Inhale,** lifting your straight arms and clasped hands overhead with palms turned upward. Lengthen your spine as you soften your shoulders.

4. **Exhale,** releasing your hands as your arms sweep open and back behind you.

5. **Inhale** and reclasp your hands behind your back, lifting your chest gently.

6. **Exhale,** releasing the clasp and circling your arms forward, bringing your palms together once more.

7. **Inhale,** returning your hands to your heart.

Repeat the full sequence two more times. When finished, rest your hands on your knees, soften your shoulders, and breathe into the warmth and openness you've created.

Ananda Mandalasana truly earns its name. This simple heart-opening sequence can refresh your energy at any time of day and is especially powerful in the morning, setting the tone for mindfulness, ease, and joy.

*If you would like to practice *Circle of Joy* and more postures with me, you can find my practice CD, *Yoga for Deep Relaxation*, on many streaming services including CDBaby, iTunes, and Spotify.

Child Pose (Balasana)

Balasana is one of yoga's most grounding and restorative postures. Rooted in the Sanskrit words *bala* (child) and *asana* (pose), it resembles a resting infant and carries that same sense of surrender and humility. This gentle fold reminds us to pause, soften, and allow ourselves to be held by the moment.

Though it appears still, Balasana is an active release. As the torso folds toward the thighs and the breath deepens, the parasympathetic nervous system (PSNS) engages—slowing the heart rate, quieting stress responses, and inviting the body into true "rest and digest" mode. It's a simple shape with profound influence, offering a safe return to presence whenever life feels overwhelming.

Who couldn't use a dose of that childlike ease?

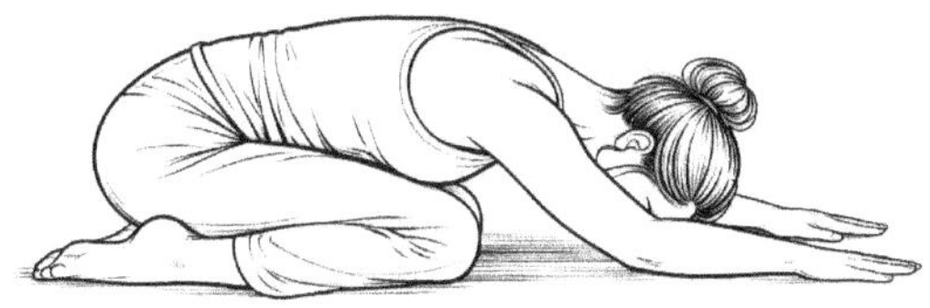

Fig.5 Balasanna (Child Pose)

Benefits—Child Pose (Balasana)

Balasana offers both physical and emotional grounding. It naturally promotes diaphragmatic breathing, which supports lung capacity, calms the mind, and stabilizes the core. This inward-turning shape also encourages mindful awareness by creating clear physical sensations—especially along the spine, hips, thighs, and ankles—as the body gently folds forward.

The soft compression of the abdomen can support digestion, and the overall release of tension may improve sleep quality and help ease stress-related discomfort. For beginners, Balasana provides a comforting entry point into the breath–body connection; for seasoned practitioners, it remains a place of refuge and reset.

CAUTIONS

While Balasana is supportive for most bodies, a few considerations will keep it safe:

- Avoid the pose if you've recently had abdominal, hip, knee, or ankle surgery or injury.
- If your hips or knees feel tender, place a cushion or blanket between the thighs and calves, or elevate the ankles with a rolled towel.
- Pregnant practitioners may widen the knees or use props for space, though the pose is generally best avoided after the second trimester.
- If you experience high blood pressure, headaches, or inner-ear concerns, the head-down position may not be appropriate—consult your healthcare provider.
- Practice on an empty stomach or wait two to three hours after eating to avoid discomfort.
- Tight hamstrings may benefit from additional support under the torso or between the legs.
- Always listen to your body. Comfort is not optional in Balasana—it's the point.

EXERCISE—Child's Pose (Balasana)

Below are step-by-step instructions for safely entering and exiting Balasana (Child's Pose):

1. **Begin on hands and knees** in a tabletop position. Place wrists under your shoulders and knees under your hips.
2. **Bring your big toes together** and widen your knees to create space.

3. **Sit your hips back toward your heels**, adjusting knee width to your comfort.

4. **Extend your arms forward with palms down** and rest your forehead on the mat. Alternatively, you can place your arms alongside your body with palms facing up by your feet. Another option is to place your stacked hands under your forehead, palms facing down, slightly elevating your forehead. This lessens the intensity of the stretch.

5. **Close your eyes and breathe deeply.** With each exhale, feel your body soften and settle. Stay as long as you are comfortable.

6. **To exit, press into your palms** and slowly lift your torso back to seated. Use your abdominal muscles to support your spine as you lift.

7. **Bring your knees together** (if separated) and return to tabletop—or transition into your next posture.

Balasana is a powerful reminder that slowing down is not the same as stopping. It reconnects you with breath, body, and present-moment awareness. Whether used as a morning grounding ritual, a midday reset, or a calming bedtime practice, Child's Pose is always there to welcome you home to yourself.

Cat–Cow Pose (Marjaryasana–Bitilasana)

Marjaryasana–Bitilasana, or Cat–Cow Pose, is a gentle, rhythmic flow that warms the spine, eases tension, and invites breath-led movement. A staple in Hatha yoga, this sequence mirrors the subtle arching and rounding of a stretching cat and the soft belly-drop of a grazing cow. For simplicity, I'll refer to it as Cat–Cow Pose.

Don't be fooled by its ease. Cat–Cow is deceptively powerful. By moving the spine through flexion (cat) and extension (cow), this sequence increases mobility, builds support in the back muscles, and reconnects you with your natural rhythm of breath. Each flowing movement invites a deeper sense of fluidity.

In Cat Pose, the spine rounds upward as the belly draws in and the chin tucks toward the chest. In Cow Pose, the spine gently dips while the chest opens and the tailbone lifts. Flowing between these positions helps unlock stiffness, increase circulation, and restore balance in the spine and nervous system.

Fig. 6 Cat-Cow Pose (Marjaryasana-Bitilasana)

Benefits—Cat-Cow Pose (Marjaryasana-Bitilasana)

Cat–Cow Pose strengthens and nourishes the entire spine, making it an excellent daily practice. The movement stretches the muscles of the back, shoulders, and torso, easing stiffness and improving posture. As the spine moves in its full range of motion, blood flow increases, which can reduce pain and promote long-term spinal health.

This sequence is also a wonderful morning ritual. Its soft, wave-like motion wakes up the body, stimulates circulation, and delivers fresh oxygen to the brain and muscles. Many students tell me it gives them more energy than a cup of coffee—and I agree. The gentle "pump" created by the spine's movement also massages the abdominal organs, supporting digestion and metabolic balance.

Emotionally, Cat–Cow has a playful, freeing quality. Its steady rhythm soothes the nervous system, eases anxiety, and encourages mindful breathing. The movement naturally opens the chest, supporting emotional release and cultivating a sense of spaciousness in the heart. This simple flow supports presence, grounding, and ease.

Cat–Cow has been part of my daily practice for years, and I include it in nearly every class I teach. Its fluidity drops me out of my head and into my heart, helping me meet each day with energy and openness. Let this sequence become one of the ways you reconnect to your body's wisdom.

CAUTIONS

Because Cat–Cow focuses on spinal movement, anyone with neck or back injuries should proceed carefully and consult a health-care provider or experienced instructor. Conditions such as herniated discs, osteoporosis, or severe scoliosis may require customized guidance or avoidance of deep flexion and extension.

The pose also places weight on the wrists. If you experience wrist pain or conditions like carpal tunnel syndrome, practice on fists or use props to reduce pressure. Recent wrist surgery is a clear reason to avoid the pose until fully healed.

Cat–Cow can be very supportive during pregnancy, but modifications are key—especially in later trimesters. Avoid excessive arching in Cow Pose to prevent strain in the lower back. Props under the knees or chest can add comfort and stability.

As always, listen to your body. If the movement creates discomfort or pain, adjust or pause. Mindful practice is safe practice.

EXERCISE—Cat-Cow Pose (Marjaryasana-Bitilasana)

Follow these steps to practice Cat-Cow Pose:

1. **Begin in a tabletop:** Place your wrists under your shoulders and your knees under your hips. Keep your spine and neck neutral. Take a few natural breaths.

2. **Move into Cat Pose (exhalation):** Tuck your tailbone, draw your navel toward your spine, round your back upward, and let your head release toward your chest.

3. **Move into Cow Pose (inhalation):** Lift your tailbone and chest, letting your belly lower toward the mat. Gently lift your chin and gaze forward or slightly upward.

4. **Flow with the breath:** Continue alternating between Cat (exhale) and Cow (inhale), moving slowly and mindfully. Feel your spine soften and lengthen.

5. **Repeat for several rounds:** Notice how each cycle deepens your breath and increases your sense of ease.

6. **Return to neutral:** After a few rounds, come back to tabletop and observe how your body feels—lighter, looser, and more awake.

Cat–Cow Pose is approachable, versatile, and profoundly effective. Practiced regularly, it enhances spinal health, reduces stress, and strengthens the connection between breath, body, and awareness. Whether used as a warm-up or a standalone practice, Cat–Cow encourages fluid movement and mindful presence in every part of your day.

Mountain Pose *(Tadasana)*

Tadasana, or Mountain Pose, comes from the Sanskrit words *tada* (mountain) and *asana* (pose). Rooted in ancient yoga, it embodies steadiness, clarity, and inner strength. Standing in Tadasana invites you to ground your energy, align your body, and connect with a sense of unwavering stability—much like a mountain rising from the earth. With mindful awareness, you learn to refine your posture, settle your energy, and step into the present moment with quiet confidence.

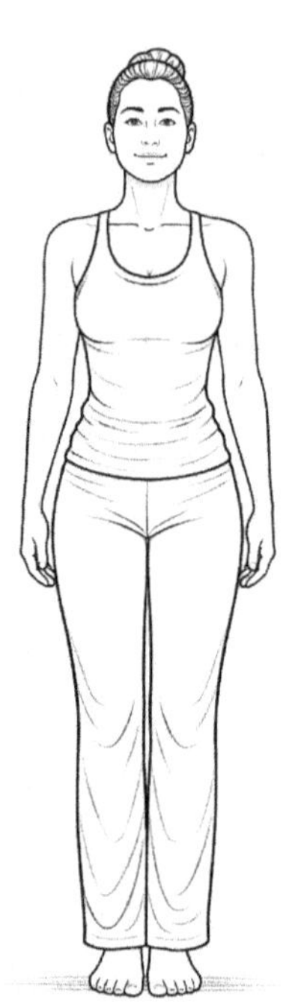

Fig. 7
Mountain Pose (Tadasana)

As a foundational posture, Tadasana anchors nearly every standing pose in yoga. It gathers your attention and helps you transition with intention, much the way a mindful pause can shape the course of your day. Practicing Mountain Pose at the beginning of class—or at the beginning of anything—sets the tone for clarity and purpose.

Tadasana is especially helpful when life feels uncertain or overwhelming. By rooting your feet and steadying your breath, you draw on the metaphor of the mountain: calm, grounded, and unshakably present. This pose reminds you that strength doesn't always mean force—sometimes it simply means standing your ground and feeling fully here.

Benefits—Mountain Pose (Tadasana)

Standing may seem ordinary, but in Tadasana it becomes a conscious act of alignment. While trees and animals stand from instinct, humans can choose to stand with awareness. Some people naturally carry themselves with uplifted energy, while others round forward from stress, fatigue, or years of habit. Mountain Pose helps you reconnect with your inherent ability to stand tall—physically, emotionally, and spiritually.

Tadasana improves posture by bringing your attention to the spine and encouraging subtle adjustments that promote stability and ease. With your feet rooted, core lightly engaged, and heart lifted, the body organizes itself into a strong yet relaxed stance. Over time, the pose strengthens the legs, core, and back, and gently supports bone health through conscious engagement. This grounded awareness invites a sense of trust, resilience, and mindful presence.

CAUTIONS

While Tadasana is simple and accessible, a few precautions are worth noting. If you've recently had surgery or injury to your spine, hips, knees, or feet, consult your doctor before practicing prolonged standing. Those with low blood pressure, dizziness, migraines, or vertigo may need to proceed gently. Extended standing can also contribute to varicose veins for some individuals.

Avoid locking your knees in this pose. A slight bend keeps circulation flowing and helps prevent faintness, allowing the posture to remain supportive rather than rigid.

EXERCISE—Mountain Pose (Tadasana)

Tadasana can be practiced almost anywhere. Whether you are at work, at home, or out with friends, when you need a moment of balance and strength, stand up and reconnect.

1. **Stand with your feet together** or hip-width apart, toes facing forward. Soften your knees and lightly draw your navel toward your spine.

2. **Lengthen your spine** as you lift through the crown of the head. Keep your chin parallel to the floor and relax your shoulders down your back.

3. **Gently engage your core**, allowing the tailbone to drop slightly as your body finds natural alignment.

4. **Soften the face and jaw**, releasing unnecessary tension while keeping your body alert and present.

5. **Breathe deeply and evenly**, adjusting your posture as needed to stay balanced and stable. Remember—stillness does not mean stiffness.

6. **Hold for several breaths**, noticing how your body organizes itself around this subtle, steady alignment.

7. **Release the pose with a slow exhale.** Shake your arms and legs gently, or transition into your next posture.

Mountain Pose may appear simple, but its power lies in its subtlety. Practiced regularly, Tadasana strengthens the body, refines posture, and nurtures a grounded sense of mindfulness. When you stand with intention, you embody steadiness—not just on your mat, but in every moment of your life.

Warrior II Pose (Virabhadrasana)

Virabhadrasana—Warrior II Pose—embodies strength, stability, and clear focus. Though not explicitly found in early yogic texts, this posture was shaped by influential teachers such as Krishnamacharya, B.K.S Iyengar, and Pattabhi Jois, who helped refine the modern versions practiced today.

The pose draws inspiration from the mythic warrior Virabhadra, a fierce manifestation of Shiva who rose out of grief and devotion. Warrior II captures that story *not* through aggression, but through unwavering presence—an inner steadiness that remains calm even when life feels chaotic. In yoga, the "warrior" is not one who fights, but one who meets challenge with clarity, grounding, and courage.

There are three Virabhadrasana variations—Warrior I, II, and III—each offering its own level of intensity. While Warrior III is more advanced, Warrior I and II are accessible to most practitioners and offer profound physical and mental benefits when practiced with mindful intention. We will specifically focus on Warrior II in this section.

Fig. 8 Warrior II Pose (Virabhadrasana)

Benefits—Warrior Pose (Virabhadrasana)

The Virabhadrasana trio shares similar qualities, but all have their own unique focus.

Warrior I, with its forward hip position and wide leg stance, builds foundational strength. It focuses on strengthening the legs, stretching the hip flexors, and enhancing balance. The overhead arm position stretches the chest and shoulders, encouraging upper-body flexibility and heart opening.

Warrior II, continues the theme of leg strength, but focuses on the muscles of the inner thighs and groin. The wider and more open stance encourages a deep stretch in the quadriceps, inner thighs, and the hips while building endurance through the outstretched arms.

Warrior III demands deep core engagement. Balancing on one leg, extending the upper body and arms forward and the back leg behind, the practitioner engages core muscles and relies on the strength of their back, glutes, and standing leg. Engaging the shoulders without tensing the neck requires deep breathing and focus. Not to be taken lightly, this pose improves strength, balance, and concentration, intensifying the benefits of Warrior I and II.

The series of Warrior poses increases stability, mobility, and stamina. They strengthen the legs, open the hips and chest, and cultivate a sense of spaciousness in the spine and joints. The sustained breathing required in these poses sharpens focus and calms the mind, often leaving the practitioner feeling centered, energized, and quietly confident.

Regular practice proves that yoga *can* build strength comparable to traditional athletic training—while simultaneously developing presence, concentration, and emotional resilience. Over time, these postures encourage an inner fortitude that naturally extends into daily life.

CAUTIONS

As with any physical practice, honor your body's current condition. Recent injuries or surgeries involving the knees, ankles, hips, spine, shoulders, or neck require caution—and often rest—before attempting any Warrior pose.

Monitor hip and shoulder tightness and don't push past your level of flexibility. With regular practice and focus on deep breathing, you should notice improvement.

Those with high blood pressure or heart conditions should ease into Warrior I and II and avoid Warrior III unless cleared by a doctor. If you experience vertigo, migraines, or balance challenges, use props or a wall for support, and avoid Warrior III during active episodes.

Pregnant practitioners should modify stances and rely on props to maintain comfort and stability. Individuals with scoliosis, osteoporosis, or herniated discs should consult a physician or knowledgeable yoga teacher to determine appropriate variations.

Note: Practicing weight-bearing yoga postures has proven positive effects on osteopenia, osteoporosis, and scoliosis. Research, including the work of Dr. Loren Fishman, suggests that weight-bearing yoga can support bone health. If you're navigating osteopenia or osteoporosis, exploring his work may be especially beneficial.

EXERCISE — Warrior II Pose

1. **Begin in Tadasana** (Mountain Pose) at the front of your mat. Stand with your feet together. Take a breath to center yourself.

2. **Step your right foot back** about one-leg length as you open your torso to the right. Your front foot faces forward; your back foot turns in, roughly 70 degrees.

3. **Bend your left knee** so it aligns over the ankle, creating a strong, grounded lunge.

4. **Inhale and extend your arms out to the sides** at shoulder height, palms down. Relax your shoulders. Exhale.

5. **Lift through your spine** while keeping the hips level and the legs engaged.

6. **Turn your head to the left** and softly gaze past your fingertips without straining your neck.

7. **Breathe steadily**, maintaining relaxed shoulders and a long spine as you hold the pose.

8. **To release, straighten the front knee** and lower your arms.

9. **Turn your torso forward** and step back into Mountain Pose.

10. **Pause** and feel the after-effects of the posture

11. **Repeat** on the opposite side.

Warrior II deeply opens the hips, strengthens the legs, encourages spaciousness across the chest and shoulders, and promotes circulation and mental clarity. Though strong and energizing, it often leaves the mind calmer and more focused afterward.

Practice Warrior II whenever your confidence wavers, when you feel scattered, or when you need to reconnect with the steady presence at your core. Over time, this pose cultivates grounded courage, inner resilience, and a mindful determination that supports you well beyond the mat.

Fig. 9 Vrksasana (Tree Pose)

Tree Pose *(Vrksasana)*

Vrksasana, or Tree Pose, comes from the Sanskrit *vrksa* (tree) and *asana* (pose). Long associated with balance, stability, strength, and flexibility, it has appeared in yoga traditions for centuries. Early depictions—some dating back to the seventh century—show Hindu sadhus meditating in this posture to cultivate discipline, stillness, and devotion. Standing in Tree Pose symbolized grounding in the earth while reaching upward toward clarity and enlightenment.

Like a tree weathering shifting conditions, this posture teaches us how to remain steady amid life's uncertainties. Balancing on one leg mirrors the mental and spiritual balance we strive for: to stand firmly in our truth while staying flexible enough to adapt. Whether practiced in ancient temples or modern studios, Tree Pose offers a reminder of resilience, mindfulness, and the quiet strength that comes from rooting deeply within ourselves.

Benefits—*Tree Pose (Vrksasana)*

Tree Pose, known for its simple elegance and stability, is one of my favorite yoga postures. Its simplicity holds remarkable power. Practiced regularly, Vrksasana builds both physical strength and mental steadiness. Balancing on one leg activates the core and leg muscles, strengthening the ankles, calves, thighs, and abdominal muscles. This engagement supports healthy posture and overall stability, and with the help of props or modifications, Tree Pose can be especially beneficial for those managing osteopenia or osteoporosis.

Beyond the physical work, the pose sharpens concentration and cultivates inner awareness. Standing tall and rooted invites the qualities of a tree—strength, flexibility, grace, and presence. As balance improves on the mat, many people notice a parallel improvement in their ability to stay centered amid daily challenges.

Key benefits of Tree Pose include:

- Improved balance and stability

- Strengthened legs, ankles, and core

- Better posture and alignment

- Increased mental focus and concentration

- A gentle stretch for the hips, groin, and sides of the torso

Tree Pose becomes even more valuable as we age. Good balance is essential for long-term mobility and confidence, and Vrksasana supports both physical steadiness and mental clarity. With consistent practice, this grounding posture helps you meet life with resilience, poise, and a calm, centered presence.

CAUTIONS

Vrksasana is generally safe and accessible, but mindful alignment is essential. Keep your standing foot facing forward, avoid pressing your lifted foot into the knee joint, and maintain balanced hips by engaging your core. If you are pregnant, recovering from surgery, or dealing with balance challenges, practice near a wall or chair.

Those with ankle, knee, or hip issues should modify the pose to avoid strain. Practitioners with arthritis—especially in the lower body—may find the posture uncomfortable; avoid it if pain arises. Individuals with vertigo, dizziness, or significant balance difficulties should skip Tree Pose.

If you have blood pressure concerns, keep your hands at heart center rather than overhead. Beginners should start with the lifted foot low on the standing leg and gradually move it higher as balance improves.

With mindful care and appropriate adjustments, Tree Pose can be practiced safely and effectively, supporting both physical alignment and inner steadiness.

EXERCISE — *Tree Pose* (Vrksasana)

1. **Begin in Tadasana** (Mountain Pose). Stand tall with weight evenly distributed across both feet. Focus on your relaxed and steady breath.

2. **Shift your weight.** Ground into one foot and engage the standing leg.

3. **Lift the opposite foot**, turn the knee outward, and place the sole of your foot against the inner thigh or calf of your standing leg. Avoid placing it directly on your knee. *Beginners may keep the toes of the lifted foot on the ground with the heel resting at the ankle.*

4. **Place your hands** in the prayer position (Anjali Mudra) at your heart or, if you wish to deepen the pose, reach your arms overhead like tree branches.

5. **Set your gaze.** Focus on a steady point in front of you to support balance.

6. **Align and breathe.** Keep your hips level and maintain a straight, standing leg. Avoid locking the standing knee. Engage your core and lift through your spine. Maintain a soft, steady breath.

7. **Hold the pose** for five deep breaths (longer if comfortable). Use a wall or chair for support as needed. Gently release and return to Tadasana.

8. **Repeat** on the other side.

The beauty of Vrksasana lies in its simplicity. Accessible to practitioners of all levels, it encourages balance, stability, and grace—qualities that extend far beyond the mat. Practice Tree Pose whenever you feel unsteady or overwhelmed. Like a tree bending with the wind yet rooted in the earth, you too can remain strong, centered, and resilient, no matter the storms you face.

Corpse Pose (*Savasana*)

Savasana—derived from sava (corpse) and asana (pose)—is the essence of yogic rest. Often called the "king of relaxation," it represents profound stillness, surrender, and the integration of practice. First recorded in the fifteenth-century *Hatha Yoga Pradipika,* Savasana has long been regarded as a doorway to deep restoration and inner awareness.

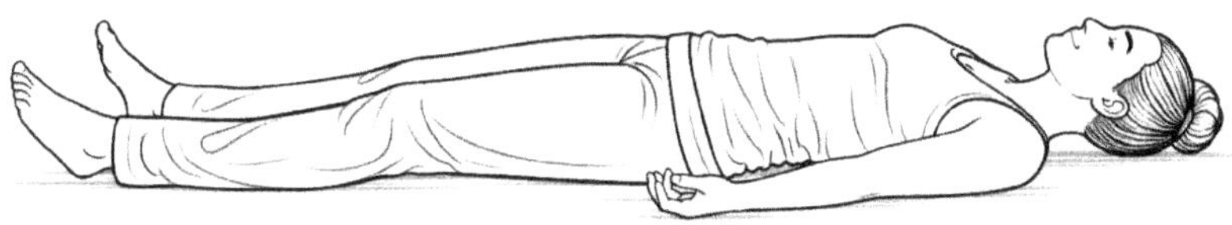

Fig. 10 Savasana (Corpse Pose)

Although its English translation can sound stark, the yogic meaning is far more expansive. Savasana reflects the natural cycle of life, inviting a symbolic "death" of the ego so we can touch the spaciousness of higher consciousness. By releasing the need to control, to perform, or to strive, we reconnect with the quiet, unchanging presence at the center of our being.

More than a resting pose, Savasana is a vital part of every yoga practice. It offers the body time to absorb the benefits of practice, while the mind settles into clarity and ease.

Benefits—Corpse Pose (*Savasana*)

I cannot stress enough, the immense benefits of practicing Savasana. If you can only do one yoga pose, choose Savasana. It is one of the most healing tools in yoga. By activating the parasympathetic nervous system, it shifts the body out of stress mode and into deep relaxation, easing muscle tension, quieting mental chatter, and lowering overall anxiety.

Because of its complete stillness, Savasana allows you to turn inward, building subtle mind–body awareness and giving space for emotional and physical healing. This simplicity—lying down, breathing, letting go—creates profound calm, clarity, and a renewed sense of connection to your inner Source.

With consistent practice, Savasana enhances overall well-being, improves focus, and supports long-term nervous-system health.

CAUTIONS

Savasana is generally safe, but a few adjustments can make it more comfortable and supportive.

Pregnancy: Especially in the later trimesters, it is best to avoid lying flat on your back for long periods of time. Instead, lie on your side or use props to rest in an inclined position. This helps to avoid vena cava compression.

Neck or back discomfort: Place a pillow or rolled towel under the neck and a bolster or folded blanket beneath the knees to ease spinal pressure. This position supports the natural curves of the spine.

Digestive concerns: Recline with the head and torso elevated to reduce reflux.

Emotional sensitivity or trauma recovery: Savasana may feel unsettling for some individuals. Those recovering from trauma or depression may find the deep surrender challenging or triggering. Work with a mental-health professional if needed and communicate privately with your yoga instructor before class.

For the best experience, practice Savasana in a quiet, dimly lit space. Stay warm, use a blanket if needed, and choose the position that allows your body to fully relax. Your comfort is the key to receiving the most benefit.

EXERCISE—Corpse Pose (Savasana)

Savanna can be transformational, though beginners often find stillness surprisingly challenging. With patience, it becomes a gateway to presence and inner peace.

1. **Lie on your back** with knees bent. Press your feet into the floor and lengthen your tailbone away from your head. Extend your legs, one at a time, letting the feet fall open naturally. *If you have low back issues, place a pillow or rolled blanket under your knees to take pressure off your low back.*

2. **Rest your arms alongside your body**, palms facing up. Soften the shoulders and allow your breath to deepen.

3. **Gently tuck your chin** so your neck aligns with your spine. Relax the jaw, eyes, and facial muscles.

4. **Close your eyes** and let your attention drift inward, observing your breath without controlling it.

5. **Practice Ujjayi Breath**, following its rhythm until you surrender into pure awareness.

6. **Remain in the pose** for five to ten minutes (or longer). Some practitioners stay for extended periods when deeply relaxed.

7. **To awaken, begin with small movements**, wiggling fingers and toes, extending into a full-body stretch. Draw your knees toward your chest, roll to one side, and pause.

8. **Press into your hands** and rise to a comfortable seated position.

9. Before reentering your day, **sit quietly for a moment**, noticing the lingering stillness and clarity.

Savasana reminds us that profound shifts often come from stillness rather than effort. By surrendering the body and quieting the mind, we align ourselves with the spacious, timeless awareness that yoga invites us to remember.

Journaling

My introduction to journaling began when I was nine. I don't remember who gave me my first diary, but I remember filling its pages each night—documenting the day, my feelings, and usually a few lines about the cute boy who sat one aisle over in fourth grade. Since then, journaling has been a loyal companion. It has carried my thoughts, dreams, disappointments, gratitude, and questions when I didn't yet have the words to speak them aloud. Writing has helped me process complicated emotions, organize ideas, and release stress that might have otherwise spilled into my relationships.

Over the years, I've completed hundreds of journals. Looking back, I can see how they shaped my ability to write clearly and think more calmly. Journaling has offered me a meditative, creative space to discover who I am, what I want, and where life is calling me—one mindful entry at a time.

Journaling is a simple yet powerful tool for mindfulness and emotional well-being. It gives your inner world a place to land, providing structure and perspective. When you put thoughts on paper, emotions become easier to understand and patterns become easier to see. This clarity allows you to make choices aligned with your values instead of reacting from habit or stress.

Journaling also opens the door to creativity. When you write freely and without judgment, new ideas and solutions begin to surface. The mind softens, the heart opens, and unexpected insights appear—sometimes quietly, sometimes in bold strokes of revelation.

Science supports this. Writing helps calm the amygdala—the brain's emotional alarm center—and shifts activity toward the prefrontal cortex, the area responsible for clarity, reasoning, planning, and decision-making. This simple act of transferring thoughts from mind to page can reduce anxiety, regulate emotions, and create a healthier balance between emotion and logic.

Journaling encourages you to slow down, reflect, and respond thoughtfully rather than react impulsively. It can soften anger, ease fear, elevate your mood, and help you revisit meaningful memories with gratitude. It is a private, judgment-free space to be honest with yourself.

While journaling may not resonate with everyone, I encourage you to try it. Your journal is for you alone—unless you choose to share it. Let your writing be imperfect, spontaneous, and real. These words are reflections of your life, illuminating what matters most and helping you understand yourself more deeply. Over time, this practice strengthens the relationship between your emotional and rational mind, creating greater mindfulness and emotional resilience.

In the pages that follow, you'll find three journaling practices— Gratitude Journal, Morning Pages, and Evening Release. All you need is a pen and paper. Set aside your electronic devices if you can. Long-hand writing encourages memory, presence, and a tactile connection to your thoughts. It invites you to slow down, breathe, and be with yourself in a way that screens rarely allow.

Incorporating these journaling practices into your routine can bring more clarity, balance, and meaning to your life. Each one offers unique benefits, and you can shape them in whatever way best supports your journey.

Gratitude Journal

A gratitude journal is a simple but powerful practice: Each day, you write down what you're thankful for. This gentle shift—from what's missing to what's already present—cultivates a more positive, resilient, and appreciative mindset. Over time, it strengthens emotional well-being, deepens relationships, and helps you recognize the abundance already woven through your daily life.

Set aside a few minutes each day to list at least three things you're grateful for. (Three is a starting point—I often write five to eight.) Many people find evenings the best time to write. Keeping your journal by your bed allows you to reflect on the day's bright spots before sleep. Ending your day in a state of gratitude supports better rest, steadier mood, and greater overall health.

Some days, gratitude comes easily. Other days, especially when life seems to be serving up one challenge after another, it may feel like searching for light through thick clouds. In those moments, remember that gratitude doesn't have to be grand. It may be as simple as a warm cup of tea, a quiet sunrise, your first deep breath on the yoga mat, or a moment of affection from someone you love. Of course, include the big blessings too—milestones, opportunities, and the people who anchor your life are definitely worth grateful recognition.

A simple process for your gratitude practice

Before writing, take a few slow breaths and let your shoulders soften. When a grateful thought arises, write it in a clear statement such as *"I am grateful for ..."* or *"I am thankful for ..."* Speak it aloud if you can, letting the feeling of gratitude move through you. Add details if they help you reconnect with the moment. Repeat the process for at least two more reflections, noticing how your body and breath respond. With each entry, your mind settles and your heart opens just a little more.

As this practice becomes part of your routine, you may notice gratitude sparking more often throughout the day—a hummingbird passing by your window, the aroma of fresh coffee, your dog's happy tail wag. Even if you can't write them down right away, allow these tiny moments to lift your mood and remind you of the beauty threaded through ordinary life. Gratitude expands the more you acknowledge it, gently guiding you toward a life lived with presence, appreciation, and joy.

Morning Pages

Julia Cameron introduced *Morning Pages in The Artist's Way* as a simple yet powerful practice of three handwritten, stream-of-consciousness pages written first thing in the morning. This unfiltered writing clears mental clutter, softens anxiety, and opens pathways to creativity by giving your mind space to release whatever it has been quietly holding.

I first turned to Morning Pages in 1995, shortly after moving to Nashville to work in the music industry. I was struggling with writer's block, and a friend urged me to try Cameron's twelve-week program. The idea of filling three full notebook pages every morning felt overwhelming at first—but surprisingly, it wasn't difficult at all. My handwriting was barely legible and my thoughts scattered, but when I finished, I felt lighter, as if I had released years of tension in a single sitting. While I can't promise the same dramatic shift for everyone, I can say that Morning Pages consistently restored my creativity and confidence during a time when I needed both.

The power of Morning Pages lies in their freedom. Writing without censoring or judging your thoughts helps you bypass the inner critic and allows fresh ideas to emerge. The process brings you back to the present moment, clears mental noise, and builds self-awareness. Over time, the ritual becomes an anchor—something that steadies your mind before the day begins.

If you're ready to try Morning Pages, here's how to begin:

1. **Write first thing in the morning.** Before your day gathers momentum—ideally as soon as you wake up—sit down with your journal and give yourself enough time to write without rushing.

2. **Write by hand.** Sorry tech folks, no phones, tablets, or laptops allowed. Longhand writing slows your thoughts and makes the experience more personal and grounding.

3. **Fill three notebook pages.** Write anything that comes to mind—messy, repetitive, nonsensical, emotional, or mundane. The goal is release, not perfection.

4. **Be consistent.** Do them daily, especially on days when you feel uninspired. Consistency teaches discipline, strengthens creativity, and deepens self-trust.

Morning Pages are more than a writing exercise—they are a daily clearing of the mind, a gentle invitation to creativity, and a grounding practice in mindfulness. Three simple pages can help you reconnect with yourself, uncover new insights, and start each day with a fresh and open mind.

Evening Release

The Evening Release is a simple journaling practice that helps you process the day so you don't carry its emotional weight into tomorrow. By reflecting on your experiences—both uplifting and difficult—it provides an opportunity to reflect, identify lessons learned, and release any lingering negative emotions you've been holding onto from the day's events. It isn't meant for making long lists of grievances, however, some days may call for it. Ultimately, it's about gaining perspective and acknowledging moments of gratitude and growth.

Like gratitude journaling, this practice supports better sleep by easing mental tension and clearing unsettled thoughts. It nurtures mindful awareness and sets a calmer, more balanced tone for the next day. Over time, reviewing your day increases emotional clarity and helps you respond—rather than react—to life's challenges. Evening Release gently guides you toward mindful living, one day at a time.

Let's give Evening Release a try:

1. **Find your space.** Choose a quiet, comfortable spot where you can write without interruption. You might do this before bed or anytime in the evening when the day is winding down.

2. **Reflect on the day.** Take a few minutes to mentally walk through your day. Notice what felt good, what felt challenging, and how your body responds as you recall each moment. This simple awareness prepares you to write with honesty and clarity.

3. **Write what stands out.** In your journal, capture the moments that truly stayed with you. How did they make you feel? Did they teach you something or did they feel random? Highlight what supported you and what you'd like to improve moving forward.

4. **Release what felt heavy.** If anything left you tense, frustrated, or unsettled, write it down with the intention of letting it go. Acknowledge your emotions without judgment. This is your chance to clear internal clutter and soften any lingering stress.

5. **Name three things you're grateful for.** End the reflection by noting three meaningful moments from your day. This shifts your mind away from negativity and reconnects you with what is nourishing and supportive.

6. **Set an intention for tomorrow.** With your mind clearer and your heart lighter, write how you want to feel or what you hope to bring into the next day. Setting a simple intention helps you wake up with purpose and optimism.

Sweet dreams.

Nature

Nature is a powerful teacher of mindfulness, continually inviting us into the present moment. Its rhythms—serene or wild—hold a primal wisdom that has guided humans since the beginning of time. Whether we're savoring the hush of a summer twilight or listening to the fierce winds of a winter storm, nature draws our attention back to what is happening *right now*. Observing the plants, animals, and elements around us help us see life from different perspectives, opening us to understanding and compassion—the very roots of inner peace.

Curiosity is a natural doorway into this awareness. How does a wren experience its world? How does a maple tree know when to release its leaves? What motivates creatures who thrive at night versus those who come alive with the sunrise? These questions deepen our connection with nature and with ourselves.

Plants evolve through life nourished by water, earth, and sunlight. Animals follow their own patterns of play, protection, and survival. Watching an ant carry a crumb or listening to birdsong can gently pull us out of mental clutter and into quiet presence. The cycles of day and night, the turning of the seasons, and the ebb and flow of weather reflect our own inner cycles—sometimes peaceful, sometimes turbulent, always moving forward.

Nature offers a sanctuary where the mind softens. Its sensory richness—color, sound, texture, movement—grounds us in the here and now. It encourages reflection, stillness, and a deeper connection with our inner being. When we're outside, pretenses fall away. We simply are, in relationship with something far larger than ourselves.

One experience that brought this truth home to me happened on a visit to the Highlands of Scotland a few years ago. I was driving along a quiet little mountain road when I saw a pair of black lambs frolicking along the side of the road. The fence beside them looked damaged and they had apparently jumped across to explore what was on the other side. Stopping the car across the road, thinking it was a good photo opportunity, I quietly stepped out of the car with my camera to find the right angle, but these two little imps heard me and took off, jumping back across the fence to find their mother. Unfortunately, one of the lambs didn't quite get enough height to clear the fence and landed squarely on the barbed wire. It kicked its back legs and bleated for help to no avail.

Since it seemed I was the one to cause the lamb's plight by interrupting its play, I felt compelled to help the little darling out of its predicament. Leaving my camera in the car, I looked both ways and cautiously crossed the road to the scared creature. As I approached, I sent Reiki energy and gently cooed to it as if it was the family pet. Approaching, I could see the barbed wire was poking into its scruff, so I stepped one boot onto the wire, lowering it away from its neck and I scooped my arms around the lamb's body, hugging it to my chest.

Feeling its wooly and sturdy body in my arms, I realized this little creature felt much differently than I had imagined. My brain suddenly realized I was doing something completely out of the ordinary. I exclaimed to myself, *"You are holding a little black lamb next to your chest!"*

Nothing else in the world mattered in that moment as I fully experienced the unexpected weight of its body and the connection of two beings. It stopped bleating and seemed to relax against me as I leaned forward to deliver it across the wire. Its mother and twin strode to the fence in time to receive their wayward relative. As if to say, "thank you," the mother sheep looked into my eyes and gave a little nod and a bleat before the family trotted away, finding their next patch of green grass for grazing.

Left to consider what had just happened, all I could think about was the fact that I had hugged a little black lamb, quite possibly saving its life! I felt more awake and present in that moment than I had felt during the past year. The air smelled fresher, the green of the countryside seemed more vibrant, the sky overhead echoed a coming thunderstorm, and I could still feel the weight of that precious little life pressed against me as I watched it trot away. Reflecting on the unexpected experience, I realized I had just participated in the most natural exchange of presence, connection, and care. It was a moment that pulled me completely into the aliveness of *now*.

Nature often brings us back to ourselves like this. It reduces stress, clears mental fog, and offers space to release what we cannot control. When we let the natural world hold our attention, curiosity grows and our busy minds settle into deeper awareness.

Profound experiences don't require a trip across the globe. Something as simple as hugging a tree in your backyard or planting a balcony garden in your fifteenth-story apartment can foster a sense of wonder that compels present moment contemplation. The natural world is always offering an invitation.

What small moment of nature could help you reconnect with clarity today?

Take a step outside—however briefly—and let Mother Nature hold your attention, your breath, and your sense of wonder.

Negative Ionization

Nature's uplifting effect isn't just poetic—it's physical. One reason we feel so restored outdoors is negative ionization, a natural process that cleanses the air and supports overall well-being. Negative ions attach to pollen, dust, and other airborne particles, causing them to fall out of the air we breathe. Cleaner air supports easier breathing, a stronger immune system, better sleep, a brighter mood, and greater mental clarity—all of which naturally deepen mindfulness.

Have you ever wondered why you feel so good in nature? Negative ionization plays an important role in making you feel better. Think back to a time when you were hiking in a forest, standing at the ocean's edge, swimming in a mountain lake, or strolling through a neighborhood park. Did you breathe more deeply or move more slowly so as to take in the fresh air, aromas, and views of the setting?

Could you sense a feeling of calm and confidence settling in? Perhaps your mind felt clear or your body completely relaxed, letting go of tightness and stored stress. That refreshed, grounded feeling was more than an emotional state of mind. You were inhaling millions of tiny, negatively charged particles that help lift your mood and quiet your mind. These positive experiences were brought to you, in part, by negative ionization.

To understand this phenomenon, we must remember back to middle school science class when we learned about the properties of atoms and ions. That introductory to chemistry and physics can help to explain negative ionization and how it promotes mindfulness and peace of mind. If you will recall, atoms are microscopic particles that are the building blocks of all matter. They consist of a nucleus with protons, neutrons, and electrons that orbit the nucleus. Protons have a positive charge, neutrons are neutral, and electrons carry a negative charge.

When an atom gains an extra electron, it becomes a negatively charged ion. Nature generates these ions constantly. Sunlight, wind, waterfalls, ocean waves, thunderstorms—even the spray from a garden hose—can all energize the air and create negative ions.

Forests, mountains, oceans, and countryside are especially abundant with negative ions, and this abundance is part of why these places feel so cleansing and restorative. Research shows that negative ions can also increase serotonin levels, helping to regulate stress and enhance feelings of happiness, clarity, and relaxation. No wonder warm sunlight after a storm or the sound of rushing water can shift your whole mood.

While negative ionization is strongest outdoors, especially near moving water, simply spending time in nature increases your exposure. This, in turn, supports mindfulness by helping you slow down, breathe more fully, and experience the present moment with greater ease. Clean air, natural rhythm, and beauty all work together to create a deeper sense of connection—to nature, to life, and to yourself.

Ultimately, negative ionization is one of nature's quiet gifts. It purifies the air, sharpens awareness, and helps us return to a centered, calm way of being. Immersing yourself in outdoor environments—even briefly—can uplift your mind and body, making mindfulness more natural and accessible.

What are you waiting for? Get outside and fly a kite, take a walk, go for a swim, or just sit on your front porch, breathing in those negative ions and enjoying the richness of the present moment.

Savoring

"Savoring" is a wonderfully rich word, often used in the culinary world to describe the act of slowing down to enjoy and appreciate the taste and aroma of food and drink. We've all had moments of savoring things like the taste of a juicy ripe peach or catching the scent of barbecue as it wafts through the neighborhood on a summer afternoon. Yet savoring goes far beyond flavor. At its heart, savoring is the practice of *feeling good about feeling good*—recognizing that we're content, present, and fully engaged in the moment.

As a mindfulness practice, savoring requires focused attention and a deliberate intention to enjoy what is happening right now. It means tuning into the positive aspects of an experience, quieting distractions, and meeting the moment with openness rather than judgment. Mindfulness teachers often describe savoring as fully engaging with and appreciating life's pleasures with awareness and gratitude. It invites us to immerse ourselves in the sensations, emotions, and thoughts that arise in moments of joy or peace.

Nature is one of the easiest places to practice savoring. When we allow ourselves to sink into the glow of a sunset, feel a brisk wind on our cheeks, or listen to a distant foghorn echo over the water, we discover details that enrich the present moment. Perhaps the sunset stirs awe, or the wind makes you feel fully alive. Maybe you simply feel grateful for a warm coat. Savoring gives us permission to experience these moments with a deeper appreciation for the present moment.

Imagine watching an enthusiastic hound race across a park to fetch a ball, tail wagging wildly. As you observe the dog's joy, do you feel your own body soften? Does the playful scene make you smile or breathe more deeply? Allowing yourself to feel these small ripples of delight is part of savoring. Even as an observer, you can absorb the joy unfolding around you.

Buddhist teachings take savoring a step further: appreciating each moment without attachment. This means appreciating the moment, no matter how insignificant, understanding that all experiences are worth celebrating no matter how fleeting they are. While not always easy, this outlook can reduce our suffering and open the door to profound inner peace.

Consider waking up on a camping trip in the mountains to a leaky tent and a soaked sleeping bag. Comfort may not be your first thought, but could you still savor the sound of rain on the forest canopy? Could you appreciate the nourishment the storm brings and find an element of amusement for your predicament? Understanding the temporary nature of all things, and knowing that our experiences are what we make of them, can invoke a deeper appreciation for the present moment. Even difficult situations offer something meaningful to notice—gratitude for warm boots, humor in an unexpected mishap, or simple appreciation for being alive and aware.

Savoring does not mean ignoring unhealthy or unsafe situations. Instead, when we can step away from judgment and clearly witness our present moment, it is possible to be grateful for our rain jacket and waterproof boots even though our tent was flooded. Savoring invites us to find what can be appreciated within an experience, no matter how small. Nature naturally supports this practice. Without judgment or expectation, it invites us back to presence again and again. Through this lens, savoring becomes a powerful path toward inner peace.

Ways to savor nature are as unique as we are. You might relish lying beneath a star-filled sky, sketching a landscape, eating a simple meal outdoors, or walking a trail with a loved one. You might savor the silence between birdsong, the texture of moss under your fingertips, or the way a warm breeze lifts your hair. These moments, when noticed with intention, become small anchors of peace.

Savoring also strengthens mindfulness in practical ways:

1. **Focused attention:** By concentrating on one experience at a time, savoring sharpens awareness and grounds us in the present moment.

2. **Emotional development:** Savoring amplifies positive emotions and helps build emotional intelligence by teaching us to recognize and nurture joy, gratitude, and contentment.

3. **Reduced stress:** Shifting attention toward uplifting experiences decreases stress and encourages physiological calm, balancing the effects of cortisol.

4. **Enhanced gratitude:** Reflecting on what makes a moment meaningful naturally cultivates gratitude, resilience, and a positive outlook.

5. **Better relationships:** Shared moments of savoring strengthen connection, deepen appreciation, and foster more mindful communication.

6. **Lasting memories:** Savoring imprints youthful moments more clearly, creating memories that can later restore peace and perspective.

7. **Non-attachment:** Enjoying a moment without clinging to it, we honor the beauty of the present without resisting the truth that everything changes.

Savoring seamlessly enriches a mindfulness practice and deepens our appreciation of life. It helps us notice what nourishes us, even in unexpected situations.

One late autumn evening, I experienced this firsthand. A friend and I set out for a late afternoon hike, certain we had enough daylight left. We lingered along the trail, mesmerized by the golden sunset shining through the bare trees. Half way through the loop, the light faded faster than we had anticipated and we found ourselves navigating the woods in complete darkness. The forest that had felt peaceful, even magical, minutes before suddenly tested our confidence and imagination.

We stumbled through the pitch black woods, trying to stay calm as we guessed our way toward the trailhead. Both of us wondered whether we had taken a wrong turn but tried to reassure each other.

Then, out of nowhere, a ghostly white figure appeared. At first, I thought my eyes were playing tricks on me, but my friend saw it too and called out, *"Hey!"* A young man in a white T-shirt and jogging shorts, accompanied by his white malamute, stopped immediately. After exchanging quick hellos, we admitted we were lost. He told us to turn around and walk about a mile back the way we'd come. He assured us we would find our way back where we parked our car.

We followed his directions, turning our blind trek into an adventure. Holding hands, we eased forward one cautious step at a time, feeling almost as if we were floating in space. When we finally reached the comfort of the car, we collapsed into laughter and wrapped each other in hugs of relief. Seeing one another under the dome light made everything feel real again.

In that moment, I savored everything at once: safety, friendship, trust, and the kindness of a stranger and his dog. Even the fear became part of the story—one that reminded me how alive and connected I felt.

Now, it's your turn. What moments in nature have you savored, and how have they shaped your sense of inner peace? Savoring invites awe, deepens mindfulness, and brings you back to the present, allowing you to feel good about feeling good, wherever you are.

The next time you're in nature, slow down. Linger. Use all your senses to take in the colors, textures, sounds, scents, and tastes around you. Let yourself appreciate your connection to the natural world as you mindfully savor your unique path to inner peace.

Gardening

Planting, tending, and watching things grow is a meditative practice. It slows us down, anchors us in the present moment, and offers simple joy through the act of caring for something alive. Beyond the beauty of flowers or the nourishment of fresh herbs and produce, gardening eases stress, lifts mood, and nurtures emotional well-being. It invites patience, gratitude, and acceptance as all of our senses engage with the natural world.

I don't know about you, but the combination of sunshine, fresh air, dirt, and water sparks my excitement and curiosity. There's nothing quite like placing a seed in the earth and later watching it emerge with a quiet little announcement: *I'm here!* Nurturing seedlings can feel deeply fulfilling and therapeutic, providing a sense of accomplishment, and a surprising sense of inner peace.

Although I grew up pulling weeds in my parents large garden, as an adult, I've rarely had much land to plant. Still, I've always found ways to grow things on the various patios and balconies where I've lived throughout my life.

Once, I planted five Meyer lemon trees, nurturing them in tiny pots on a sunny windowsill until they were strong enough to transplant into larger pots on my patio. I planted two or three seeds per small pot and treated them as if they were priceless gems. I checked on them daily, watered them weekly, and imagined the unseen work happening beneath the soil. Those little pots became a cherished ritual. I'd greet each one, inspect the soil for signs of life, and read everything I could about lemon trees so I could offer the best care possible. It may sound simple, but nurturing those seeds gave me purpose and strengthened my self-confidence. I even learned the art of non-attachment, watching each seedling grow in its own way and on its own timeline.

Two weeks in, the first shoot appeared—small, determined, and full of promise. Upon morning inspection, I felt grateful and amazed to witness such tenacity. Within a month, all five pots held saplings at different stages of growth. Three grew quickly; two needed more time; all became healthy little lemon trees. That experience expanded my mindfulness practice by awakening my curiosity, compassion, and appreciation for the miracle of life. As I cared for my plants, I found myself improving my own self-care.

If gardening feels out of reach for you because you live in an apartment or believe you don't have a "green thumb," let me offer some reassurance. Gardening is less about expertise and more about connection. Whether you grow a few herbs on a windowsill, tend to a container garden on a balcony, or join a community plot, you can cultivate presence, reduce stress, sharpen focus, and improve your overall well-being simply by interacting with the natural world.

A garden begins as an idea—an invitation to slow down, breathe, and reconnect with what is real. Beyond the beauty of blooming plants or the reward of homegrown food, a garden offers tranquility, contentment, and a grounded sense of presence. Time in nature is proven to increase happiness and reduce stress, and gardening amplifies these benefits by placing our hands—and our attention—directly in the earth.

Even the soil itself supports our wellbeing—literally. Contact with dirt exposes us to *Mycobacterium vaccae*, a naturally occurring bacterium that boosts serotonin and strengthens immunity. Paired with sunshine, movement, and repetitive tasks like digging and weeding, this earthy companion acts like a natural antidepressant, improving mood and decreasing tension. The simple focus required for gardening—planting, watering, pruning—draws us into the present moment and invites the nervous system to unwind.

Gardening also reflects the rhythms of life. We plant, nourish, prune, and support our gardens much like we tend to our relationships, aspirations, and personal growth. Whether caring for a plant or a person, offering our best attention is a meaningful act of love. And when we recognize the impermanence woven through each cycle of growth, it becomes easier to greet every moment as a gift rather than something to cling to.

Surrounded by plants and natural elements, all of our senses come alive. The cool crunch of a freshly picked cucumber, the scent of rich soil, the sound of wind moving through leaves, the warmth of sunlight on our skin—each becomes a small meditation in gratitude. When we truly pause to savor these experiences, we cultivate not only a garden, but a deep well of gratitude and inner peace.

If you'd like to begin or deepen a mindful gardening practice, here are some helpful ways to get started:

1. **Create a simple Zen garden.** If traditional gardening feels daunting, try a small arrangement of sand, stones, and minimal greenery for a meditative space. This can be an excellent option if space, natural light, or confidence is an issue.

2. **Start small with easy plants.** Choose forgiving plants like herbs, succulents, or cacti to build confidence. These

plants require less care, making them ideal for beginners.

3. **Use indoor plants.** Houseplants bring calm, beauty, and a breath of nature into any space.

4. **Focus on the process,** not the outcome. Let gardening be about presence—not perfection. Enjoy the process of tending to your plants without focusing on the outcome.

5. **Learn and adapt.** Every mistake is a lesson. Gardening, like life, involves trial, error, and growth.

6. **Include other mindful activities.** Pay attention to your breath while working in the garden. Try meditating in your garden or practice yoga next to your houseplants.

7. **Practice patience and compassion.** Acknowledge that gardening is a journey. Both you and your plants grow at your own pace. I once had an orchid that didn't bloom for seven years until one day, after I moved to a new home, it bloomed and continued producing numerous blossoms year-round.

8. **Use gardening as a restorative break.** Similar to using mindfulness or stretching at your desk, a few minutes with your plants can reset your mind.

9. **Appreciate the small stuff.** Celebrate small successes in your gardening journey. Notice the new leaf, the budding flower, the subtle changes. These details are invitations to joy.

10. **Join a community garden.** Shared spaces offer connection, education, and a deeper sense of belonging.

Gardening nourishes more than the body; it nurtures inner peace. It pulls you into the present moment, awakens your senses, and strengthens your connection to the natural world. By tending to a garden—no matter the size—you tend to yourself. And that is something to be truly grateful for.

EXERCISE: Sensory Engagement

The next time you're in your garden, slow down and explore it through each of your five senses. Use the suggestions below or let them inspire your own mindful discoveries.

Sight: Instead of taking in the whole garden at once, choose a single plant and study it closely. Notice the shape and color of its leaves, the structure of its stem, and any blossoms or fruit it may hold. Observe it with curiosity.

Hearing: Close your eyes and breathe steadily. Listen for distinct sounds—the call of birds, the hum of bees, the rustle of leaves. Let the garden's natural rhythm anchor your attention.

Touch: Put your bare hands in the soil. Feel its texture, temperature, and moisture. Notice the grounding sensation of touching the earth directly.

Smell: Lean in and inhale the scents around you—the sweetness of a flower, the sharpness of an herb, the richness of the soil. Explore how each fragrance makes you feel.

Taste: If you grow edible plants, mindfully taste something you know is safe—an herb leaf, a ripe berry, or a fresh vegetable. Before tasting anything, make sure you're familiar with what's edible and what isn't. Let the flavors connect you more deeply to the garden's gifts.

After exploring each sense individually, take in your garden as a whole. How does your experience shift when you absorb all the sensory details together? How do you feel after giving yourself this mindful moment?

Gardening becomes transformative when we engage with it fully. Through simple sensory awareness, we learn to be present, patient, and connected to the natural rhythms around us. As we tend our plants, we're reminded of life's beauty, impermanence, and resilience—lessons that nurture inner peace as surely as sunlight nurtures growth. Now, that is something to savor with gratitude.

Walking and Hiking:
Stepping into Mindfulness

Imagine stepping outside, leaving behind the hum of daily life, and feeling the solid earth beneath your feet. Spending time in nature is an invitation to slow down, to notice, to arrive fully in the present moment. Every step along a path, every inhalation of fresh air, every rustle of leaves beneath your feet, can be an opportunity to find calm, clarity, and inner peace.

As you move through the world, the rhythm of your footsteps becomes a meditation. The gentle exertion of hiking, the rise and fall of your breath, and the warmth of sunlight on your skin work together to calm the mind and soothe the spirit. Studies show that these simple acts reduce cortisol, ease anxiety, and relieve mental fatigue. Even brief exposure to natural light can regulate sleep patterns, while time spent moving through trees, trails, or hills can leave you feeling calm, focused, and restored. The body, too, responds with resilience. Your heart grows stronger, your legs develop more powerfully, and your immune system becomes more robust with each step.

There's a reason humans are drawn to nature. Research consistently shows that being active outdoors, whether in a city park or in rugged back country, improves well-being. Walking along a forest path or through a quiet green space can be grounding in a way that nothing else can. Your senses awaken to the rustle of leaves under foot, the distant trill of a whippoorwill, and the earthy scent of soil and moss. Each sound, color, and texture bring you fully into the moment, inviting mindfulness in its purest form.

Science confirms what we intuitively know. In a 2008 study at the University of Michigan, participants were split into two groups. One walked through a wooded park, the other along a busy urban street. Afterward, those who walked in nature performed 20% better on memory and attention tests—and reported greater mood and mental clarity. Nature, it seems, doesn't just refresh the body—it sharpens the mind and nurtures the soul.

We are drawn to the great outdoors for more than its physical beauty and emotional support. Biology plays a role in our need to commune with nature.

One helpful way to understand this concept is through the **Biophilia Hypothesis**. *Biophilia* comes from the Greek *philia*, meaning "love of life," and the concept suggests that humans are naturally drawn to connect with nature and other living beings. This instinct isn't accidental—it's part of our evolutionary story. For thousands of years, our ancestors relied on the natural world for food, safety, and shelter. Because of this long relationship, we're biologically wired to feel calmer, safer, and more at home when we step into a natural setting.

The term *biophilia* was first introduced in the 1960s by German psychologist Erich Fromm, who described it as "the passionate love of life and all that is alive." His perspective came from psychology and humanistic philosophy, emphasizing that a genuine love for living things is part of a healthy and fulfilled human personality.

Two decades later, Biologist Edward O. Wilson expanded on the idea in his 1984 book *Biophilia*. Wilson approached the concept from an evolutionary and ecological angle, proposing that our attraction to nature is not just emotional but biological—a built-in affinity shaped by millions of years of living closely with the natural world.

Though Fromm and Wilson came from different scientific disciplines, their ideas beautifully complement each other. Fromm highlights the emotional and psychological nourishment we receive from nature, while Wilson explains the biological roots of that connection. Together, their work offers a holistic understanding of why being outdoors—walking, hiking, or simply sitting under a tree—feels so profoundly grounding. Their shared message is clear: reconnecting with nature supports our well-being, strengthens our sense of belonging, and reminds us of our place in a larger living world.

Consider the way nature has nurtured you throughout life. From childhood summers running through sprinklers, to traipsing across new landscapes on family vacations, to quiet evenings watching the sun dip below the horizon, we inherently find comfort in and trust the wisdom of the natural world. There's something in these moments that reassures and restores us. Nature invites reflection, encourages gratitude, and awakens a sense of wonder.

Simply walking through a park or forest while paying attention to the sights, sounds, and smells around us can be a deeply grounding experience. No matter where we walk or hike, whether in an urban or natural setting, these activities are good for promoting overall wellness and mindful contemplation. However, the facts clearly point to nature's invaluable contribution to our well-being. Hiking and walking in natural environments engage our senses and provide a calming effect on mind and body, which leads to inner peace and a mindful way of experiencing life.

What are some of the ways in which spending time in nature affects your life? Besides the obvious feelings of relaxation and stress relief, how does walking and hiking in nature foster inner peace in you?

Here are a few examples of some of the benefits I have experienced from walking in nature:

- **Stress reduction:** Nature lowers cortisol and releases tension, easing both body and mind.

- **Mental clarity:** A walk through trees or along a quiet path provides a break from intense focus required in urban settings, and restores attention, clears mental fatigue, and refreshes creativity.

- **Emotional well-being:** Natural beauty inspires joy, peace, and resilience. Elevated dopamine levels reduce symptoms of anxiety and depression, contributing to more balanced emotions.

- **Physical vitality:** Navigating varied terrains strengthens muscles, builds stamina, and supports cardiovascular health. Also a great form of aerobic exercise, hiking increases lung capacity.

- **Breath awareness:** The physical exertion of hiking encourages deep breathing, which causes me to focus on the quality of my breath. Remembering my breath encourages mindfulness and present-moment awareness.

- **Sensory engagement:** Nature provides a rich sensory environment. Sights, sounds, smells, textures, and tastes are more intense and can deepen present-moment awareness.

- **Personal growth:** Walking in solitude allows reflection, new ideas, and personal insight to emerge. Have you ever noticed how you can quickly clear your thoughts or an inspiration just comes to you when you're taking a walk in nature?

- **Social connection:** Essential for emotional well-being, shared walks foster meaningful interactions and deepen bonds with others. Nature provides a more relaxed setting for connection.

- **Present-moment awareness:** Each rhythmic step is an invitation to be present, and the beauty and grandeur of nature encourages even greater focus on external surroundings and internal sensations. In nature, we realize, the now is all there is.

- **Gratitude:** Observing the natural world invites appreciation for life's gifts, cultivating inner peace.

Pause and reflect for a moment. Imagine standing at a trailhead after a long week, inhaling the crisp mountain air. *Gratitude.*

Look over a ridge at a valley dotted with alpine lakes. *Gratitude.*

Stroll along a quiet beach as the sun melts into the horizon. *Gratitude.*

These moments, small and fleeting, are also powerful. Gratitude underpins mindfulness, making the peace found in nature enduring.

Even a simple walk in a nearby park can offer these gifts. Notice the way grass bends underfoot, the hum of insects, or the play of sunlight on leaves. Each moment of attentiveness strengthens your connection—to yourself, to life, and to the quiet wisdom of the world around you.

Enjoy a simple guide for mindful walking and hiking:

- **Find a time of day** when you can walk or hike without feeling rushed. Early morning or late afternoon can be particularly peaceful times.

- **Choose a location** that feels safe and inviting.

- **Set an intention** to notice your surroundings, your breath, and the sensations you experience as you walk.

- **Engage all of your senses:** listen, feel, see, and breathe. Listen to the sound of your footsteps, feel the breeze on your skin, watch birds flitting from tree to tree, taste the salt in the air, and smell the coming storm.

- **Focus on your breath:** Practice full, intentional breathing as you walk. Inhale deeply through your nose and exhale slowly. Allow yourself to sigh. This helps to release tension in the body.

- **Move at your own pace:** There's no need to rush, so walk at a pace that feels comfortable and allow yourself to fully engage with your surroundings.

- **Take a moment afterward to reflect:** How do you feel now, compared to when you began your walk? Do your thoughts feel more organized and is your mood lighter? Does your body feel stronger and more relaxed?

Walking and hiking are more than exercise—they are practices of presence. They cultivate mindfulness, gratitude, and inner peace, step by step. Nature invites us to slow down and notice each step we take. It invites us to feel alive in each present moment, connecting with the splendor and peace of the natural world. With each trail walked, each path explored, we reconnect with the rhythms of life itself. Step outside. Breathe. Notice. With each step, allow yourself to arrive fully into your body, your mind, and the restorative embrace of the present moment.

Sunrise / Sunset Meditation

Sunrise and sunset are natural thresholds—quiet openings and closings of the day—that gently invite us to pause, breathe, and arrive fully in the moment. Sunrise offers the promise of beginning again, while sunset encourages release and unwinding. Both create spacious opportunities for reflection and mindful awareness. Simply witnessing these daily shifts can spark a sense of awe and deepen your connection to nature's steady, ever-changing rhythm.

Meditating during sunrise or sunset aligns you with the earth's natural cycles. Sunrise invites intention-setting, gratitude, and a calm start to the day. Sunset offers a chance to unwind, digest the day's experiences, and let go of accumulated stress. Some people gravitate toward the stillness of early morning, while others prefer the quiet exhale of dusk. You may even choose to meditate at both times, bookending your day with awareness and returning to yourself with each transition. These moments hold distinct energies—freshness at dawn and spacious release at dusk—each offering its own kind of peace. These times are often quieter, providing a peaceful environment for meditation and reflection.

Years ago, when I was living in Phoenix, my partner and I would take what we called "mini vacations" around town to meditate together. One evening, we drove to the top of South Mountain for a sunset meditation. Others had arrived with the same intention, so we made our way to the mountain's edge and settled separately into our own quiet spaces.

I found a flat rock facing the western sky, just perfect for sitting cross-legged. A warm, gentle, warm breeze brushed against my skin as the sky deepened into purples, fiery oranges, and soft gold stretching along the horizon. With half-opened eyes, I slipped into that sweet, spacious place where thought fades and presence expands—where nature, breath, and awareness all merge.

A slight movement drew my attention. A fox had padded toward me, watching curiously as I sat completely still. When our eyes met, there was no fear—just simple recognition. After a moment, it continued on its way and disappeared. I returned my half-lid gaze to the unfolding sunset, feeling myself dissolve into color and light. My body grew light and quiet, as if I was released from the earth's gravity. In that silence, a soft flute melody floated through the air, weaving itself into the changing sky.

That meditation remains one of the most profound moments of my life. The colors, the music, the warm breeze, and the unexpected appearance of that fox lifted every worry from my mind. What remained was pure gratitude—quiet, steady, and complete.

(If you're curious about the flute, I eventually met the musician. He had seen me sitting on the rock and walked a little farther down the ridge to begin his own meditation. Nature truly is its own orchestra.)

Your sunrise or sunset meditation doesn't need to resemble mine. It can be five minutes or forty-five, in your backyard or on a mountaintop. What matters is that you choose a peaceful spot with a clear view of the horizon—somewhere you feel comfortable and safe.

Once you settle in, set an intention. It may be as simple as "to be present," or you may choose to focus on gratitude, peace, clarity, or release. Focus on your breath, inhaling and exhaling slowly through your nose. Let your breath carry stress out of your body and create space inside you.

As the sun rises or sets, notice the shifting colors, the play of light and shadow, the quiet movements of earth turning toward or away from the day. Let the sky itself be your meditation anchor. Listen to what surrounds you—birds greeting the morning, waves meeting the shore, wind rustling leaves. Even distant traffic can become part of the landscape of awareness when you listen without judgment.

When your meditation feels complete, gently stretch and observe how you feel. You might journal your reflections or simply offer a moment of gratitude for the experience—gratitude for the sun, for the quiet, for your own willingness to pause.

Sunrise and sunset meditations offer profound support for inner peace. Dawn brings clarity and fresh possibility; dusk provides a moment of reflection and rest. In these moments of transition, we join the natural world in its constant movement, and in doing so, we reconnect with the stillness within ourselves. By embracing the beauty and calm of these daily rituals, we strengthen our sense of presence, deepen our connection to the world around us, and nurture a lasting foundation of peace and well-being.

PART FOUR

More Mindfulness

Now that we have explored the foundations of mindfulness and its role in cultivating inner peace, it's time to go deeper—beyond understanding and into daily living. Mindfulness is more than a concept to be grasped; it is a way of being that unfolds moment by moment. What makes it so remarkable is that it belongs to everyone. It doesn't matter where we come from, what we believe, or what stage of life we are in—mindfulness meets us exactly where we are. It's a personal journey of consciousness that ripples outward, touching the lives of others in quiet yet powerful ways.

In my own life, I've seen how mindfulness spreads effortlessly. A simple smile or kind word shared with a stranger has often turned a passing moment of acknowledgment into the beginning of a genuine friendship. When you begin to live with more awareness and calm, the people around you notice. They may not have words for it at first—they simply sense that your presence feels different. Perhaps you listen more deeply, speak with more care, or simply radiate a steadier kind of energy. In that sense, mindfulness is contagious. It doesn't need to be preached or promoted; it is shared by example. When we cultivate peace within, we give silent permission for others to do the same.

Contagious Calmness

ere's a story about a woman—let's call her Mara—who began a simple mindfulness practice after a particularly stressful year. Her work had become overwhelming, patience with her child was wearing thin, and she often found herself losing her temper over small things. One morning, after reading about mindful breathing, she decided to try it. For five minutes before getting out of bed, she simply sat and breathed, noticing each inhale and exhale. She didn't expect much—but over the weeks that followed, something began to shift.

Her mornings felt less frantic, her words were kinder, and she felt more accepting toward her life. When her son spilled his cereal, instead of reacting with frustration, she paused, took a deep breath, and helped him clean it up with a smile. Soon, her husband began sitting quietly beside her in the mornings, just breathing too. Within months, the energy of their home felt different—not because the world outside had changed, but because peace had started to grow within its walls. That's how mindfulness works—it begins with one person, one choice, one breath, and then spreads outward, quietly transforming relationships, spaces, and the self.

When we practice mindfulness, we don't just change ourselves; we influence our environment in subtle yet profound ways. Our energy—the calmness, patience, and compassion we cultivate— becomes a form of teaching without words. Think of how you feel when you spend time with someone who is genuinely calm and centered. You might breathe a little slower, soften your voice, and notice your nervous system is relaxing in response. That is the contagious nature of mindfulness. It doesn't demand; it invites. It doesn't convert; it connects.

Free for Everyone, Everywhere

Another remarkable truth about mindfulness is that it is completely free. In a world where self-improvement often comes with a price tag—retreats, memberships, apps, or expensive workshops—mindfulness stands apart. You don't need special equipment, fancy cushions, or a quiet mountaintop to begin. All you need is your breath, your awareness, and a willingness to be present.

You can practice mindfulness while walking the dog, washing dishes, or waiting at a traffic light. Every moment of your life is an opportunity to awaken to the present. The cost is not measured in dollars but in dedication and the willingness to pause and notice, again and again. In that way, mindfulness is the most accessible tool for personal transformation available to anyone, anywhere.

A friend once told me that some of his most peaceful moments come during his daily commute. Instead of fighting traffic and growing steadily more frustrated, he began to use those moments to practice mindful awareness. He turned off the radio, silenced his phone, and simply drove—breathing deeply, noticing the rhythm of the road, the color of the sky, the feeling of his hands on the steering wheel. He said those drives became a kind of moving meditation, transforming something ordinary (and sometimes stressful) into something sacred.

The beauty of mindfulness doesn't ask for extra time in your schedule, it simply asks for your awareness in the present moment. Whether you're standing in line at the grocery store, folding laundry, or sipping your morning coffee, you can practice awareness. These small moments, strung together, create a mindfulness practice and become the foundation of inner peace.

The Practice
that Grows

Like any meaningful skill, mindfulness flourishes through steady practice and gentle persistence. It isn't something that can be forced or achieved overnight. Instead, it grows quietly within you, one moment of awareness at a time. It's more like learning to play a song on the piano—at first, your hands may fumble and the notes feel uncertain, but with patience and repetition, the melody begins to flow effortlessly. In the same way, mindfulness becomes second nature through repetition. Regardless of your background or beliefs, you can learn to be more present. The only requirement is a willingness to show up and practice, even on days when your mind feels scattered or restless. Mindfulness simply asks that you show up, again and again, to the present moment.

At first, sitting still or staying present can feel uncomfortable. Our minds are used to racing ahead to future plans and to-do lists or falling back into worries and memories, but every time we gently bring our attention back to the present moment, we strengthen our capacity for peaceful presence. Over time, this effort is transformative. We begin to notice that we respond to life differently. Breathe through challenges instead of reacting impulsively, we listen more, rush less, and find that ordinary moments carry unexpected joy.

One afternoon, I found myself stuck in long grocery line behind an elderly man who was counting his coins one by one. The line was moving slowly, and I could feel impatience bubbling up inside me. Then, I remembered my practice. I took a breath and softened my shoulders. Instead of being anxious, I watched the man count his coins—shaky, but careful and deliberate. I saw the smile he gave the cashier and the gratitude in his eyes when she waited patiently for him to hand her his payment. In that simple moment, mindfulness turned my anxiety into compassion. The situation didn't change, but I did.

This is the quiet miracle of mindfulness. It doesn't remove the challenges of life, but it changes the way we meet them. With each moment of awareness, we reclaim our power to choose peace over reaction and presence over distraction.

Universal, Not Religious

One of the most profound truths about mindfulness is that it belongs to no single faith or philosophy. While its roots stretch back thousands of years to Hindu and Buddhist traditions, the practice itself transcends religion. At its heart, mindfulness is simply the art of being fully present. It is an act of awareness and acceptance that is universal.

Anyone can practice mindfulness, whether you identify as deeply religious, spiritual, agnostic, or none of the above. It asks nothing of you except that you pay attention to your breath, your thoughts, and the moment unfolding around you. In this way, mindfulness becomes a bridge that connects people of all beliefs. It encourages compassion, patience, and understanding, the values that every faith and moral philosophy upholds.

For those who do follow a particular religion, mindfulness can deepen that connection. A Christian practitioner might experience mindfulness as a form of contemplative prayer, a way of resting in God's presence without words. A person of Jewish faith might find it mirrors the awareness cultivated in Sabbath rest, where one fully embraces stillness and gratitude. In Islam, mindfulness resonates with the practice of *dhikr*—remembrance of the Divine. Even in secular life, mindfulness can awaken a deep sense of reverence for existence itself.

For those who consider themselves spiritual but not religious, mindfulness offers a direct path to self-understanding and communion with the Divine Self. It helps to reveal one's true nature, without judgment. It brings awareness to the stories we tell ourselves, the emotions we carry and the ways we respond to life. Through this awareness, we move closer to our true self.

Awareness, presence, and acceptance transcend doctrine and unite all spiritual and religious perspectives. No matter your chosen creed, mindfulness is not about changing who you are or what you believe. It's about waking up to what is right in front of you and living with more attention, greater intention, and compassion for all beings.

Living Mindfully in the Real World

It's easy to imagine mindfulness as something practiced in serene settings such as mountaintops, in meditation halls, or during long silent retreats. But the truth is, the most powerful mindfulness happens in the middle of everyday life. It is in the moments when your child is fussing, your phone is buzzing, or the traffic is unbearable. These are the real opportunities to practice and bring presence into the chaos.

Take a moment to pause right now. Notice your breath. Feel the weight of your body where it rests. Listen to the sounds around you. This simple act of coming back to the present is mindfulness in motion. You don't have to close your eyes or retreat from the world. You simply have to notice the world as it is, without rushing to change it.

Mindfulness instills a quiet sense of purpose and ease. It doesn't mean you never get upset or distracted—it means you know how to return to yourself when you do. Over time, with practice, this awareness becomes a natural way of living, reflected in subtle and quiet ways. Perhaps you eat more slowly, savoring each bite, or you listen to others without planning your response and take your time to think through a solution before blurting a thought out off the top of your head. Each of these moments are opportunities for mindful connection.

My teacher Thich Nhat Hanh, would always suggest that mindfulness is not a way to escape life, but to be fully present in it. Mindfulness is about engaging with life more deeply, even during the challenging moments. When we are truly present, even in the simplest moments— watching sunlight move across a window, laughing with a friend, a deep breath after a long day—they become profoundly meaningful.

The Ripple Effect

Living mindfully transforms more than just our own life—it naturally extends its influence outward, like light spilling gently into the world. When awareness deepens, every interaction becomes an opportunity to share peace. Listening with genuine attention, speaking with kindness, or simply showing patience in a moment of tension creates quiet waves that travel farther than we can imagine.

Imagine dropping a pebble into a still pond. The ripples spread outward in widening circles until they reach the farthest edges. Mindfulness works the same way. Each mindful act—listening, breathing, forgiving, pausing before reacting—creates waves that move outward, touching lives you may never even see. A calm voice in a heated conversation can steady the emotions of others. A single act of kindness might brighten a stranger's day and inspire them to do the same for someone else. The small ripples of awareness are not insignificant; they are seeds of collective healing.

One of the most profound truths about mindfulness is that the more it's shared, the stronger it becomes. The peace cultivated within naturally expands outward, returning again like an ocean tide. Compassion grows from awareness, and awareness deepens through compassion. Each mindful action, no matter how small, reinforces the connection between inner peace and outer harmony. In this way, mindfulness is both a personal practice and a collective gift—a living web of calm and care that unites us all.

A Lifelong Journey

Mindfulness is not a destination to reach but a relationship to nurture—a steady companion that grows and changes as life unfolds. Some days the mind feels crowded and restless, while other days, it is still and clear. Both states belong to the practice. What matters most is not the condition of the mind, but the gentle willingness to return again and again to the present moment.

Over time, mindfulness reveals that peace is not something you find, it is something you uncover. Beneath the constant noise of thought and distraction lies a deep reservoir of calm that has always been there. With every breath of awareness, you come closer to it.

The beauty of mindfulness lies in its simplicity and inclusivity. It requires no special belief system, no teacher, no perfect conditions—only your attention. It costs nothing and can be practiced anywhere. It does not demand perfection or ritual, only presence. Whether you follow a spiritual path or none at all, mindfulness asks you to show up and welcomes you exactly as you are. In doing so, you discover that inner peace isn't a distant goal, but a natural state that has been waiting for you all along.

So begin where you are. Take a breath. Notice this moment. Let mindfulness take root, and watch as it grows, not only within you, but all around you. The more you practice, the more your life becomes a living reflection of peace. In a world that often feels hurried and divided, mindful presence is not just healing, it's revolutionary.

Coming Home to Yourself

———

Mindfulness: *A Do-It-Yourself Guide to Inner Peace* was created with one simple intention: to help you return to yourself. Not to a different or improved version of yourself, not to a flawless or perpetually calm ideal, but to the deeper awareness within you—the one that has always been present, always available, always capable of meeting life with clarity, compassion, and presence. As you reach the end of these pages, you have traveled through ideas, practices, reflections, and invitations that all lead back to a single truth: **Mindfulness is a practice of paying attention without judging, of accepting what is without needing to change the outcome.**

This practice, simple yet profound, is the thread that weaves through every chapter of this book. It calls you toward a life rooted in awareness rather than distraction, groundedness rather than reactivity, and intentionality rather than habit. You have explored multiple ways of living mindfully—from meditation and breath work to gratitude practices, mindful walking, emotional awareness, deep listening, body-centered presence, journaling, and more. Each technique has offered a unique doorway into the present moment. And yet every doorway ultimately leads to the same place: the quiet steadiness within, the place where peace begins.

This concluding chapter is not simply a summary—it is a reflection on the journey you have taken and an invitation to carry its essence forward into your daily life. It is here to remind you that the power of mindfulness does not live in the concepts but in the practice; not in thinking about awareness but in embodying it; not in striving for perfection but in gently returning to the present, again and again.

Mindfulness as a Way of Being

Throughout this book, you have learned that mindfulness extends far beyond structured practices. While meditation, journaling, mindful walking, and similar techniques strengthen your awareness, the deeper purpose of mindfulness is to transform how you live every moment of your life. Mindfulness becomes less something you *do* and more something you *are*. It becomes a way of seeing, a way of listening, a way of relating to yourself and others. It becomes a shift in how you approach every experience—especially the difficult ones.

To live mindfully is to make peace with the truth that life unfolds moment by moment. The past is unchangeable, the future is unknowable, and the present is where your power, your clarity, and your peace reside. When you learn to inhabit the present with openness instead of judgment, something remarkable happens: you begin to experience life more honestly, more vividly, and more compassionately.

Mindfulness means paying attention to your life as it happens. It means noticing the feel of your breath, the sensation of your feet against the ground, the rise of an emotion before it becomes overwhelming, the story your mind is telling you, the habits that shape your reactions, and the space that appears when you pause long enough to observe instead of judge.

Mindfulness is not about trying to change the outcome. It is about accepting the outcome as it is, then responding with clarity and purpose. This is the heart of inner peace.

Some people believe mindfulness means pushing away unpleasant emotions or achieving a permanent state of calm. But mindfulness does not ask you to become passive or detached. It asks you to see clearly. To be with what arises. To acknowledge without resisting. When anger comes, mindfulness allows you to observe it. When grief appears, mindfulness helps you hold it gently. When joy spills into your life, mindfulness invites you to savor it. Through this simple awareness, you begin to notice that every emotion, every thought, every moment has a beginning, a middle, and an end. Nothing remains fixed. Everything moves.

And with that realization, life softens.

You soften.

The Power of Awareness in Everyday Life

Some of the most profound moments of mindfulness do not happen during meditation sessions but within ordinary experiences. When you paid attention as you drank your morning tea, folded laundry, listened to someone you love, or simply stepped outside to breathe fresh air, you were practicing presence. When you paused before reacting to frustration, counted to ten before responding in a heated moment, or created space in your day to reflect before rushing forward, you were discovering the transformative power of conscious awareness.

Mindfulness helps you see your circumstances with greater clarity and respond with wisdom rather than automatic patterns. It steadies you when life becomes chaotic, guides you when decisions feel overwhelming, supports you when relationships become strained, and comforts you when emotions grow heavy.

Even the simple act of noticing your breath brings coherence to the mind and body. You learned how this gentle practice calms the nervous system, reduces stress, illuminates unconscious habits, and strengthens your capacity to remain centered in challenging moments. When you breathe with awareness, you anchor yourself to the present—the only place where peace and clarity are possible.

This book has taught you that you are not your thoughts. You are the awareness behind them. In this spacious awareness, you gain the ability to make conscious choices, to break patterns that no longer serve you, to listen deeply, and to treat yourself and others with patience and kindness.

The present moment—the one you are living right now—holds all the potential for inner transformation.

The Wisdom of Great Teachers
and the Wisdom within You

The teachings of Thich Nhat Hanh, Jon Kabat-Zinn, Deepak Chopra, Wayne Dyer, the Dalai Lama, and many other mindfulness pioneers have shaped modern understanding of presence, compassion, and mind–body awareness. Their voices echo throughout this book because they have spent lifetimes learning how to quiet the mind and open the heart.

Yet the true purpose of studying their insights is not to imitate them—it is to listen to the teacher within yourself. All mindfulness ultimately returns you to your own inner wisdom. You may have begun this journey believing you were learning something new, but in truth, you were remembering something ancient. Presence is your natural state. Awareness is your birthright. Peace lives within you, not outside of you.

The techniques and perspectives you explored throughout this book are simply tools to help you rediscover what has always been there. They are stepping stones on a path that now becomes uniquely your own. You are not here to replicate anyone else's journey, but to honor your own unfolding.

Your Mindfulness Toolkit

By now, you have gained more than a set of practices. You now hold a complete toolkit—a way of seeing, thinking, responding, and living that can transform every layer of your experience.

You have learned:

- how to observe your thoughts rather than becoming entangled in them

- how to connect your mind and body through breath

- how to navigate emotions with openness rather than fear

- how to slow down long enough to make conscious choices

- how to strengthen relationships through deep listening and presence

- how to meet discomfort without collapsing or resisting

- how to savor joy without clinging to it

- how to cultivate gratitude, clarity, and compassion

- how to come home to yourself

These are not small achievements. They are life-changing realizations.

Mindfulness has shown you that peace is possible—not because life stops being challenging, but because you become the kind of person who can meet those challenges with steadiness and grace.

Life Is a Playground of Presence

As you practiced bringing awareness into your daily experiences, you may have noticed a subtle transformation: The world became richer. Colors appeared brighter. Conversations felt more meaningful. Ordinary routines became opportunities for connection. This is one of the quiet miracles of mindfulness—when you pay attention, your life becomes more vivid.

Moments that once seemed mundane now offer depth. Tasks that once felt mechanical now become grounding. And situations that once appeared overwhelming now begin to lose their power over you. You are no longer sleepwalking through your life; you are awake, engaged, and participating fully in every unfolding moment.

Mindfulness allows you to experience beauty in places you once overlooked. A gentle breeze, a shared smile, the sound of children playing, the weight of your body settling into a chair—these small moments become invitations to reconnect with yourself and the world.

Presence turns life into a playground of wonder and possibility. It gives coherence to chaos and clarity to confusion. It does not eliminate difficulty, but it brings light to the moments when you most need guidance.

Mindfulness as a Daily Practice

If there is one truth that echoes throughout every chapter of this book, it is this: **mindfulness must be practiced to transform your life.** Awareness is a muscle that strengthens through repetition. Even a few mindful minutes a day create profound shifts over time.

You do not need long periods of stillness or elaborate rituals. What you need is willingness—the willingness to begin, to continue, to return, and to trust the process even when your mind feels restless or distracted.

Some days your practice will feel effortless; other days it will feel challenging. This fluctuation is natural and expected. The goal is not perfection. The goal is presence.

Mindfulness asks only this: *keep showing up.*

Show up for your breath.

Show up for your body.

Show up for your emotions.

Show up for the people you love.

Show up for your challenges.

Show up for your joy.

Show up for yourself.

This is how mindfulness becomes a way of life—one breath, one moment, one conscious decision at a time.

A Mindful Life Awaits

As you pause to reflect on your journey through this book, consider what you now know: **inner peace is not something you pursue—it is something you cultivate.** It is something you choose. With every mindful breath, every moment of awareness, every act of compassion, every pause before reacting, you build the foundation of a peaceful, intentional, meaningful life.

You are now equipped with tools that many people spend years searching for. You have learned how to slow down enough to sense the wisdom within your body, how to access clarity beneath the noise of your thoughts, how to open your heart to deeper connections, and how to navigate uncertainty with steadiness.

You have awakened a part of yourself that will never again be fully asleep.

Mindfulness is a homecoming.

It invites you to breathe more fully, love more deeply, listen more intently, and live more consciously.

It invites you to trust yourself—to trust your inner rhythm, your inner wisdom, your inner truth.

It invites you to walk through the world with a lighter step and a more open heart.

The life that awaits you is not a perfect life. It is a present life. And that is far more valuable.

Mindfulness Is Calling You

Now comes the most important moment of this entire book—the moment you choose how to carry these teachings forward. The moment you allow mindfulness to move from theory into lived experience.

The invitation is simple, powerful, and transformative:

Begin now.

Not tomorrow.

Not someday.

Not when life feels easier.

Begin now—with one conscious breath.

Let this breath be your anchor.

Let the next breath be your choice.

Let the breath after that be your awakening.

Carry presence into your mornings and evenings.

Bring awareness into your conversations, your decisions, your relationships, your movements, your rest.

Let mindfulness shape the way you speak, listen, love, and respond. Allow your presence to become a gift—to yourself first, then to everyone around you.

And remember:

This is your life.

You are the one living it.

You are the one shaping it.

You are the one who chooses how awake, open, compassionate, and peaceful you become.

You have everything you need.

You always have.

So step forward.

Walk with awareness.
Meet each moment with your whole heart.
Let mindfulness be the way you come home to yourself—again and again, for the rest of your beautiful, unfolding life.

A mindful life is calling.
Answer it with your whole heart.
You are ready.

Bibliography

Acevedo, Bianca, T. Hammond, and Sarah Kraft-Feil, et al. "Smiling Sincerely or Grimacing Can Significantly Reduce the Pain of Needle Injection." Health. UCI School of Social Ecology, 2020.

Albrecht, Karl. "The (Only) 5 Fears We All Share." Psychology Today, 2012.

Ashley-Farrand, Thomas. *Healing Mantras*. New York: Wellspring/Ballantine, 1999.

Benson, Herbert. "Mindfulness Training May Help Lower Blood Pressure, New Study Shows." Brown University, funded by the National Institutes of Health, 2019.

Berman, Marc G., John Jonides, and Stephen Kaplan. "The Cognitive Benefits of Interacting with Nature." Psychological Science 19, no. 12 (2008): 1207–1212.

Berry, Jeffrey. "Mindful Arguing." Psychology Today, January 22, 2016.

Brown, Kirk Warren et al., "Contemplating Mindfulness at Work: An Integrative Review." Journal of Management 41, no. 4 (2015): 1056–1090.

Cameron, Julia. *The Artist's Way: A Spiritual Path to Higher Creativity*. New York: Tarcher Publishing, 1992.

Cherry, S. et al., "Exploring the Health Benefits of Bhramari Pranayama (Humming Bee Breathing): A Comprehensive Literature Review." Indian Journal of Physiology and Pharmacology (2024).

Chopra, Deepak. *How to Know God: The Soul's Journey into the Mystery of Mysteries*. New York: Harmony Books, 2000.

Cording, Jessica. "Why Mindfulness Matters for Healthcare Professionals." Forbes, August 29, 2024.

Creswell, J. David, and Bassam Khoury. "Mindfulness Meditation: Psychologists Have Found That Mindfulness Meditation Changes Our Brain and Biology in Positive Ways." Washington, DC: American Psychological Association, 2019.

Dyer, Wayne W. *Change Your Thoughts, Change Your Life*. Carlsbad, CA: Hay House, 2007.

Epstein, Mark. *Going to Pieces Without Falling Apart*. New York: Broadway Books, 1998.

Fishman, Loren, and Ellen Saltonstall. *Yoga for Osteoporosis: The Complete Guide*. New York: W. W. Norton & Company, 2010.

Fowler, James H., and Nicholas A. Christakis. "Acts of Kindness Spread Surprisingly Easily: Just a Few People Can Make a Difference." University of California San Diego, 2010.

Fox, Kieran C. R., Matthew L. Dixon, et al. "Functional Neuroanatomy of Meditation: A Review and Meta-Analysis of 78 Functional Neuroimaging Investigations." Cornell University, 2016.

Frankl, Viktor E. *Man's Search for Meaning*. Boston: Beacon Press, 1959.

Fromm, Erich. The Heart of Man: His Genius for Good and Evil. New York: Harper & Row, 1964.

Gladwell, Malcolm. *Outliers: The Story of Success*. New York: Little, Brown and Company, 2008.

Gokhale, P., V. Lakshmeesha, S. Shetty, S. Rani, and R. Kumar. "Influence of Kapalabhati Pranayama on Oxygen Saturation and Blood Pressure." International Journal of Medical and Health Research, September 2018.

Goleman, Daniel. *Emotional Intelligence: Why It Can Matter More Than IQ*. New York: Bantam Books, 2005.

Grossman, Paul, Lars Niemann, Stefan Schmidt, and Harald Walach "Mindfulness-Based Stress Reduction and Health Benefits: A Meta-Analysis." Journal of Psychosomatic Research 57, no. 1 (2004): 35–43.

Harvard Medical School. "6 Ways to Use Your Mind to Control Pain." Harvard Health Publishing, 2015.

Hicks, Esther, and Jerry Hicks. *Ask and It Is Given*. Carlsbad, CA: Hay House, 2004.

Hölzel, Britta K., James Carmody, Markus Vangel, Christy Congleton, Sita Yerramsetti, Tim Gard, and Sara Lazar. "Mindfulness PracticeLeads to Increases in Regional Brain Gray Matter Density." Psychiatry Research: Neuroimaging191, no. 1 (2011): 36–43.

Iyengar, B. K. S. *Light on Yoga: Yoga Dīpikā*. New York: Schocken Books, 1966; rev. ed. 1977.

Kabat-Zinn, Jon. *Mindfulness for Beginners: Reclaiming the Present Moment and Your Life*. Boulder, CO: Sounds True, 2016.

Khalsa, Dharma Singh, and Cameron Stauth. The Pain Cure: The Proven Medical Program That Helps End Your Chronic Pain. New York: Grand Central Publishing, 1999.

Kraft, Tara L., and Sarah D. Pressman. "Grin and Bear It: The Influence of Manipulated Facial Expression on the Stress Response." Psychological Science 23, no. 11 (2012): 1372–1378.

Kriakous, Stephanie, Rebecca Elliott, Simone Lamers, and Rachel Owen. "The Effectiveness of Mindfulness-Based Stress Reduction on the Psychological Function of Health Care Professionals: A Systematic Review." Journal of Occupational Health Psychology (2020).

Kumar, Amit. "A Little Good Goes Farther Than You Think." University of Texas at Austin, 2022.

Laplane, Sabine. *15 Days of Prayer with Brother Roger of Taizé.* New York: New City Press, 2010.

Leavitt, Sarah. "Mindfulness: The Tuition of Intuition." Psychology Today, 2024.

Lieberman, Matthew D., et al. "Putting Feelings into Words: Affect Labeling Disrupts Amygdala Activity in Response to Affective Stimuli." Psychological Science 18, no. 5 (2007): 421–428.

Luskin, Fred. *Forgive for Good: A Proven Prescription for Health and Happiness.* San Francisco: Harper San Francisco, 2001.

Maddocks, Fiona. *Hildegard of Bingen: The Woman of Her Age. London*: Faber & Faber, 2013.

Malhotra, Varun, Danish Javed, et al. "Study of Immediate Neurological and Autonomic Changes during Kapalabhati Pranayama in Yoga Practitioners." Journal of Family Medicine and Primary Care 11, no. 2 (2022).

Mann, Denise. "Negative Ions Create Positive Vibes." WebMD, May 2002.

McCraty, Rollin. "The Science of HeartMath." HeartMath. https://www.heartmath.com/science/#

Merriam-Webster. Merriam-Webster Dictionary. Springfield, MA: Merriam-Webster, n.d.

Nardi, Wendy, et al. "Mindfulness-Based Blood Pressure Reduction: Stage 1 Single-Arm Clinical Trial." PLOS ONE 14, no. 6 (2019).

Nash, Steve. "The History of Meditation: Its Origins & Timeline." Positive Psychology.com, 2019.

Newsonen, Erica. "Why Does Gardening Feel So Good?" Psychology Today, April 25, 2024.

Peale, Norman Vincent. *The Power of Positive Thinking.* New York: Prentice Hall, 1953.

Pert, Candace. *Molecules of Emotion.* New York: Simon & Schuster, 1999.

Random Acts of Kindness Foundation. "The History of Random Acts of Kindness Day." January 26, 2023. https://www.randomactsofkindness.org.

Salzberg, Sharon. *Lovingkindness: The Revolutionary Art of Happiness.* Boston: Shambhala Publications, 1995.

Satchidananda, Sri Swami. *The Yoga Sutras of Patanjali.* Buckingham, VA: Integral Yoga Publications, 1978.

Satyananda Saraswati, Swami. *Yoga Nidra.* Munger, India: Yoga Publications Trust, 1976.

Škobalj, Maja. "Mindfulness and Critical Thinking: Why Should Mindfulness Be the Foundation of the Educational Process." U.S. Department of Education, 2018.

Sodeman, Tracy. "Use Mindfulness to Cope with Chronic Pain." Mayo Clinic, 2024.

Taizé, Brother Roger of. *Seeds of Trust.* Chicago: GIA Publications, 2006.

Taizé, Brother Roger of. *The Rule of Taizé.* London: S.P.C.K. Publishing, 2012.

Tavoian, David, and Laura Craighead. "Deep Breathing Exercise at Work: Potential Applications and Impact." 2023.

Thich Nhat Hanh. *Peace Is Every Step: The Path of Mindfulness in Everyday Life.* New York: Bantam Books, 1991.

Thich Nhat Hanh. *Peace Is Every Breath: A Practice for Our Busy Lives.* New York: HarperCollins, 2011.

Tseng, Yu-Chih. "Scientific Evidence of Health Benefits by Practicing Mantra Meditation: Narrative Review." International Journal of Yoga 15, no. 1, 2022.

Urlacher, Julie. *Yoga Nidra Meditation Scripts.* Boulder, CO: Sacred Nature Press, 2023.

USC San Diego Health Sciences. "Brain Scans Reveal That Mindfulness Meditation for Pain Is Not a Placebo." 2024.

Walker, Matthew. *Why We Sleep: Unlocking the Power of Sleep and Dreams.* New York: Scribner, 2017.

Weir, Kirsten. "Nurtured by Nature: Psychological Research Is Advancing Our Understanding of How Time in Nature Can Improve Our Mental Health and Sharpen Our Cognition." Monitor on Psychology 51 no. 3, 2020.

Wilson, Edward *O. Biophilia.* Cambridge, MA: Harvard University Press, 1984.

Wood, Bliss. *ChantDance—Sonic Bliss.* CD Baby, 2008.

Wood, Bliss. *Empowering Your Life with Yoga.* New York: Alpha Books, 2004.

Xiao, Li et al., "Biological Effects of Negative Air Ions on Human Health and Integrated Multiomics to Identify Biomarkers: A Literature Review. Environmental Science and Pollution Research, May 2023.

Index

About the Author

Bliss Wood has devoted her life to guiding others toward greater harmony, self-awareness, and inner peace. A certified holistic wellness coach, she has spent decades helping individuals transform their lives through mindful living and compassionate self-care. Her deep commitment to the healing arts shines through her work as the author of the acclaimed *Empowering Your Life With Yoga*©, as well as through her widely appreciated yoga-focused CDs, ChantDance® and Yoga for Deep Relaxation©.

With over twenty-five years as a Reiki Master, Bliss blends ancient wisdom with modern understanding, creating an approach to wellness that is both accessible and profoundly transformative. Her expertise has made her a nationally recognized educator in the fields of yoga and holistic wellness. Through her involvement with organizations such as NCBTMB, Yoga Alliance, and AMTA, she offers high-quality education and coaching that reflect her passion for empowering others to live more balanced and meaningful lives.

Bliss's creativity extends far beyond the classroom and studio. An avid traveler with a keen eye for beauty, she captures striking images from around the world and pairs them with stories that invite readers into her journeys. Her love of expression also finds its voice—quite literally—in her flourishing career as a voice-over artist. Whether she is narrating audiobooks, voicing commercials, or bringing characters to life, she brings the same grounded presence and heartfelt intention that define her work in wellness.

Whether teaching, writing, creating, or traveling, Bliss embodies the mindful, intentional living she inspires in others. Her work continues to touch countless lives, offering guidance, encouragement, and a path toward a more peaceful, centered existence.

Connect with Bliss at www.blisswoodvo.com, on Facebook, or on Instagram to explore more of her work, teachings, and artistic pursuits.